SECURITY (cyber & non-cyber) IS NO LONGER THE EFFECTIVE STRATEGIC FOCUS - "SURVIVABILITY" IS.

SURVIVABILITY

Confronting the Unmitigated Risks & Unprecedented Threats of Today's Geo-Poli-Cyber™ Warfare to Survive and Competitively Thrive into the 21st Century

At a time when cybercrime has become endemic and with the onset of quantum computing, Khaled is spot on in his contention that if you can't name the threat, you cannot mitigate the threat.

It is noteworthy that he created the term Geo-Poli-Cyber™ way back in 2012 differentiating financially motivated cyber attacks from devastating and destructive political, ideological, extremist, and geopolitical cyber threats.

The notion of the need to shift strategic mindset focus from cyber security to *Survivability* is key. A must read in this ever changing political and economic landscape.

Anthony, Lord St John of Bletso.

Survivability should be read by every tech-savvy person, every economic professor and advisor, every cyber-security expert, every government official, and every company executive.

The author combined his in-depth knowledge, years of professional experience, and his unique abilities to foresee the future and its gravest of risks to present a very valuable risk and mitigation awareness book.

Survivability should also be used by universities and training agencies to widen business, economics and cyber-security students and top executives' knowledge, perspectives, and awareness.

Dr. Imad Hoballah

- Minister of Industry, Government of Lebanon.
January 2020-September 2021.
- Provost/Chief Academic Officer, American University in Dubai (AUD).
March 2017 - January 2020.
- Chairman/CEO, Telecom Regulatory Authority, Lebanon.
March 2007 - August 2015.

Survivability by Khaled Fattal will surely be the classic introduction to the interwoven yet complex relations between politics, economics, security, especially geopolitics in our global world.

Based on a wide and comprehensive glo-calised field studies ranging from banking to aviation, Khaled alludes to the most acute and unmitigated threats that might prohibit an organisational "Survivability".

In this fast-moving world where technology creates the strongest links to opportunities and vulnerabilities to national sovereignty, corporate security, health, safety, and profit, the author astutely challenges conventional thinking. He also explores the most crucial trajectories that society is facing today and in the newly established multipolar world while he courageously provides admirable solutions moving forward.

Prof. Dr Makram Khoury-Machool
Director of the European Centre for the Study of Extremism, Cambridge, UK. (Specialist in International Relations and Mass Media Communications).

SECURITY (cyber & non-cyber) IS NO LONGER THE EFFECTIVE STRATEGIC FOCUS - "SURVIVABILITY" IS.

SURVIVABILITY

Confronting the Unmitigated Risks & Unprecedented Threats of Today's Geo-Poli-Cyber™ Warfare to Survive and Competitively Thrive into the 21st Century

KHALED FATTAL

NEW YORK

LONDON • NASHVILLE • MELBOURNE • VANCOUVER

SURVIVABILITY

Confronting the Unmitigated Risks & Unprecedented Threats of Today's Geo-Poli-Cyber™ Warfare to Survive and Competitively Thrive into the 21st Century

Published in New York, New York by Morgan James Publishing in partnership with Survivability New Publishing. Morgan James is a trademark of Morgan James, LLC.
www.MorganJamesPublishing.com

SURVIVABILITY NEWS PUBLISHING

Proudly distributed by Publishers Group West®

2nd printing

ISBN 9781636982250 paperback
ISBN 9781636982274 ebook
ISBN 9781636982267 hardcover
Library of Congress Control Number: 2023938376

Cover and Interior Design by:
Survivability News Publishing™

CONTENTS

FOREWORD

While Khaled was writing his book *Survivability*, he never told me he was writing about our great debates and engagements while he was my student at the University of Southern California (USC) +40 years ago.

Back then, Khaled distinguished himself in the manner he critically and constructively argued and debated. Only after *Survivability* was published did I discover that he wrote a tribute to me as a special mentor who contributed to his life's successes and impacted his way of thinking forever. This gives me a great sense of gratification and accomplishment as a teacher.

The fact that, over many decades, Khaled contributed to the global internet infrastructure becoming the Multilingual Internet it is today — and having created the term Geo-Poli-Cyber™ in 2012 to distinguish financially motivated cyber-attacks from devastating and/or destructive political, ideological, extremist and geopolitical ones in damage impact — is testament to his vision. However, having created strategies and solutions to mitigate such risks and threats that today remain unmitigated speaks volumes about his mind and creativity, and especially his perseverance.

His argument that national leaders and top business decision makers who seek competitive advantages today and into the 21st century need to make the strategic mindset shift from security (cyber and non-cyber) to survivability is worthy of a serious consideration.

Consistent with Khaled's truest self, what he did in my class +40 years ago is exactly what he is doing today for the world — particularly with his book *Survivability*. I would not be opposed to working with him to find a way to factor his "Social/Societal Responsibility" into Supply Side Economics to deliver a sounder and more robust Capitalism model for the 21st century. After all, and to quote Khaled's own words, "agility in adaptability is critical to effective and competitive survivability".

Dr. Arthur B. Laffer.
Recipient of the U.S. Presidential Medal of Freedom in 2019 for his contribution to Capitalism in the 21st century | Laffer Curve Creator | Often referred to as "Father of Supply-Side Economics"

INTRODUCTION

Those of you who do know me, or of me—who decided to get a copy of my book to read after months of anticipation—might feel justified in wanting to know what I have to say.

Of course, there are those of you who aren't as aware of me, and you might not even know that I exist. For you, I imagine there was some intrigue by virtue of the title, the cover, or any press surrounding my book. Now, you're probably wondering what in the world this book is about, why I wrote it—and why I am perhaps uniquely qualified to talk about Survivability, let alone a Geo-Poli-Cyber™ (GPCyber™) threatened world.

At that, if you are already wondering, *What the hell is Geo-Poli-Cyber™?* then prepare to enter a globally growing club of the better informed. On second thought, in a different context, prepare to remain in an ever-shrinking club.

Before I continue, let me also warn you to be ready to have some of your conventional thinking, opinions, beliefs, and concepts—which you may have assumed would stand the test of time—challenged, if not politely massacred. If you are not ready for this, feel free to close the book now and go back to whatever you were doing.

I'd like to begin with a very important detail regarding my professional journey. I'll surely share a little about who I am, where I was born, how I got where I am today, the adversities of my life that led to the topic of "Survivability," and if you're lucky, whether I was bottle- or breast-fed as a baby. There's something you ought to know about me first. It might compel you to want to read and learn more about what I am saying. In fact, your very own survivability—personal, economic, along with your life and livelihood—may be riding on it.

I have been involved in the infrastructure of the global internet (its resiliency, stability, and security) since the mid-'90s. I championed, led, and actively contributed at the highest levels in making it the Multilingual Internet it is today. This was done through international institutions and forums such as the United Nations (UN), International Telecommunications Union (ITU), Internet Corporation for Assigned Names and Numbers (ICANN), UN Internet Governance Forum (IGF), along with many other local, regional, and international fora and processes. In fact, I was one of the few international experts to be invited by United Nations Secretary-General Kofi Annan to its New York headquarters in 2004 for the UN's first-ever consultations on internet governance.

My vision had always been to help deliver a digitally empowered citizen and information society that would create more informed and tolerant people for a better world and humanity. The dream, however, has turned into today's nightmare, warranting the need for many interventions. Are you wondering what kind of interventions are needed? Are you asking yourself what we need to fix, specifically?

Well, a new "Era of the Unprecedented" is already upon us, and cyber warfare—more specifically, GPCyber™ warfare, which I address in detail often in this book—has been ongoing since 2010. The most lethal GPCyber™ attackers have no direct financial motivations. They are driven by political, ideological, extremist, terrorist, and twisted religious goals toward the devastation and destruction of others. Citizens and decision makers across the world have little or no clue as to the depth of this new reality, how it impacts them, or how to deal with it.

In recent years, too many financially and GPCyber™ motivated attacks that compromised governments and businesses could be classified as "unprecedented," despite many of the targets already having cyber security, strategies, solutions, policies, and procedures in place. Yet, the status quo continued failing to defend nation-states, governments, corporate structures, and above all, the lives and livelihoods of citizens all over the world.

In 2020, the COVID-19 pandemic showcased Western democracies' systematic failure to prepare for a "precedented" threat. It cost too many lives that could have been saved, along with damaged societies and economies that may take decades to turn around. Moreover, the pandemic exposed the malfunctions of current economic, regulative, legislative, and democratic institutional models. The poor got poorer and the rich got richer on never-before-seen scales. The pandemic also crystalized that the cyber security, resiliency, and continuity strategies, structures, solutions, and defenses accepted as gospel today are no longer fit for the purposes of defending the nation nor protecting its citizens.

You will discover in my book why I am fully justified to give special attention to Western democracies' failures, instead of treating all models' failures equally. While reading my book and after, every reader anywhere in the world will have the opportunity to start considering—better still, questioning—their own government's failures to prepare for a mere virus that was highly and imminently expected.

How ready is your government for more than a billion devices entering the internet every quarter, with little or no attention to security or patching? How ready are they for fake news, false narratives, Purposed Disinformation™, special interest, corruption, election meddling, extremism, cyber and non-cyber terrorism, biotech warfare, the quantum computing supremacy race, and the devastation and seismic consequences of ever-growing and unrelenting GPCyber™ attacks, all happening at the same time?

For those of you who think your government is ready for all these risks happening simultaneously, I have a certain bridge from Brooklyn to sell you ...

From experience, I truly believe all of them are totally unready. And guess who ends up paying the price of such failures? The citizens of the world.

As an ordinary citizen, what are you going to do about it?

As a top business or government decision maker, what will you do about it?

Are you willing to bet your house that your national sovereignty or corporate security and your competitiveness and effectiveness are well protected by continuing to exclusively rely on strategies and solutions that keep failing?

Are you willing to bet your own nest egg and the kids' college fund that becoming compliant with laws and regulatory requirements and following "best practices" are sufficient in helping you mitigate GPCyber™ threats? Will they be enough to avoid you being devastated by their attacks?

This book explores all these very scenarios with fact-based cases and specific chapters that focus on key sectors and stakeholders that are under clear and present danger. Along the way, I also delve into possible ways forward. But most of all, to cement the point that safeguarding nation-states, governments, organizations, and citizens today has less to do with cyber security, know now that it has everything to do with Survivability.

A MUCH-NEEDED PIVOT (AND A POLITELY REFUSED OPPORTUNITY)

In the early '90s, I was headhunted and hired by an American multinational corporation to join its senior executive management team to fix major issues it was having in its operations in Middle East countries. The company was RJR Nabisco, a global, fast-moving goods company. Just imagine, they hired a cigarette nonsmoker and put him in charge of their tobacco business operations (although I will admit I was an occasional cigar smoker).

My out-of-the-box thinking, problem-solving, and management style resulted in great successes in a very short time. This also turned some dinosaur-thinking bosses into enemies worrying about their own jobs because of a new rising star. Something else was also happening. Inadvertently, I became known as a tobacco expert instead of an international market development expert.

I did not like being in the tobacco sector despite the great rewards and successes I was experiencing. My role was very well paid and rewarded, as I was managing existing markets and creating new distribution channels, not only in the Middle East but also in Eastern Europe. Then one day something happened ...

My son, who was born and raised in Los Angeles, was about five years old at the time. When he saw me smoke a cigar, well, he was very unambiguous in what he told me. He said that smoking would kill me and that he did not want me to die on him.

It was at that time that I decided I needed a new focus and challenge in my life and career. By the mid-'90s, I had decided to give up first-class corporate travel, amazing perks and bonuses, and a phenomenal senior executive salary, not knowing yet where I would get involved. That's right, I made my exit without knowing where I was going next. However,

I decided my new direction needed to have the following criteria at its core:

1. It needs to have an innovation and technology focus.
2. It must give me the ability to have my finger on the pulse of people/citizens/consumers on an international scale.

I decided to travel the world and attend shows, conferences, and events having to do with these focuses, not knowing what I would find. I attended many regional and international technology shows in Europe, the Far East, the Middle East, and the US. One of those key shows was the Consumer Electronics Show (CES) in Las Vegas. My first one was in 1994 or 1995. Back then, part of CES was the porn expo. Yes, you guessed it—businessmen walking the CES halls looking for the latest tech gadgets while stumbling upon porn stars promoting their latest movies and businesses. Most people may or may not know that the porn industry was one of the first adopters and enablers of the internet in its early days.

Later that year, new friends came to me proposing I join some of the very lucrative new ventures they had started. They were already making millions of dollars and wanted me to join them as both an investor and a leading executive. As tempting as it was, I declined their offers, wishing them well, saying that neither the sector nor the businesses they were in were for me.

Have you guessed what the businesses were?

They were in online porn.

Many of them ended up making not just millions but hundreds of millions. Some were even making billions as they were creating new industries. My reasons for saying, "No, not for me, thank you" were clear, and I do not regret that decision for a moment regardless of the untold financial wealth it was creating. I told them that although I am not a religious man, I consider myself a spiritual person. I said that I could not profit and feed my son from money that was generated at the expense of the exploitation of many of the women who worked in that industry.

I recall one of them saying that they were creating opportunities for many of these women who did this type of work out of choice. My clear rebuttal was that, while that may be the case, many of these women may not have chosen porn careers if they had better choices, environments, education, homes, and role models in their lives. To me it was a moral issue I imposed only on myself. I was and remain now clear-minded not to judge others on choices they make. I politely declined their proposal, and we moved forward in our separate ways with good wishes.

In those days, the internet was also known as the "information superhighway." This became a key initiative of the White House of the Clinton administration in the mid-'90s. It was President Bill Clinton's initiative that resonated strongly with me.

Back then, the internet was a military defense project that worked with a handful of universities to create a communication model and mechanism for the military. That system was based on the ASCII character set (that's American Standard Code for Information Interchange). For the non-techie, ASCII is in essence a version of the English alphabet. It was designed in the early '60s as a standard character set for computers and electronic devices. ASCII is a 7-bit character set containing 128 characters. It contains the numbers 0–9, the upper- and lower-case English letters from A to Z, and some special characters.

I talk about such concepts and my involvement in more detail in Chapter 2 (specifically, important developments in 2012). Nonetheless, as I looked deeper into the Clinton White House's vision and plan, I realized that the internet architectural design would essentially exclude people in countries all over the world who do not speak English.

None of the early internet pioneers foresaw it becoming what it is today. Neither did President Clinton or leaders in his administration. I did, and I also had an impossible, improbable dream and vision. I asked myself, *What if this internet thing can be made accessible to people all over the world so they can have information at their fingertips—in their own native language? What benefits can it offer them and their local societies?*

Let me confess, I had no answers for these questions—not yet, anyway. Then in 1999, a new not-for-profit organization was set up by the White House to be overseen by the US National Telecommunications and Information Administration (NTIA). This function was established within the US Department of Commerce—the Executive Branch agency that is principally responsible for advising the US president on telecommunications and information policy issues. And its new created nonprofit got called "ICANN" (Internet Corporation for Assigned Names and Numbers).

The US administration created it to become a private-sector-led organization and initiative to manage the names and numbers of the internet functions. It would specifically manage the IANA functions

(Internet Assigned Numbers Authority), the crown jewels of the global internet functions that the US managed and controlled. The IANA entails the global DNS Root, IP addressing, and other internet protocol resources that the White House wanted ICANN to manage. Its core functions include domain names management of the DNS Root Zone as well as assignments of countries of their own country code top-level domain (ccTLDs)—like .uk for United Kingdom, or .fr for France, as well as generic top-level domains (gTLDs) like .com, .net, and a few others back then. Recently, new gTLDs have reached a thousand or so.

Nevertheless, ICANN's mandates were clear—

To only manage internet names and numbers.

That's all. It was given clear mandates *not* to get involved in the content of the internet.

I hope I did not lose you too much with all this tech lingo. But I think this background is important. And I can confidently tell you that very few people can call themselves founders, fathers, mothers, or early stewards of this new organization called ICANN. It is with humility that I tell you I am one of those few.

WE CAN ...

In the early ICANN days most, if not all, participants were techie geeks. This included some amazingly smart women. The beginning of my ICANN engagement made me learn that the internet was built on a technical architecture that could not function to serve anyone who did not speak English, or a European language that uses Roman letters (aka, the English alphabet). In layperson's terms, back then, the URL you typed in your internet browser could work only if the letters you typed were from the English A–Z set. This flaw meant that billions of the world's non-English-speaking users would be left outside of the human empowerment tool (this was about a decade before Steve Jobs, another fellow Syrian, would invent Apps and revolutionize the internet with his little finger).

I started looking deeper. And that's when I saw major flaws that needed to be addressed if this new tool would help people and communities around the world whose languages were not English- or Latin-based (such as Chinese, Korean, Arabic, Urdu, Farsi, and many others that are used round the world) and who need empowering most. In essence, I recognized that two things needed to be addressed for the internet to become effectively multilingual: (1) its domain naming and addressing, and (2) the way it ought to govern itself.

The internet needs to give local communities the empowering tools and transparencies to govern themselves locally, regionally, and internationally. My ideas and motivations opened the door for me to launch an international drive in 1999–2000 to turn the internet into a Multilingual Internet. The motto was simple:

The world had one of two options to make the internet global and multilingual.

1. Teach the world English
2. Multi-lingualize the internet, based on the values of local empowerment

Option 1 would be a colonial revival that everyone would naturally reject outright. Option 2 was clearly what I had in mind. I made this strategic push not only within ICANN but also within the United Nations and the International Telecommunication Union (ITU), a UN family member. ITU and the UN were also the global leaders, hosts, and organizers of the UN's World Summit on Information Society (WSIS) 2001–2005.

I became a key player and outspoken spokesman and visionary at the UN and its WSIS forum. I was a champion of the cause of a Multilingual Internet that has local empowerment of these communities at its core. My argument was that without local, transparent, and democratic representations of these communities as a core value, we would not be able to claim it as being either democratic or truly representative of their people.

To be frank, in conversation with world leaders and government ministers and ambassadors at WSIS events, I seldom got any pushback on the noble aspirations I was putting forth for this imaginary "Global Multilingual and Interoperable Internet" I was calling for. Many could not believe that I had no vested interest in its creation. In fact, many became stronger believers upon knowing this was pure philanthropy for me to make the world a better place.

I also recognized that something else had to be done. The world needed a charter, a document like the Declaration of Independence in the US (or the Magna Carta a few hundred years prior). A global mandate was missing. One that would be underwritten and legitimized by the

United Nations. One that would have governments of the world not only sign up to it—but just like internationally binding treaties are today—one that they would be committed to.

In December 2003, one of my proudest moments was securing a critically important clause on multilingualism of the internet be included in the United Nations Declaration of Principles. To put this achievement in its proper value and context, it is worth noting the requirements established. For the entire declaration and any of its clauses to pass and be adopted by the United Nations, all participating governments must agree on the full text without any one single government objecting to any part or word it contains.

Suffice it to say that Clause 48 of this UN declaration states:

> The Internet has evolved into a global facility available to the public and its governance should constitute a core issue of the Information Society agenda. The international management of the Internet should be multilateral, transparent and democratic, with the full involvement of governments, the private sector, civil society and international organizations. It should ensure an equitable distribution of resources, facilitate access for all and ensure a stable and secure functioning of the Internet, taking into account multilingualism.

That last part—"taking into account multilingualism"—brings to mind a significantly special story that is worth telling one day as to how I got a major obstructing nation to change its position that made the clause and the declaration possible. The fact is, I achieved what I set out to accomplish. What is now part of human history is that this Declaration of Principles became part of human history the moment it had over 100 countries sign it.

Many asked me then and continue asking today, "What's the big deal about it? Why was this so important?" The UN Declaration of Principles is no less important than the first-ever declaration of human rights that was decreed 4,000 years ago by Assyrian King Hammurabi. This is because it recognized and established the right of local communities for their self-determination and their democratic representation on the internet.

In essence, it is the first-ever human rights "self E-determination" declaration. And my fingerprints were all over it being born. This very "multilingualism" clause in the Declaration of Principles became the mandate for ICANN to internationalize itself and its functions, and to multilingualize the Domain Name System (DNS) to start being able to accept non-ASCII domain names as part of a locally managed and operated Multilingual Internet.

I served and still serve on many committees within ICANN, such as the President's Advisory Committee on International Domain Names (IDN). I'm sad to say that I truly believe ICANN failed miserably to fulfill on this original mandate and its obligations and responsibilities given to it by the WSIS Declaration of Principles of 2003 and its outcome documents of 2005. In and of itself, perhaps this will need a deep-dive, reveal-all book down the line.

Fundamental, and at the core of all my engagements, was making sure that all technical standards and architecture of the global internet and all changes we were considering ensured that the security, stability, and resiliency of all internet function and architecture were maintained. From my roots, there were many factors driving me in this cause. And on that note, let's take another step back through time for readers who are keen to know about my heritage and childhood.

MY PAST

I can tell you that before I turned 16, my family was forced to leave the country we were in and uproot ourselves, twice. Both times, we left out of fear for our lives. And before I was 21, a third move was in my tarot cards.

I was born in Syria. My father was a prominent journalist and publisher. He was also the youngest to be elected to a newly formed parliament when Syria and Egypt briefly united as one country in the '50s.

My mother's uncle was the former president of Syria, Nazem Al-koudsi. Nazem was democratically elected. He had also served as prime minister, speaker of the House of Parliament, and leader of a political party.

My mother's side of the family were large feudal landowners for centuries. All their land was nationalized in the '60s. My immediate family was what would be considered today as middle class.

I was raised in a highly intellectual household thanks to my father's influence. He was a journalist and publisher in days when Syria was going through coups d'état as frequently as seasons. This meant that he was in and out of prison routinely and had the torture marks on his body for the remainder of his life.

In 1963, he was taken to prison, but this time not just torture awaited. He was to be summarily executed within a day or two. Overnight, a new group of military officers organized another coup against the government that was in power, overthrew it, and took over control of the government in Syria. It was Dad's luckiest day of his life.

The new prison commander turned out to be a best friend from high school. He told Dad that he was going to cause a mistake that would get him released—and that this mistake wouldn't be discovered for another 24 hours. He arranged a passport for my father and told him not to go home but escape straight to Beirut, Lebanon, immediately.

So it was in late 1963 that Dad escaped and arrived in Lebanon. My mom, my sisters, and I left Syria permanently in 1964, with the clothes on our backs, to be reunited with him. I was only four.

In Lebanon, we had the most amazing life you could imagine. We attended schools that would rival the best in UK, Switzerland, or the US. I was raised in our intellectual household in what was known as the Paris of the Middle East. Then the Lebanese civil war started in 1974.

Our home was in an affluent Beirut suburb. It got shelled and burnt to the ground in 1975. Luckily, my dad was already established in London, England. That's when my parents made the decision for us to permanently leave the Middle East and move to London.

As a Mediterranean teenager, growing up in London was good but not easy. I was used to daily sunshine and warmth, like what people are used to in Los Angeles or San Francisco. Now, in the winter, the sun would not rise until after 9 a.m., when I had risen, dressed, and arrived at school. That's if I was lucky. The dark would set in by 3 p.m. or thereabouts. Added to that, the cold and constant wet weather made for damp experiences imprinted in my memory banks. Don't start feeling sorry for me—I loved growing up in London and had amazing experiences. Nevertheless, somewhere else was calling me.

I always dreamt that one day I would go to the US—Hawaii, surely, and Los Angeles specifically, to visit Malibu's beaches. I remember seeing Malibu in TV shows in the '60s and '70s. I never thought this would really happen one day.

I had friends who lived in LA. I asked them to advise me on how to apply to go to university in California, and they did. So, in 1979, I started sending applications to California universities. I got accepted by Stanford and UCLA to start in September 1981. However, USC had accepted me to start nine months earlier, in January 1981. I picked USC because I could get to the US sooner, and I consider myself fortunate that my dad was willing and able to cover it.

MY PRESENT

So, before turning 21, I had embarked on two forced life-changing moves, and I chose to pursue a third. All of which meant saying goodbye to people in one place to start a new life somewhere else. Today, I am the founder and chairman of the MLi Group. And for those who see it already, yes, you guessed it! MLi stands for Multilingual Internet. We started using MLi exclusively more than a decade ago because people assumed we were only a translation company. On that note, I actually did own a translation company called Live Multilingual Translator, more than 15 years ago (a story for another time).

Long before Google or Facebook, MLi was the first to allow users to read English news and other websites translated into Arabic with full grammar and syntax, and better than 90% accuracy, at the click of a button. Arabic readers could start reading such front pages as those found in *Time* magazine, *The Guardian*, and many others, and they would read entire articles. In comparison, Google translator's results would make the reader give up after reading two lines due to its incoherence.

In 2012, MLi Group was conducting a major study of the internet usability of the communities that use the Arabic script worldwide. The total size of that market was 1.2 billion users. Of them, 27% were already online. That's more than 300 million internet users who contributed zero to their local digital economy, let alone the global one.

I often talk in great detail about the seminars we conducted in many capitals around the world and the many ministers and regulators I personally interviewed, as well as the online surveys we conducted in many languages. But above all, I often share our eureka moment (more on this in Chapter 2), the discovery that we made during that study that would change not only my future but perhaps the immediate future of the world and the challenges it is struggling to mitigate today. This more than influenced the strategies, solutions, and services MLi Group has been able to develop and offer to businesses and governments ever since.

Today, the MLi Group is the creator and worldwide leader in Cyber- and Non-Cyber Survivability and Security Mitigation Strategies, Solutions, and Services. We help and guide government and business top decision makers in mitigating the latest national and corporate risks—especially GPCyber™ attacks and threats. GPCyber™ motivations are political, ideological, extremist, geopolitical, and "religious." They differ from financially motivated cyberattacks in magnitude, impact, and damage, as well as mitigation strategies and solutions. Some of the key perpetrators of GPCyber™ devastation/destruction-motivated cyberattacks are the new breed of extremist and terrorist groups—lone wolves who are often directed or backed by not only enemies but by presumed allies. The latter can often be more damaging than threats from rogue states.

I will talk in great detail about GPCyber™ risks in upcoming chapters. For now, know that we predicted where everything has changed on society. That's why Survivability Strategies™ and GPCyber™ were created back in 2012–2013. Since then, we have developed to the forefront of mitigation across many different industries. Today, MLi Group and many of its subsidiaries offer an array of strategic and operational services, such as:

- National Cyber-Survivability Strategies with a Legislative Road Map™
- Comprehensive Cyber-Security & Survivability Risk Audits & Pen Testing™
- Corporate Cyber-Survivability™ Strategies with Operating Plan™
- Geo-Poli-Cyber™ Vulnerability Risk Assessment & Training™ Levels 1 to 5
- Geo-Poli-Cyber™ Risk Audits
- Geo-Poli-Cyber™ Incident Response & Communication Audits
- Chief Survivability Officer™ (recruitment and training)
- Financial Institutions Due Diligence Processes Audit™
- IoT, Smart Cities & Buildings Survivability Risk Audit™
- Cyber-Survivability™ vs. Cyber-Security – Government & Board Private Briefings

- Survivability Cyber Insurance Risk Audits
- Thought Leadership keynotes at major expos and conferences as well as private board briefings

In 2020, we launched *Survivability News.* Soon after, in 2021, we launched *Survivability Wealth Management*™ as the only place for Geo-Poli-Cyber™ Risk Mitigation for M&A (mergers and acquisitions), Sovereign, Wealth, Hedge Funds and Private Equity, Geo-Political International Property Investment Portfolios, and other Investment Vehicles, which cyber security alone cannot mitigate. Also in 2021, we started *Survivability Recruitment*, because strategic survivability awareness, and the necessary leadership, expertise, and human talent, are critically missing at the top of government and corporate decision-making.

> **NOTE:** More offerings regarding business subsidiaries, operations, and disciplines are to be announced soon after this publishing. Also, at the end of the book, I will share more on my investigative program "The Era of the Unprecedented," which I created in 2016–2017.

Today, from my time with MLi, I can tell you that the era of the dinosaur mindset and management style never went extinct. It remains the current mode of operation in the 21st century, putting us all under unprecedented threat. Business models are still unashamedly implementing what continues to fail routinely. And regulation is as effective as wet lettuce, while our focus is on the wrong things.

Although our clients are corporations and governments, I make a concerted effort with significant budgets used to inform and educate the general public. To me, it is not about profitability but ensuring the survival of our humanity. While preventing human extinction is a very worthy goal, ensuring humanity does not lose its humanity hits a little closer to home for me. If anything, I would like to see this book change the mindset at all levels of society. Only then can we salvage the cherished democracy from its stage four cancer and the wars we claim to have launched many times in the past to allegedly safeguard and protect it back home.

Leaders in politics and corporations (i.e., top decision makers) need to recognize that serious change is needed, not tweaks. Beyond that, we also require prompt action with truly new directions. Whether citizens feel the pain or not, their lives and livelihoods are directly affected first and foremost. And they look to leadership to keep their best interests in mind.

Leaders reading this book will face serious questions throughout the chapters ahead. I want them contemplating this during their experience:

How can you convert the unprecedented risks explored in this book into a competitive advantage for your nation, organization, or your people?

COMPLEX YET OPTIMISTIC

As far as the structure of my book, it has been set into three parts:

I. The New Era of the Unprecedented (A Seismic Shift in the Global Cyber and Non Cyber Threat Landscape)
II. Modern Vulnerabilities (Ten Sectors Under Unprecedented Threat)
III. An Unprecedented Threat to Humanity and Democracy

In Part I, I will address the New Era of the Unprecedented. It begins with moments that changed everything (events of 2010 and 2012). I then dig deeper into what changed after those moments. I specifically address how organized cybercrime and GPCyber™ terrorism converged, putting us all "nine meals from anarchy." This part ends on the emergence of technological breakthroughs (artificial intelligence [AI], machine learning, and fake news), as well as the new phenomenon I've coined as "Allyversaries™." As our relationships change, country to country, we continue a silent and undeclared WWIII through such events as quantum computing and the false narrative of cyber supremacy.

In Part II, I've researched ten sectors under unprecedented threat. This includes Critical National Infrastructure (CNI) as a whole, IoT and "smart" technology, Smart Environments and Cities, the cloud itself, Banking & Financial, Telecommunications, Transport, Marine & Shipping, Aviation, and Cyber Insurance. By the end of this part, my goal is making it abundantly clear that the leadership behind regulations and mitigation are putting their stakeholders (including us, the citizens) "three meals from anarchy."

Part III is where I address how the aggregate of Parts I and II is a compelling argument that both humanity and democracy are now under unprecedented threat. Survivability becoming the very concern of every citizen on this planet, not just for top decision makers, is vital. This is even more so for those of us who are citizens of the US and Western democracies.

Why? you might ask.

It is because we live in nations where our civil liberties and all kinds of freedoms—including free speech and the right to peacefully dissent against our own governments—are enshrined by constitution and/or guaranteed by laws and regulations. If we don't step up to protect these rights and liberties while we enjoy all these constitutional guarantees, then we do not deserve to have them in the first place. Nor can we expect others who live under oppression to fix this cancer for themselves or us.

If we do not become better informed about some of the symptoms of special interest, we will never be able to see how and why they are a threat to democracy, nor how they corrupt leaderships. My hope is that Part III will drive the point home. We are told our concerns should lie with obvious enemies. Unfortunately, our problems are far more domestic than we'd like to believe. Left to its ongoing failures, the broken system will only further perpetuate cycles of destruction and devastation.

All of this said, I would like to close on the following thought. Before I leave you to start reading Chapter 1, please let me tell you that I am a true realist and an eternal optimist. My realism stems from knowing the facts that I will share with you in this book. I would not have taken the huge time and effort to write and document these unprecedented failings I am observing if I did not believe that there is hope. Moreover, my optimism is not based on mere hope but on a real way forward to benefit people, society, and humanity combined.

The challenge facing each and every one of you is whether you can accept the new reality or if you can afford to accept the consequences. The present is dire, and the future seems to be more of the same, or worse, unless we do something different. Together, informed and active—but above all, capable of critical thinking—we can in fact bring the real change we need to see to save ourselves and so much more. Let us acknowledge the past, understand the present, and build the survivability of many tomorrows to come.

Throughout the book, I've created these text boxes to provide further reading and opportunities for you to connect with MLi Group and *Survivability News*. My intention is to help us all become more engaged citizens, and through these resources, I hope we can create the real change needed by the world today.

survivabilitythebook.com

PART I

The New Era of the Unprecedented

(A Seismic Shift in the Global Cyber and Non Cyber Threat Landscape)

1

Moments That Changed Everything

(The Birth and Rise of Systematic, Politically Motivated Cyberattacks)

IN 1989, NASA was about to launch its *Galileo* spacecraft with the ambitious goal of studying Jupiter and its moons. At the time, *Galileo* was seen as highly controversial for being a nuclear-powered satellite. Bear in mind that the world was just emerging from the Cold War, so anxiety over nuclear weapons would be understandably high—plus, the added stress of the mid-launch explosion of the *Challenger* shuttle less than four years previous. With prospects of another shuttle disaster carrying nuclear cargo, there were fears that an explosive launch could cause radioactive fallout over Florida.

In the midst of debates and concerns, NASA announced multiple cancellations of the much-anticipated launch. Concerns were valid, and research and precautions were well worth taking. However, what became clear after the fact was that days before the final launch date, NASA's DECnet computer network had been compromised by the WANK Worm. The creation of this virus is attributed to Melbourne-based hackers; the Australian Federal Police attributed its creation to two monikers, Electron and Phoenix.

Many readers might fall into the trap of linking "WANK" to British slang, "wanking." Wrong, you dirty-minded people. In this case, WANK was an acronym for "Worms Against Nuclear Killers." The hack itself was an apparent attempt to cause mayhem in advance of the controversial launch of the *Galileo* spacecraft. It succeeded. Many believe one of the hackers may have been none other than Julian Assange, which he denies to this day.

WANK may have first appeared in NASA, but it did not stay there. Workers soon found their computers affected across the world, including:

- The US: Department of Energy
- Switzerland: The European Organization for Nuclear Research (CERN)
- Japan: Institute of Physical and Chemical Research (RIKEN)

Overall, the effects of this worm could be compared to vandalism. At worst, it appeared to delete files, but this was revealed to just be a visual trick. While it was concerning, WANK was an inconvenience, with political statements and snippets of lyrics and quotes spliced throughout its code. As New Zealand was the only nuclear-free zone, according to the hackers, it was the only country spared of chaos. And beyond the scope of WANK's international spread, there is something that makes it and its creators unprecedentedly unique:

It was the first known non-financially, Geo-Poli-Cyber™ (GPCyber™) motivated attack.

WATERSHED MOMENTS

Decades after 1989, in 2010 and 2012, two more watershed moments occurred, kickstarting a seismic shift in the global threat landscape. In 2010, an Iranian nuclear power plant was cyberattacked. Two years later, this event was followed by another cyberattack on a Saudi Arabian oil company, Aramco.

These most recent attacks correspond with the early days of one of the most horrific extremist and terrorist organizations, by the name of Daesh (or as you would know it, ISIS). I'll share more on this in Chapter 18, in Part III. For now, I will say that Daesh rose to Western infamy in 2013. During the Iraq War, seemingly out of the blue, an unknown force mobilized tens of thousands of fighters out of Syria and coordinated with other followers in Iraq. In a matter of a few weeks, Daesh occupied a third of Iraq, including its second largest city, Mosul.

The 2010 and 2012 watershed moments, in combination with the rise of Daesh, amounted to the perfect storm of everything to come for the next decade. This created a new trend of cyberattacks motivated by politics, ideology, extremism, or "religion." And the regional communities were not prepared for this development—nor was the rest of the world, as we can see from the last eight years. However, before I get ahead of myself, let's dive into the specifics of 2010.

In early January, the inspectors of the International Atomic Energy Agency were visiting the Natanz uranium enrichment plant in Iran. They noticed centrifuges used to enrich uranium were failing at a significant rate. It was a complete mystery to the inspectors, as it was to the Iranian technicians themselves. A few months later, an Eastern European security company was called in to troubleshoot what was going on. They discovered a handful of malicious files were installed on one of the systems.

The Iranian nuclear power plant was infected with the Stuxnet Worm. While it is widely believed that Stuxnet was developed by the US and Israel, neither of them has admitted to this officially. Nevertheless, where the WANK Worm of 1989 seemingly deleted files through visual gags, Stuxnet not only accessed information, it could steal it. At that, this worm could start and reboot targeted computers.

In this case, with computers crashing and rebooting repeatedly, the hacking of the Iranian plant caused the centrifuges to act erratically, creating excessive heat, which caused serious damage. In turn, this effect delayed Iran's ambitions for nuclear power by at least ten years. Similarly to WANK, if the Stuxnet hackers' goal was to delay or disrupt Iran's plans, they succeeded. One could say that Stuxnet itself was in fact the first digital weapon of its kind.

DESTRUCTION & DEVASTATION MOTIVATION

The unprecedented trend of Stuxnet and the Iranian hack (as well as the Aramco attack, plus the birth of Daesh) exhibits a clear destruction motivation. These events created a seismic shift in cyber warfare whereby financial motivation was no longer the primary cause for why these things were happening. Now we have new political, ideological, "religious," and extremist motivations—including the desire to perpetrate maximum damage/destruction of the target wherever possible.

It is worth noting that both the hack of Iran's nuclear reactor and the cyberattack of Aramco could not have happened without the direct involvement of nation-states. Again, these attacks were in 2010 and 2012. This is significant because until then, while extremist groups may have had the motivation, they did not have the expertise or resources to actually cause havoc on such a large scale through cyberattacks.

This is a serious concern, and its degree of real terror is rising. Even more significant is the rise of ISIS and its desire to cause maximum damage or destruction through cyber means on its targets for political purposes. Initially, this left many of us embracing the thought that all of this was temporary and quickly fading out of the big picture. Such unfounded optimism is understandable—but unacceptable. Despite any recent defeats in which ISIS suffered significant setbacks and defeats in Syria, Iraq, and many other parts of the world where they were previously quite prominent, the US and its allies' unprecedented and embarrassing failure in the shambolic withdrawal from Afghanistan left a huge vacuum for the group to resurge and wreak havoc upon the world by all means available.

Here, I must caution decision makers and readers alike: Do not fall into the above false sense of security. I want you to imagine a husband and wife with a child. The child is diagnosed with an advanced case of cancer. What will this husband and wife do? Well, they will more than likely commit to doing their utmost to attempt to save their child and provide as much comfort as possible. But then the cancer reaches extremes, metastasizes, and the child dies. What do you imagine happening next? It's not as if the parents suddenly return to a normal life. In fact, what made these parents focus on the child is the metaphor I use regarding this subject when making presentations to corporate and government leaders around the world.

ISIS was focused on fulfilling its version of an Islamic Caliphate in its evil quest throughout Syria, Iraq, and other parts of the world. Historically, the Islamic Empire was ruled by a Caliphate (like a king) and, much like rulers of many historic empires, the Caliphates came in dynasties. ISIS wanted to resurrect the glory days of an Islamic Empire through a Caliphate system. For perspective, the Islamic Empire extended as far as Spain in the early eighth century for seven centuries—where most science, literature, astronomy, etc., used in the West today originated.

At peak Islamic influence, the world gained algebra as well as astronomy, improved medicine, and improved hygiene via indoor plumbing.

However, at peak resurrection, ISIS wanted to rebrand Islam to be associated with beheadings. Nevertheless, ISIS's vision of a Caliphate materialized by way of force and high numbers. If ISIS is the parents, then the Caliphate is their cancered child—and parties all over the world have been attempting to kill their baby. In the last couple of years, while it would appear that local and international forces have soundly defeated the ISIS-made Caliphate, the failures of Western allies in Afghanistan significantly undermined this. Do you think these people will stop what they're doing in the wake of a military defeat? If you do, then you're seriously mistaken.

In fact, even before its "defeat," ISIS already woke up to discover that the most impactful way it could cause damage or wreak havoc on the world was through cyber means. And that's exactly what it has been doing. Over the years, there were numerous cases of attacks on soft or vulnerable targets. In most cases, while hackers repeatedly claim their attacks on behalf of the "Digital Caliphate" (or ISIS), I believe many of the perpetrators are in truth lone wolves who want to associate with ISIS. And, contrary to any optimism on the subject, our risk of such cyberattacks will not decrease now that the Caliphate has been destroyed. The "parents" are in violent grief, and the risk will increase in number and sophistication owing to their thirst for revenge against all parties involved with the death of their "baby."

These events have led to a very important cataclysm: the birth of systematic, politically motivated cyberattacks. This phenomenon should force a prompt rethink of risk, mitigation, and remediation considerations by government and corporate leadership. As of 2010, destruction-focused, non-financially motivated (ideological, political, religious, extremists, etc.) cyberattacks are the new norm, for which society has no effective solutions. Unfortunately, even by 2020, the world still lacked necessary mechanisms or regulatory frameworks.

How do nation-states mitigate these threats from other nations? Most often, upon any suspicion of another nation-state perpetrating cyberattacks, many leverages can be exerted including economic sanctions, cutting off political ties, exerting pressure with their allies, and so on. Within certain political corridors, traditional strategies could actually push the perpetrator to recognize that their methods won't be tolerated. However, how can nation-states mitigate these threats from hidden or otherwise inaccessible organizations when there is no feasible way of impacting or retaliating against them?

I want you to imagine a rogue group. You have no idea where they're established. There is no information by way of headquarters, membership, or leaders. All you know is that they are inspiring digital lone wolves to become perpetrators for their cause. How do you enforce such a thing? How do you stop their attacks? Well, in blunt terms, you can't.

Destruction-motivated cyberattacks are a new threat. Due to modern perpetrators' abilities to stay hidden, these attacks aren't mitigatable through the traditional approaches—be they cyber security, resiliency, or continuity solutions/strategies. Good luck to us all. The world stands to endure more damage and carnage than what we've seen with financially motivated attacks. This is especially so when assaults are aligned with propaganda, fake news, or misinformation storylines that could actually create a new way of thinking within the general population. And this is where the threat is magnified.

In terms of lives and livelihoods, the cost is too high for humanity to bear. And that cost is driven by the stubbornness of 20th-century dinosaurs insisting on the continual use of their strategies and solutions in the 21st century. After 2020, I imagine most citizens around the world can see that the problem is systemic and these issues lead to catastrophic ramifications. We continue to witness unprecedented failures in the methods used by our leaders to defend government installations, critical national infrastructure, and organizations. The results of this systematic failure are debilitating to citizens and consumers all over the world, and this new form of cyberattack will only continue to be on the rise.

THE WATERSHED CONTINUES (FROM IRAN TO SAUDI ARABIA, WITH SHAMOON)

In 2012, two years after the Stuxnet attack in Iran, Saudi Arabia's national oil company, Aramco, was targeted. The cyberattack was set in motion when one of its employees simply clicked on a fake link in a mysterious email. They came face-to-face with the Shamoon virus, which promptly infected more than 30,000 company computers of the Saudi oil giant. From August 1 through August 15 of that year, the attack retrogressed company operations back to the Dark Ages. With screens going black, there was no communicating by email. Contracts would need to be faxed and signed page by page. Departments were no longer able to interface. One of the largest oil suppliers in the world had officially been curtailed.

The Shamoon virus is capable of spreading through stealing and erasing information. Once the hackers were inside, there was no stopping them on the original terminals. Aramco worked hard to get back to some form of normal. Ten days after their systems went dark, on August 25, they announced that business was resuming. This was premature. Throughout Aramco's attempts to rally, the hackers responsible released messages ensuring it was known that not only were they still inside, they also were well aware of sensitive information—including the CEO's password. It wasn't over just yet, no matter what the company claimed.

After allegedly using a private fleet of planes and seriously depleting worldwide hard drive inventories, Aramco did in fact accomplish some form of normal. However, even through September 1, there were lines of oil trucks unable to be filled due to the ongoing shutdown. While setting in place a safe and secure system, Aramco needed to ensure that speculation of the disruption did not affect oil prices. Meanwhile, resources were dwindling in Saudi Arabia itself, and even Qatar's oil company, RasGas, began dealing with a cyberattack of its own. In Shamoon we find a second digital weapon of its kind, following the wake of Stuxnet. In this chapter on cyberattacks, we find further examples of destruction motivation.

I want you to consider the magnitude of damage and the catastrophic implications from the cyber warfare on Iran and Saudi Arabia. Financially, there were resources required to both resolve and continue recovering from these unprecedented attacks. Over the course of the last decade, changes in infrastructure, system and mechanical repair, repeat attacks, and public relations efforts surely amounted to anywhere from $10 billion to hundreds of billions. And keep in mind, the hackers neither demanded nor received so much as a penny of that expense in the form of ransom. It was purely political. It was pure devastation. Their motivations were not financial, and the end result was as they intended. Never before had a national company or a business suffered a cyberattack on such a scale. And now, this has become the "new normal."

In the case of Aramco, speculation began surfacing as to whether or not Iran was the source of the Shamoon infection; however, no concrete evidence of that exists. By the same token, there is no concrete evidence as to Israel and the US being responsible for the Stuxnet hack of Iran. What remains conclusive is that both of these attacks did in fact take place, the damage was groundbreaking, the motivation had nothing to do with financial gain, and these events began the Era of the Unprecedented.

Of course, today and in the near future, you will still have opportunistic hackers using a denial-of-service (DoS) or distributed-denial-of-service (DDoS) hack to fund their criminal activity. Strategies against them by cyber security companies will remain the same, driving opportunity costs so high that the time and resource expenses will motivate attackers to redirect their efforts to a system that will require less time/effort to successfully hack. Such philosophies, traditions, and designs of cyber security solutions no longer serve the modern purpose. As I regularly tell clients in briefings, such old methods belong in the toilet, "and I recommend you flush multiple times."

In the new era, we now have hackers without opportunity costs or profits at the forefront of their minds. These modern perpetrators want to serve a higher goal. Some of them are aligned with the "parents" mourning their "baby." Others are merely the hands of government bodies, in which they are fulfilling a shadow role—at that, numerous agencies claim the higher goal of both freedom and democracy. Context aside, the politically motivated hacker is more than willing to do whatever it takes to serve their cause and breach targets fitting the political profile of their enemy—no matter how long it takes.

The emergence of these players should be most concerning. Their unmitigated attacks bring with them unprecedented collateral devastation. Beyond any effect on their target, in their "success" you'll soon witness drastic consequences upon people's lives and livelihoods, as well as the security and effective survivability of nation-states. The en masse arrival of such hackers has actually thrown cyber security strategies, solutions, and models into chaos. While these are no longer sufficient, it is still necessary for leaders and decision makers to implement their cyber security at the highest level of requirement and quality. However, relying solely on "gospel" cyber traditions will leave nations and organizations incapable of mitigation—and they may find themselves brought to their knees.

The 2010 and 2012 watershed moments were a seismic shift, unleashing a tsunami of Geo-Poli-Cyber™ attacks in the Era of the Unprecedented. In Chapter 2, not only will I further define politically motivated attacks and hackers, but I will name our new enemy. I will also share the intricate details of MLi Group's Internet Usability Study implemented in 2012. While we were not searching for it, we were the first in the Western world to discover early warnings of ISIS's destruction and devastation motivations through cyber means.

For more information, please visit survivabilitythebook.com/ placeholder (or scan the code below) to see articles referenced as well as my recommended reading list. We have been very lucky to have journalists with integrity on the case. I encourage you to explore how the world received this story.

2

The New Era of the Unprecedented

(What Changed After the Moments That Changed Everything?)

IN JUNE 2016, Robert Hannigan, the head of the GCHQ (UK equivalent of America's National Security Agency), spoke at the Cheltenham Science Festival. The following quote was used for headlines across the globe, including that of *The Telegraph* (UK): "Terrorists and rogue states are gaining the capability to bring a major city to a standstill with the click of a button." As more consumer goods (transport, appliances, toys, etc.) were being built to interact with "the internet of things," Hannigan was providing a warning as to terrorist groups seeking to take advantage of this technology. He said, "At some stage they will get the capability."

Later that year, in December, Alex Younger, the head of MI6 (the UK's Central Intelligence Agency equivalent), called for a press conference. Spy agency leaders are not typically in the business of being in the limelight nor do they like such public exposures. Nevertheless, as he addressed the press in his briefing, Younger specifically warned about the unprecedented threats facing the UK and its allies from Daesh/ISIS without the terrorist group "ever having to leave Syria."

These warnings were provided by the two most senior cyber, espionage, and defense figures in the UK. Hannigan and Younger were primarily focused on raising both awareness and concern levels as to attacks anticipated from ISIS via cyber developments rather than traditional terrorist activities. Together, six months apart, they made it clear that devastation was possible without ISIS crossing any borders, and this was enabled by modern technologies. However, it's worth noting that neither of them offered any solutions or remedies. Of course, they were happy to keep the narrative alive and well as to how we need to do more cyber security and what we need to implement. Their actual intention was warning government and business stakeholders of this new existential threat.

The question that should have been asked of Hannigan or Younger is how many businesses and government organizations decided to change traditional mitigation strategies in the face of new cyberthreats. The answer? Very few, if any. Also, what additional regulatory frameworks were added to mitigate these threats beyond 2016? Aside from the EU's General Data Protection Regulation (GDPR), none. And at that, GDPR specifically regards privacy, not survivability. To date, Hannigan's and Younger's warnings practically remain unaddressed.

In the New Era of the Unprecedented, the prospect of damage from these new threats will be totally different from the traditional risk exposures. Our systems are no longer exclusively menaced by financially motivated cyberattacks. From Chapter 1, the attacks in Iran and Saudi Arabia showcase how mitigation of 21st-century cyberthreats will no longer be fit for purpose if the same traditional mechanisms are followed.

Historically, organizations and decision makers operated under the belief that if the damage of a financially motivated cyberattack amounts to a few hundred thousand dollars, you don't trouble the CEO while he's playing his 18-hole game of golf. This belief is slamming the door on its way out. The damage of these new cyberattacks is much larger than hundreds of thousands or even a few million, and it affects more than the bank accounts of any business or its stakeholders.

The majority of decision makers either remain poorly advised or blissfully ignorant of this new era. The lack of innovative thinking, advice, direction, and solutions indicates to me that the models followed (be it cyber security, resiliency, or continuity) died with the dinosaurs. And the most significant concern is the manner in which budgets are appropriated in advance of any such attack.

Beyond the watershed moments of 2010 and 2012, damages are amounting to much more than mere millions, or even hundreds of millions. As I will elaborate in Part II of my book, we've seen devastation cost organizations and governments billions—which is the new normal, not the rare exception. At that, this is only measuring cost by dollars and cents, not the damage to society, people's lives and livelihoods, or business survivability.

AN UNEXPECTED DARK BLOB

On April 9, 2015, a significant event unfolded in France. Viewers around the world have access to a network of around a dozen French television stations—and this story begins with Channel 5. TV5 Monde was preparing for the launch of a new high-fashion station aimed at the Middle East market. From any behind-the-scenes specials and shows about making shows, you might be able to visualize preparation, arrangements, efforts, and the huge cost involved in their launch—only to be derailed by a virus. This unfortunate intrusion not only shut down the new TV channel that was to be launched—it literally shut down all 11 stations, along with their website.

I'm sure you can imagine the panic at their organization. One minute, they were enjoying the euphoria and adrenaline rush of launching a channel for half a billion viewers, and the next, they were a dark blob on a TV screen. And it didn't stop. The next minute, it was discovered that the perpetrators had breached their website as pro-ISIS and Cyber Caliphate images and messages were displayed for all to see—calling for Western forces to remove themselves from Syria.

On first glance, this appeared to be directly from the infamous terrorist organization. Later that year, by June, there was a media frenzy regarding French authorities investigating leads to APT28, a Russian hacker group. In 2016, this investigation/suspicion was confirmed by the BBC in its interview with Yves Bigot, the director-general of TV5 Monde. Much like the watershed moments of Chapter 1, real answers as to whodunit are still lingering on the cloud.

What we do know is the aggregate of methodology, result, and motivation made this a monumental incident. The hackers were already in TV5 Monde's system, as they were scouting through servers in January 2015. Using their intel, the perpetrators tailored a distributed-denial-of-service (DDoS) virus specific to their target. They took advantage of multiple entry point vulnerabilities, including a remote-controlled camera company operating from the Netherlands. And, similar to the attacks in Iran and Saudi Arabia, the endgame did not involve any form of ransom.

This was not just a cyberattack. This was a politically and ideologically motivated hack. If this were truly arranged by ISIS, the motivation was showcasing its devastation goals in an effort to stop France from further interfering in the Middle East. Simply put, this would qualify as an act of retaliatory warfare against Monde's home nation, regardless of whether you agree with it or not. At that, the scenario brings with it a secondary goal. The attack acts as a showcase of their ability to bring down major players of the Western societies, launching war upon them. In fulfilling a David and Goliath narrative, this creates opportunities for recruitment and inspiring further digital lone wolves.

If the perpetrators were Russian, as French authorities suspect, motivations behind the hack would remain non-financial. Much like their alleged US election interference, the goal of this incident would be destabilization. Such an event would inspire further suspicion upon Syrian and Middle Eastern refugees seeking asylum in Europe. In that context, it could also inspire some form of rebellion by way of turning these parties against each other to the point of domestic warfare. Nevertheless, the chaos would be destructive.

In either case, the motivation was pure devastation. And there was no way for TV5 Monde to prepare for mitigating the attack. Yves Bigot later explained that a few weeks prior to the DDoS appearing, the organization carried out a comprehensive cyber security audit on its entire network—and everything came out fantastically well. Clearly, that was not up to scratch. Despite a 10-out-of-10 result from their audit, the hackers managed to not only penetrate the system—rendering their regularly scheduled programming into a black screen blob—but they also caused unprecedented damage to its operations, to its bottom line, and to its reputation.

The end result for TV5 Monde should not be surprising. The comprehensive audit was following best practices according to the standard traditionally followed in securing your digital fortress. And according to that methodology, everything looked hunky-dory. If you implement dinosaur strategies, you get dinosaur tar pits ...

Yves Bigot and TV5 Monde can surely be forgiven in hindsight. Outside of Chapter 1's watershed moments (four to five years previous), these non-financially motivated attacks were still on the rise—and people should not be held accountable for failing to mitigate the unknown. Since then, warnings have been plentiful. After the attack on TV5 Monde, in 2016, we received numerous valuable insights, wrapped around words of caution from the likes of Alex Younger and Robert Hannigan. And yet our methods, strategies, and solutions received no adaptation or reform. Just as a nuclear power plant, a national oil company, and an international TV station crumbled, organizations and nation-states will face similar fates until something different is recognized, adopted, and followed.

The fundamentals have clearly changed. Here we now have a new breed of destruction- and devastation-motivated hackers who have no opportunity cost, and no ransom to be fulfilled. Their motivations are political, ideological, and religious—and they are willing to target specific organizations and nations for political ramifications. These perpetrators are more than capable, and their attacks cannot be mitigated through old cyber security, strategies, and models. In fact, more devastation is on the line, as a complete lack of opportunity cost means they will remain focused on their breach until their impact is delivered, their goal is satisfied—and their reward awaits them in heaven.

A WARNING (THE BYPRODUCT OF SEARCHING FOR A COMMON DENOMINATOR)

MLi Group and I have been involved in the global infrastructure of the internet since the '90s. My fingerprints are all over our contributions to making it the Multilingual Internet that it has partially become today. In 2012, unrelated to the watershed moments, we were conducting an internet usability study to identify common denominator opportunities pertaining to Arabic script communities around the world. Communities that use Arabic script include approximately 400–450 million Arabic speakers, 600 million Urdu speakers, and 100–125 million Farsi speakers (Iranian), as well as other languages like Pashto. In total, the Arabic script speaking population around the globe is estimated at between 1.1 and 1.2 billion people. Out of this, close to 300 million were already online in 2012.

Part of our motivation was driven by the fact that from that 300 million, practically no contributions were being made to the local/global digital economy; they were using it for social media, at best. The goal of the study was determining the common denominator, digital services that we could offer to these communities. Not only could we find a way to serve those populations, we could also gain access to untapped markets and unprecedented opportunities. This was about creating a new breed of entrepreneurs, improving local businesses, and empowering locals in improving their lives—all while developing even more opportunities. In short, social impact was at the core of our vision and strategy.

Our study included online questionnaires in six versions: Arabic, Urdu, and Farsi—and for each segment, there was a respective English option. MLi Group arranged events hosted by local partners and universities, and I conducted them. These took place in different capitals of each market, such as Beirut, Amman, Cairo, Tunis, Dubai, and many others. Outside of in-person events, we also organized many online events in order to receive feedback from important stakeholders.

Over the course of our events, I also interviewed many high-profile leaders. In every country hosting us, I personally met with local telecom regulators and ministers to ascertain their governments' sense of direction as to how they saw new phases of internet technologies and the regulatory framework they planned on implementing. Nevertheless, our study was quite comprehensive.

Eighty percent of what MLi Group learned, we already knew in advance. This was accounted for, as I was looking to identify the 20% outside of our awareness. My instinct was that it could be the distinguishing factor in any form of competitive advantage. And that's where the shock of my life presented itself. We uncovered a jaw-dropping, new, and unexpected revelation. Before any attack resembling that upon TV5 Monde, we identified an early form of Daesh (later to be known as ISIS), and their aspirations and plans to launch destruction-motivated cyberattacks on targets all over the world.

Discovering this daunting, gloomy reality was a game changer. If cyber warfare was headed toward destruction and devastation over financial gain, as perpetrated by extremist groups like Daesh, then nobody would be immune. Moreover, no organization was ready to survive this onslaught, and none of the current mitigation standards and models were capable of putting it in check.

I decided that the services we originally aimed to launch for these Arabic script communities would become a second priority. We immediately began formulating new cyber strategies as to how we could mitigate this new, unprecedented era. Thankfully, some of our existing services (such as analysis and briefings) could be repurposed and infused with what we started developing. Much of this was not new to me; however, initiating it would require morphing into the company we are today.

NAME IT (GEOPOLITICAL THREATS OF THE NEW ERA)

Do you recall the virtual breaches of Yahoo! and Marriott? I will share more on these stories in Part II, but let's take a moment to gain some perspective. For Yahoo!, the hackers were in its system for three years before it was discovered. In the midst of Verizon's purchase of the company, Yahoo!'s IT department stumbled across the ongoing attack. Both parties were in shock.

It was a similar situation for Marriott, in which the company purchased Starwood Hotels & Resorts for $13.6 billion with the best experts on due diligence. At minimum, these experts should have requested a cyber security audit as a condition of sale. Spoiler alert: they did not. So, in Marriott's case, it was after the fact when they discovered that the hackers had been sitting in Starwood's system for two years prior to the acquisition.

In both examples above, the hackers were already sitting inside, monitoring data, traffic, and usage of over 2.5 billion accounts in total. In Yahoo!'s case, the data of 2 billion customers was compromised, and for Marriott, it was about half a billion. As it was with the attacks in Iran, Saudi Arabia, and TV5 Monde, there was no ransom. Potentially, the attackers were harvesting sensitive data to be sold on the Dark Web—an anonymous and untraceable version of the internet, well used by terrorists and criminal organizations for illegal business—but any activity of such transactions has yet to be verified. Keep in mind that these companies had data from leaders and decision makers all over the world, and this would reveal confidential plans as to their whereabouts.

The destruction and devastation motivation of these attacks do not always manifest themselves in a manner that cyber security hacks often do. It is not rare that the target is a conduit for gathering intelligence or sensitive data to be leveraged in another attack altogether, where the consequences will be much more severe. For the attacks above, expert reports often misled government and corporate clients in concluding that no damage was sustained, because the stolen data did not appear to have been sold.

While these two examples do not directly illustrate the new motivations that should concern you, they do illustrate the sophistication and extraordinary qualities of attacks taking place in the New Era of the Unprecedented. Clearly, the cyber security, strategies, and solutions these companies were following—including "best of class" as well as "best practice"—were no longer fit for purpose. Both companies suffered serious losses as to their brand and share value because of the hacks. Had they been aware as to why they might be at risk, they could have at least discovered the attack sooner than during the process of acquisition. So, in simple terms, purely looking at the technical aspects of the attacks, traditional cyber security alone is no longer sufficient.

As I've stressed so far in this book, it is critical to look at the motivation of modern perpetrators targeting us; without this insight, no mitigation process will be sufficient. We need to become more proactive in methods of assessing how cyberattackers are constantly changing their approach in impacting stakeholders. If decision makers are able to measure their own risk exposure variables by way of geography, political climate, economics, and religion (and so on), it is only then that they will understand how and where they are being targeted. From there, any hope of mitigation will begin for leaders and their nation or organization.

If you can't name the threat, you can't mitigate the threat. This is exactly why MLi Group and I proceeded to create and use new labels in 2012 and 2013 based on the risk factors of geography and politics with regard to these new and unprecedented cyberattacks: Poli-Cyber™, and most importantly, Geo-Poli-Cyber™ (GPCyber™). And in terms of inspiring a clear vision for decision makers working with us, we needed it to become abundantly clear that "cyber security" is no longer the keyword. As such, we now use "Survivability" to clarify the actual goals. Please note, these terms were *not* developed for marketing purposes.

GPCyber™ attacks are perpetrated, directed, or inspired by the following:

1. Extremist ideology groups (such as ISIS/Daesh)
2. National security agencies (such as America's NSA, Russia's FSB or SVR, Britain's MI6, etc.)

3. Rogue states (as determined country to country, like US to North Korea)
4. Proxies (as in digital mercenaries working on behalf of any of the above parties)

Organizations do not fully understand to any significant depth how GPCyber™ attackers are targeting them, the extent of damage they can cause, or what motivates them to do so. Existing strategies involved in the creation of a technical fortress no longer work. In reality, no fortress remains impenetrable indefinitely, and none have remained standing in the last 2,000 years—decision makers need to stop assuming theirs will be any different. They also need to ask some vital questions:

- Where do we rank on being targeted by GPCyber™ (political, ideological, religious, etc.) extremists?
- What is the likelihood of them being able to impact/alter the political or economic direction of our nation, organization, institutions, or our people?

Many organizations are ill informed as to how all of these motivations directly and indirectly impact them. Without full awareness, governments and organizations are leaving themselves vulnerable to higher scales of damage than ever before. This directly threatens their Competitive Survivability as a complete lack of action prohibits any development of appropriate mitigation strategies, solutions, and policies. How can they act and mitigate accordingly without addressing new, external threats (meaning, beyond coding)? And without any such knowledge of those threats, how will they improve their internal or external policies, procedures, and solutions to mitigate GPCyber™ threats?

Please recall GCHQ leader Robert Hannigan's statement from the beginning of the chapter. Today, one individual can bring a city to its knees with a click of a button. Well, if they can do that to a city, odds are high that they can do the same to an entire nation. Think of the turmoil experienced by citizens and organizations at all levels of society. Outside of the five attacks I've shared with you so far (and still more to come), in the last decade, there have been dozens of incidents. Companies facing those breaches stand to lose millions, if not billions, of dollars in damages. With no mug shot or convict facing charges, no ransom note delivered or monies tracked, we are often left solely with a solid geopolitical rationale.

Our vulnerabilities to geopolitics have repercussions that go beyond just high costs. Yet, less than 5% of businesses around the world conduct a traditional geopolitical risk assessment. The other 95% remain clueless, with zero ability to mitigate such risks. But the assessed 5% are still highly exposed, as their assessments do not factor against the likes of ISIS, cyber terrorists, traditional adversaries to their nation-state, and GPCyber™ motivations.

POUNDS STERLING FOR A SLAUGHTER

In the fall of 2016, a telecom operator in Liberia, Africa, hired someone to hack its competitor. When the hacker finished breaching the competition, the hacker-for-hire inadvertently shut down the internet of the entire country. With regards to the timely and unheeded warnings from Robert Hannigan and Alex Younger, their fears were realized by this result.

The hacker is now serving his jail sentence in a British jail. Most of the attacks I'll be sharing in my book do not include such resolution. He was nothing but an ignorant mercenary hired to kill the competition for a mere £25,000 (roughly $32,000).

So, for a few thousand dollars, you can hire a hacker to not only hack your competition but completely deactivate a country's internet. Alternatively, can you imagine what a dedicated terrorist with GPCyber™ motivations of destruction and devastation could do? What if this wasn't pounds or dollars for a service? What if there was no opportunity cost? If the hacker was purely motivated to elevate their ideology to a new status, can you imagine what devastation this could cause?

Many organizations and government installations that continue believing they are well protected by current standards will be easy pickings when targeted by capable GPCyber™ hackers. This will have monumental effects on corporate and national security—and most especially on the lives and livelihoods of citizens who always end up paying the price. In fact, in Chapter 3 ("The Nine Meals"), I will share how the convergence and collaboration of organized cybercriminals and GPCyber™ terrorists are putting people not only nine meals from anarchy, but three.

At this point, I want to address the voice in the back of your mind telling you that lightning won't strike twice. That's exactly what our leaders continued believing after the attacks in Iran and Saudi Arabia. Thunder is rumbling on the horizons of the immediate past and future. Top decision makers who continue to stick their heads in the sand are volunteering to become the next case study of what we need to avoid doing in the future. And if you are growing concerned, you should be.

For more information, please visit survivabilitythebook.com/ placeholder (or scan the code below) to see articles referenced as well as my recommended reading list. We have been very lucky to have journalists with integrity on the case. I encourage you to explore how the world received this story.

Specific to this chapter, you will also find more information on MLi Group's GPCyber™ Risk Audits.

3

Nine Meals from Anarchy

(The Convergence of Organized Cyber Crime & Geo-Poli-Cyber™ Terrorism)

THE LAFFER CHALLENGE

IN 1982, I was a student at the University of Southern California, and I was attending a class on economics. My professor was none other than Dr. Arthur B. Laffer, inventor of the modern Laffer curve. I want to start by giving tribute to him, as he was instrumental in shaping my mind on the subject. He more than deserves the recognition he has received. In December 2017, he became the first recipient of the American Legislative Exchange Council's Laffer Award for Economic Excellence. And on June 19, 2019, he was awarded the Presidential Medal of Freedom by President Donald Trump. He also received the Distinguished Service Award by the National Association of Investment Clubs and the Daniel Webster Award for public speaking by the International Platform Association.

To put it in its proper context, Prof. Laffer was no ordinary teacher. He hated being called "Doctor." Laughing at the mention, he would tell us, "I don't fix bones."

He would lecture us on a Monday and then fly the next day to Washington, D.C., because he served as a member of the economic advisors to Ronald Reagan and was one of the chief architects of Reaganomics and supply-side economics. In fact, he also advised British prime minister Margaret Thatcher in 1978 and was a key figure for her and the conservative government in implementing supply-side economics in the UK under "Thatcherism." To put it mildly, my mind was being trained and challenged by the best of the best in the world.

Our class had more than one hundred students, and he did not know everyone's name; but he certainly knew mine. I was one of the few who was always very engaged, questioning and debating with him, which he loved. In fact, we remained in touch for many years and built a friendship after he moved to Pepperdine University in Malibu, and even when he ran for political office in California (during the mid-'80s, as I recall). Full of energy, he was a very dynamic and articulate lecturer, motivator, and professor.

I remember a very specific session in which one of our engagements turned into a heated debate. During his lecture, I specifically challenged him, saying, "Supply-side economics is flawed; it will fail when the ordinary functions of society cease to operate normally."

His reply, I recall, was a jubilant smile, "Really. Share with us what's on your mind." I imagine he was thinking, *What in the world is Khaled coming up with?*

I continued, "Dr. Laffer, the assumption of supply-side economics being the most efficient way of allocating resources in society is flawed and is missing a key variable."

He looked at me and asked me to continue.

I replied, addressing him and the entire class, "Let me explain it this way. I was raised in Beirut, Lebanon, in a most amazing city but one going through a civil war at the time." I explained that supply-side economics was certainly not effective because most of the people during the fighting were living in shelters for the purpose of safety. When a ceasefire would take place and people were able to come outside, the first thing they started doing was securing supplies (food, drink, etc.). "Here's the challenge I see: A man standing at the corner of a street with two gallons of fresh drinking water is now able to maximize his profitability by selling it at the maximum price to the highest bidder. At least, that's according to supply-side economics. Is that not correct, Dr. Laffer?"

"Absolutely right."

"But that man has a problem. Next to him are two children who have not had a drop of water for a week. What does he do? Does he volunteer to give them some water, at the cost of not fulfilling his maximum profitability? Or does he do nothing because he wants to maximize his profitability even though the kids will remain thirsty and unhelped? What does he do?"

My professor's reply surprised me. "You Syrians want to nationalize everything."

"I'm sorry, Dr. Laffer. But you've got it all wrong. You may be a guru in economics, but you clearly don't know much about Syrians. Syria is the longest continuous civilization on the planet and dates back about ten thousand years. We are the epitome of tradespeople. We are the original entrepreneurs, the subject you actually teach here at USC. In fact, nothing in what I said to you relates to socialism, communism, or nationalization of anything. It pertains to my identification that as a model, supply-side economics is missing a critical variable."

He then asked, "What is that?"

"Social responsibility."

"How would you factor it in the model?"

I replied, "How do I know? I'm only a student!"

Over the course of the next three decades, time proved both my esteemed professor and supply-side economics wrong, and I was proven right. Twenty years later, in the midst of the economic effects following September 11, 2001, on July 16, 2002, Chairman Alan Greenspan of the Federal Reserve Board was a presenter during their semiannual monetary policy report to Congress.[1] The following words are those shared by Greenspan with the Committee on Banking, Housing, and Urban Affairs, US Senate:

> Why did corporate governance checks and balances that served us reasonably well in the past break down? At root was the rapid enlargement of stock market capitalizations in the latter part of the 1990s that arguably engendered an outsized increase in opportunities for avarice. An infectious greed seemed to grip much of our business community.
>
> Our historical guardians of financial information were overwhelmed. Too many corporate executives sought ways to "harvest" some of those stock market gains. As a result, the highly desirable spread of shareholding and options among business

> managers perversely created incentives to artificially inflate reported earnings in order to keep stock prices high and rising.
>
> This outcome suggests that the options were poorly structured, and, consequently, they failed to properly align the long-term interests of shareholders and managers, the paradigm so essential for effective corporate governance. The incentives they created overcame the good judgment of too many corporate managers.
>
> It is not that humans have become any more greedy than in generations past. It is that the avenues to express greed had grown so enormously.

Six years after the statement above, and twenty-six years after my challenge to Prof. Laffer, Greenspan spoke before US leaders once again. This time, he was two years retired and spoke as a witness on the topic of the role of federal regulators in the financial crisis, which he referred to as a "once-in-a-century credit tsunami." Below is an excerpt from his interaction with the Committee on Oversight and Government Reform at the House of Representatives on October 23, 2008:[2]

> I hope this distinguished panel will help us cut to the core of the financial problems we have encountered. At that core lies Fannie Mae and Freddie Mac: Government-sponsored enterprises that dominated the mortgage finance marketplace and gave quasi-official sanction to the opaque, high-risk investments still radiating global toxic shock waves from the epicenter of their subprime sinkhole. By the way, these were areas where we did try to regulate in some on our side and were stopped from the other side of the aisle from bringing regulation in earlier.
>
> Our earlier hearings have focused on important but, to be honest, somewhat tangential issues, a unique case bailout, a bankruptcy, flawed credit ratings, executive compensation, and the cost of corporate retreats. No one is minimizing or defending corporate malfeasance. We share the outrage of most Americans

at the greed that blinded Wall Street to its civic duty to protect Main Street.

Later during the hearing, as Greenspan was answering questions, he was specifically pressured to elaborate on what he called his "partial mistake," in which he explained: "I made a mistake in presuming that the self-interest of organizations, specifically banks and others, were such is that they were best capable of protecting their own shareholders and their equity in the firms." He also mentioned that he found a flaw in the model, which very much reflected his worldview. Upon realizing his ideology was not working, he said, "I was shocked, because I had been going for forty years or more with very considerable evidence that it was working exceptionally well."

When I originally told Prof. Laffer that supply-side economics is flawed, and that it would fail when the ordinary functions of society cease to operate normally, Greenspan's disillusionment and statement of disbelief is exactly what I was referring to. But in his heart, had he truly believed that the system could continue as it was? Or could it be tweaked?

In fact, if you look again at Greenspan's statement, "We share the outrage of most Americans at the greed that blinded Wall Street to its civic duty to protect Main Street," it proves how theories created by economic gurus had no reality on the ground. Yet, even so, these theories and resulting policies were adopted as part of the global economic order we still live under today. Such models have made the rich richer, and the poor poorer.

Do you know the civic duty Greenspan was referring to when presenting the idea of Wall Street protecting Main Street? If you're scratching your head, trying to conceive an answer to my question, you are on the correct side of history. There is no civic duty. The ethos of Wall Street never included such things; therefore, it was never blind to it. For those who might claim that "corporate social responsibility" or financial contributions to charities and good causes counts as protecting Main Street, go smoke something else.

The laissez-faire economic model shoved down our throat since the '70s created the greed of Wall Street. At that, it created a desire in the people for creating wealth on unprecedented levels. Ensuring shareholder wealth and profit maximization became the top priorities, if not the only ones. Therefore, the flawed form of supply-side economics enabled the abandonment of Main Street. For every "positive" development made toward increasing that priority profit, vulnerabilities are created and ignored, leaving the lives and livelihoods of citizens at increasing risk. And I think you'll find that these flaws are not mitigated because it's not worth the cost.

NINE MEALS FROM ANARCHY (ARE WE REALLY THREE DAYS FROM COMPLETE DEVASTATION?)

In 1906, Alfred Henry Lewis said, "There are only nine meals between mankind and anarchy." Basically, he was a journalist who coined the terminology to express that people were only nine meals away from hunger and diminishing resources, leading to civil unrest and complete chaos. Bear in mind, Lewis wrote this at the turn of the 20th century, describing how living conditions for people meant they were days away from running out of food and vital resources.

Lewis's assumptions were very reasonable, but the simplest of them was the idea that people had three meals a day by default, which was not really true back then. Most citizens likely had one meal per day, maybe. The overall point is that when we are faced with conditions wherein we are unable to ensure our personal survivability, people are capable of doing whatever they need to persevere.

Lewis clarified that it takes three days of shortages for the population to resort to violence and other means of survival. Three days, three meals each day, and therefore nine meals away from complete anarchy. To be clear, he was not stating that people were nine meals from starvation but from lawlessness and insurrection. Before people will allow themselves to starve to death, they will resort to doing something about it—after all, dying passively and quietly is never an option.

Sadly, in both developing and developed countries across the world, the social phenomenon of people facing scarcity is a common reoccurrence witnessed all too often in modern day-to-day life. During or after disasters, when supply shortages become too severe, hunting season often arrives early; people resort to other means of securing necessary resources for their families. In fact, many citizens who never considered themselves capable of brutality soon find themselves in a position where they are resorting to violence and other illegal activities to provide food for their loved ones.

Today, I'm sad to say Lewis's estimations need to be updated for a more somber reality. As I will explain further in Chapter 17, we are actually closer to three meals from anarchy, which means we are only one day away from societal chaos. Part of my estimation is due to the convergence of cybercriminals and GPCyber™ terrorists.

ENVISIONING CONVERGENCE

Modern cybercriminals and GPCyber™ terrorists have something in common. They do not give a damn about society or people's lives and livelihoods. Today, they are converging, working together to serve their respective dark goals. And neither of them fulfills the Robin Hood altruistic model; while they are stealing from the rich, they are not giving to the poor.

The advent of collaboration between GPCyber™ terrorists and cybercriminals is now gaining greater and greater traction. We're already seeing the evidence of this all over news media. These developments have taken place despite numerous (and belated) warnings from international law enforcement agencies, such as Europol in 2016 and 2017. From its 2016 announcement:[3]

> The abuse of technology and legitimate online tools and services is not an exception in the terrorism landscape. Terrorists are becoming increasingly proficient in hiding their traces and activities by using anonymising and encryption tools and services. Furthermore, the anonymity provided by cryptocurrencies, and their preferential use in the trades taking place on darkmarkets, seems to be leading terrorists to invest in this currency. Goods and services offered on Darknet such as Tor are available to different actor groups, including terrorist groups. This ranges from malware, to illegal goods like stolen weapons, to crowdfunding sites claiming to support terrorist groups.
>
> The thriving of the as-a-service industry in the digital underground provides easy access to criminal products and services that can be used by anyone, from technically savvy individuals to

non-technically skilled terrorists. This allows cyber-attacks to be launched that are of a scale and scope disproportionate to the technical capability of the actors involved.

Nevertheless, currently most internet usage by terrorists, reported by law enforcement, relates to the use of unsophisticated tools and a widespread use of social media for propaganda, communication, recruitment and knowledge dissemination. Europol's EU Internet Referral Unit (EU IRU) has also reported a limited set of techniques currently used by terrorist groups online, focusing primarily on information disclosure and disruption of service.

And from its 2017 Announcement:[4]

Counter-terrorism investigations in Europe have shown that the use of the internet is an integral component in any terrorist plot.

Key Findings

While terrorists continue to use the internet mostly for communication, propaganda and knowledge sharing purposes, their capabilities to launch cyber-attacks remain limited.

Most terrorist activity concerns the open internet; however, there is a share of terrorist exchange in the Darknet too. This concerns mostly fundraising campaigns, the use of illicit markets and advertisement of propaganda hosted on mainstream social media.

Key Recommendations

Cooperation and coordination of effort among the multitude of stakeholders in law enforcement and the private sector is required for a robust answer to the jihadist online threats and to ensure the attribution of such acts in cyberspace.

> Law enforcement must continue to engage with and support social media companies in initiatives to devise common strategies to fight their abuse by terrorist groups.

Contrary to GPCyber™ terrorists, cybercriminals remain primarily motivated by the advancement of their financial wealth; anything that might make them money, they are more than happy to engage in. Meanwhile, GPCyber™ terrorists approach this relationship with the dual goal of 1) raising funds in order to maintain their ability to carry on with their operations while also 2) fulfilling their strategy of creating cyberattacks promoting ideology and propaganda. Nowadays, both parties are exploiting the latest technologies, software, and brain power to achieve their goals. In short, cybercriminals want to make money, and GPCyber™ perpetrators want to advance their political and ideological/extremist agendas.

In the Era of the Unprecedented, this new relationship coincides with government failures, such as COVID-19 preparations and responses, cyber security regulatory frameworks, and ongoing issues with mitigation. The aggregate of this collaboration and ongoing government failures shortens Lewis's estimated nine meals to three meals. And for any chance of changing the tides, law enforcement needs to catch up—quickly.

GPCyber™ attacks aside, law enforcement continually struggles with cybercriminals, which says to me that the convergence only further complicates their efforts. In terms of regulatory models, the vulnerabilities in the systems of our businesses and nation-states ensure the success of GPCyber™ attacks; exploitation is inevitable in many sectors within many countries around the world. The possibilities of devastation are nearly infinite, and I'm only scratching the surface of conventional internet.

I would not expect nor presume that most of my readers are frequent visitors to the Dark Web. For those who research it—law enforcement and other experts alike—it is amply clear that cybercriminals and GPCyber™ terrorists are collaborating. Within the Dark Web, there are trading spaces, and both parties are sending jobs to each other in the interest of fully perpetrating their activities. For the GPCyber™ player who desires it, they can easily find access to malware as well as the know-how, illegal goods (like stolen weapons and transportation), and crowdfunding sites claiming to support terrorist groups. Such services are rampant on the Dark Web.

To put it bluntly, there is a definite business case as to why these two parties are supporting each other: ongoing success. Chat rooms on the Dark Web manifest how these parties feel safe communicating because they are clearly becoming more familiar with each other. As trust between them continues building, this leads to better synergies and efficiency, which means they grow less concerned as to who might be listening in. They exchange ideas, talk about strategies, and affirm each other as they become bolder than ever before.

While law enforcement attempts to infiltrate these chat rooms, considering the overall number of collaborations, the majority of its efforts prove inconsequential. In essence, it has no chance of making a serious dent, unless something significant changes. Knowing that the threat is only getting worse during our attempts to infiltrate and mitigate the convergence, I believe this requires a major rethink and new action plans by national governments and international bodies (such as Interpol, the UN, and others).

For any of my readers who watched the movie series *Mission: Impossible* (or even the old show), you may recall Ethan Hunt (or Jim Phelps) accepting his missions through various forms of secure communication ("This tape will self-destruct in five seconds"). Well, criminals and terrorists have accepted their mission, and they use similar methods, which ensures they are successful in remaining one step ahead of the authorities. In some cases, they rely purely on paper and pencil and other nondigital forms to ensure their communications and information are not compromised.

The flaws within our current systems and approaches to mitigation handicaps local and international law enforcement, bolstering their inability to clamp down on the activities of criminal and GPCyber™ collaboration. However, the conflict has not been resolved just yet. The mission is still on, and we have important pieces on the board that—if managed correctly—will keep us more than nine meals away from looming chaos. One such piece is the following fact:

No online criminal or terrorist activities can exist without an IP address—full stop.

The quality of management aside, no lawful or unlawful boasting, or internet activity anywhere in the world, can exist without an IP (internet protocol) number or a domain name. As surprising as it may be, this pertains not only to the everyday internet but to the Dark Web as well. Here you should be asking yourself:

- Who controls the IP addresses and domain names on the internet?
- Who manages these internet functions in order to make it operate the way it does?
- Who oversees this global infrastructure?

If you are not yet familiar, the organization in question is the Internet Corporation for Assigned Names and Numbers (ICANN), which I mentioned in the Introduction. On September 18, 1998, in order to transfer some control of global internet operations, ICANN was created by the US government through a White House initiative by the Clinton administration. You need to understand that ICANN's responsibility, at the core of its mandate, does not include content oversight. It was set up as a nonprofit organization in California with the mandate to manage the IP addresses and the domain name system under contract with the US government through the Department of Commerce.

The original intention of the US administration was to further extend its freedom of expression ethos into becoming a pillar in the online world. A serious unintended consequence of this freedom online permitted an explosion in harmful content. Toxic materials such as child pornography, terrorist propaganda, and fake news (including Purposed Disinformation™) have now become unmitigated national and corporate Cyber-Survivability™ and cyber security risks. Much like the convergence, the tremendous efforts by local and international law enforcement in their attempts to curtail this explosion are hardly making a dent.

Similar to law enforcement's results with criminals and GPCyber™ perpetrators, impacts are lacking in way of oversight on hate speech, extremist narratives, and Purposed Disinformation™. This toxic presence is spreading online and through social media despite the ushering in of new legislation specifically created to address them. The convergence continues growing, and we are now reaching the age in which people are no longer able to distinguish between fake news and truth, or fact from opinion.

I'll share further on this in Chapter 4 ("Unprecedented Threats"). For now, I want you to think about the storm surrounding us in which facts have become points of view, points of view have become facts, and partial facts are continually accepted as complete. Misinformation has already been recognized as a threat to democracy, and we continue witnessing proof of this all over the world.

Today, we can no longer afford the underestimation of the seismic power of Purposed Disinformation™. And while our cherished democracy faces its own cancer, we the people are left more vulnerable than ever. Not only is the system handled by dinosaurs, it is also working against the progress we need to ensure nine meals or more remain on society's table.

ASLEEP AT THE WHEEL (IT REALLY ISN'T HOW MUCH MONEY YOU SPEND ...)

On February 7, 2017, UK newspaper *The Independent* published an exclusive story[5] titled "Isis-linked Hackers Attack NHS Websites to Show Gruesome Syrian Civil War Images." The Defense Editor, Kim Sengupta, revealed that 11 trusts of the National Health Service (NHS) had been hacked by ISIS or ISIS affiliates. These hacks not only defaced some of the websites of the NHS trusts but destroyed some of their servers as well. The defacement included a display of gruesome images of women and children in the Syrian civil war, as well as the words "Get out of Syria." Similar to the attack on TV5 Monde, the perpetrators were making political statements regarding interventions by the UK and US.

I can go on the record now for the first time since *The Independent* published the NHS story in 2017. All of the intelligence, information, and analysis used in publishing its story came from us at the MLi Group. A few days before, one of our Cyber-Survivability™ experts actually uncovered elements of these cyberattacks on a few of the NHS trusts. But it turned out that none of them were being reported in the press.

I asked the expert to dig deeper. He later discovered that the total trusts impacted amounted to 11. When he discovered and assembled all of the factual data, he brought this directly to my attention. At that time, the MLi Group had not unveiled its *Survivability.News* platform, which we later launched in 2020.

As we were not yet a news organization, I started asking myself, *What do I do with this information? What is the responsible action?* Bear in mind, 2017 was immediately after 2016, when UK intelligence leaders made it clear that extremists could shut a city down with a click of a button. I felt that something significant needed to happen. In fact, the UK was only a couple of months from a new general election. I truly felt that putting this in the public domain—especially in a responsible and informed manner—would make this an election topic. After all, how often do we hear political leaders talk about important lessons? Then again, how often do we discover that none are ever learned?

Overall, I felt this event must be turned into a teaching moment. As a result, I contacted a few of my press connections, some of whom worked for prominent international newspapers. Eventually, I decided to offer it all to *The Independent*, and the information was provided gratis; we neither charged nor received a single penny. My sincere hope was that the awareness elevated by MLi Group working with *The Independent* as to the nature of the threat would advance the cause of decision makers and governments recognizing the need to update and adopt new mitigation strategies. After all, people's lives and livelihoods were put at risk.

The published article was referenced and repeated by news organizations all over the world. All mentions featured the MLi Group and myself as key experts; however, I specifically asked *The Independent* not to state that we were the source of intelligence. I didn't want to flash it or flaunt it; I wanted to be more responsible in addressing the information and what needed to happen next.

The hack itself showcased how poorly defended critical national infrastructures can be. The UK is the fifth-largest economy in the world. It's a superpower with a veto at the UN. While its models of threat mitigation are copied and emulated all over the world, clearly they were not working. To my disappointment, how the UK could better prepare their systems for GPCyber™ attacks, in fact, did not become a topic of the general election.

As a result of exposure, I was also hoping that the NHS would at minimum implement improved cyber security hygiene and update its systems. At the very least, I was hoping the NHS would identify how its trusts were breached at such a low level of technical expertise by the hackers. In truth, the perpetrators were able to take advantage of vulnerabilities while using outdated operating systems.

Much like general election topics, neither the updates nor the necessary analysis ever materialized. Nothing was learned, nor was anything implemented by NHS. A few months later, this proved to be a catastrophic mistake by the British government when the WannaCry cyberattack hit not only the UK but more than 150 countries.

WannaCry began its devastation on a Friday. As a result, the UK saw more than 90,000 NHS activities and operations impacted, including life-saving operations and vital treatments for cancer and other terminal conditions. The next morning, on a Saturday, British prime minister Theresa May appeared on television to address the devastating cyberattack on the UK and NHS.

Rather than talking about how the impact of WannaCry could have been prevented, if they had paid attention to the ISIS hack in February and patched their mistakes, she spoke of how the UK was leading the world. The British government had invested £1.8 billion into its new UK National Cyber Security Centre, which was ineffective in defending against or mitigating the threat after it happened. In fact, the solution ended up being quite simple, but it was not discovered by the government.

WannaCry was a worldwide attack targeting computers running Microsoft Windows operating systems. It involved a ransomware cryptoworm that demanded ransom Bitcoin payments to actually stop it. Some speculated that methods of exploiting the vulnerabilities involved were stolen from the National Security Agency (NSA) in the US.

It's worth nothing that, on December 27, 2017, the US, UK, and Australia formally attributed WannaCry to North Korea. Not only does this qualify as a geopolitically motivated cyberattack, but by the definition I created in 2012, it also qualifies as a GPCyber™ motivated attack, with unprecedented human and economic consequences.

In terms of the simple solution, cyber security expert Marcus Hutchins determined that the solution would be to create a domain name that made the virus go and terminate itself at that IP address. This cost him $10, and he singlehandedly stopped global devastation. Hundreds of thousands of computers were impacted worldwide, and over a dozen UK hospitals were shut down, and he turned the tide by purchasing a cheap domain name. Clearly, it's not about how much money you spend, it's how you spend it. For the UK, the £1.8 billion investment touted by Theresa May did not suffice in halting the attack.

Now, you would think this would be a learning moment for many governments around the world. You might be surprised in reading that it most certainly was not. WannaCry exposed the inability of governments around the world, especially Western democracies. Not only did they fail in being prepared to defend and secure their nation-states, they failed to improve their security and mitigation strategies when given the opportunity. In fact, they fell asleep at the wheel, but they surely thought they were awake.

SYSTEMATIC FAILURES (GREED IS GOOD?)

The fundamentals of capitalism are always celebrated as untouchable scripture, such as laissez-faire, free market economy, little or no government intervention, self-regulation, and—let us not forget—deregulation. If you dare to challenge any of them, you should be prepared to be labeled as an anarchist. However, these fundamentals proved to be significant contributors to the 2008 global financial crisis (if you recall the words of the Federal Reserve chairman Dr. Alan Greenspan from the beginning of the chapter).

As of late, it's clear to me that the "infectious greed" Greenspan spoke of in 2002 never stopped spreading. This was brought to the forefront of my attention on March 23, 2021, when British prime minister Boris Johnson spoke at his Downing Street news conference. In marking a full year since their first lockdown, he paid tribute to Gordon Gekko's infamous line, "Greed is good" (from the 1987 film *Wall Street*). On the record, while meeting via Zoom, he said to Members of Parliament, "The reason we have the vaccine success is because of capitalism, because of greed, my friends."

For anyone assuming Greenspan's "infectious greed" had been cured, take it from Johnson as he and Dr. Frankenstein rejoice, "It's alive!" His inner beliefs could not contain themselves, as far as I'm concerned. And while he did regret saying it, and asked for it to be forgotten, he was vindicating capitalism's fatal flaw: a complete lack of social responsibility (just as I argued with Professor Laffer as a young know-it-all). In the worst case of irony, Johnson's Freudian slip paralleled breaking reports from international news agencies regarding AstraZeneca's links to blood clots as well as its use of "outdated and potentially misleading data"[6] overstating the effectiveness of its vaccine and citing an independent panel.

Not only is "Wall Street" failing to protect "Main Street," it allows corners to be cut in the formation of solutions to detrimental problems;

it misleads "Main Street" into believing that they will be saved. How can people learn to spot fake news and misinformation when our own governments perpetrate the falsification of vital intelligence? How can we secure ourselves when leadership is still playing pretend in their fortresses?

And not only were Boris Johnson's words untimely, they were proven incorrect. AstraZeneca was not a success, and that officially makes Johnson's announcement fake news. Dozens of countries around the world are already limiting use of the vaccine after the announcements made in late March 2021. In fact, Denmark banned it altogether from its borders as of April 14, 2021 (according to *The Telegraph*[7]).

Such developments did not stop there. The greed was international and continues spreading today. In the US, the week before Johnson's fake news, a discussion among Pfizer executives was exposed. CBS News[8] and other outlets reported that it appeared Pfizer's plans were not focused on a cure for the pandemic but a perpetual solution for a continuous endemic, "as this shifts ... we think there's an opportunity here for us." More than likely, they will hike the price of their vaccine, given the chance.

Society's cancer is thriving, stronger and more prosperous than ever. Ideologically, it continues guiding many world leaders and their respective governments. Today, they are using their unprecedented economic, political, and democratic failures to fan the flames of their vaccines and other successes. Meanwhile, their citizens continue paying the ultimate price as their lives and livelihoods remain unprotected.

The cancer of flawed capitalism, supply-side economics, and ideological models has caused numerous global failures, such as the 2008 financial crisis and the COVID-19 pandemic. Our condition has only been treated with aspirin pills. Without a single dose of chemotherapy, it remains an unchecked global economic, political, and democratic (or undemocratic) world order, the "principles" of which continue to be spun as success stories and gospel.

Meanwhile, the convergence of cybercriminals and GPCyber™ terrorists means that the candle of our safety is burning at both ends. The negligence, incompetence, and corruption of our leaders is meeting their stealth, sophistication, and efficiency in the middle. Western failures will only get worse, and our leaders have yet to prove they can respond well to precedented disasters. Our situation will only improve with real change, and until then the bill for everything on the table will be left for the usual party: We, the people.

This now raises serious points of concern, which I explore in the next chapter. We need to be concerned with government decisions or lack thereof, and their failed strategies in protecting us, the citizens. How will they handle truly unprecedented events and vulnerabilities? How will they address threats from the internet of things (IoT)? How about artificial intelligence, machine learning, fake news, and other technological breakthroughs and social challenges also happening on unprecedented scales?

Our nine meals are reduced closer and closer to three meals by the day. How long until we have less than a day between ourselves and complete chaos? And once we reach that point, is there any way for us to bring the family around the table to mourn that last meal together? Ideally, that won't be the case. I believe that, beyond knowing and naming the threat, if we know our vulnerabilities, we can take the actions necessary toward real change.

For more information, please visit survivabilitythebook.com/ placeholder (or scan the code below) to see articles referenced as well as my recommended reading list. We have been very lucky to have journalists with integrity on the case. I encourage you to explore how the world received this story.

Specific to this chapter, you will also find more regarding MLi Group's Corporate Cyber-Survivability™ Strategies (including an Operating Plan), as well as the exclusive article in *The Independent* I mentioned in this chapter, along with a *Survivability News* article on Boris Johnson's statement and other vaccine developments.

4

Unprecedented Threats

(Lack of Effective Thought Leadership, Regulation & Mitigation in the Face of Speed of Technological Advancement)

OUR CONCERN TODAY in this new era of unprecedented events should not be limited to merely Geo-Poli-Cyber™ (GPCyber™) terrorists, nor should they be primarily focused on the cybercriminals who are only interested in profit at the expense of people. We need to pay special attention to the key concern that is our own governments and their failures.

As touched on briefly at the end of Chapter 3, in crises such as the 2008 financial crisis and the COVID-19 pandemic, we have seen our leaders failing to prepare for and deliver necessary mitigations. For the rest of Part I, I will now focus on the current state of the world and how international political rivalries prove to be a significant threat to stakeholders (nations, corporations, and citizens alike). At that, government decisions are seldom for the benefit of the citizen first and foremost.

CAMBRIDGE ANALYTICA AND BREXIT

In today's unprecedented times, we need to be extremely vigilant about our online activity. Most ordinary people don't think about, nor can they be bothered with, the internet of things (IoT), artificial intelligence (AI), machine learning, or even fake news. If you are reading this chapter, this paragraph, and even now embrace the thought, "Well yeah, Khaled, those things don't impact me," I assure you, they relate both directly and indirectly to your daily life. It's time to wake up and smell the hummus.

British prime minister David Cameron decided to allow for the Brexit vote. He offered it to the British people as part of the Conser-vative Party manifesto in his upcoming general election. He did so believing fully that the vote could never win. He had no idea what he was about to unleash—not only on the UK but on the world.

Apart from Cameron, there is a very specific man behind the Brexit campaign (as well as its use of Cambridge Analytica): Dominic Cummings. When Boris Johnson became prime minister, Cummings became his right-hand man. As Johnson's chief of staff, he literally became the power maker behind the prime minister until November 2020.

Dominic Cummings was the mastermind behind the Brexit vote campaign. When he was hired to lead, he brought some techies who showed him things about what could be done to influence the outcome of the election, how targeted marketing through social media and based on likes and dislikes of Facebook users could actually pivot or change the Brexit vote. This culmination would later be known as Cambridge Analytica. You may recall the scandal that engulfed this company for illegal data farming on Facebook and other platforms.

Cambridge Analytica offered surveys that were launched on social media platforms (such as Facebook) in which many people participated. Answers were gathered into a system that included respondents' data, as well as data of their friends and family. They gathered this without our knowledge or permission. This information treasure trove enabled targeted advertising toward people of specific beliefs in order to strengthen those beliefs, as well as anyone on the fence to enable them to fall on one side or the other.

Cambridge Analytica CEO Alexander Nix was caught on videotape in a press sting operation where he was bragging about how the company and its model assisted two African presidents in winning their elections. He also bragged about being involved in more than 40 US political races in 2014 and in 2015, specifically mentioning how Cambridge Analytica performed data analysis services for Senator Ted Cruz's presidential campaign in 2016. As it turns out, they worked for Donald Trump's presidential campaign in 2016 as well.

From Brexit to Trump, the manipulation of public opinion and votes was staggering. These tactics and manipulations helped Dominic Cummings become the trusted right-hand man to Boris Johnson from 2019 to late 2020. As a result of the press sting operation, Cambridge Analytica was forcibly shut down by the regulator—but Pandora's box had already been opened. Today, there may be hundreds, if not thousands, of Cambridge Analyticas operating both above and under the radar, perpetrating fake news and the manipulation of information for God knows whatever reasons.

BROKEN DEMOCRACY AND FAKE NEWS (NEW PRIORITIES FOUND IN THE ADVANCEMENTS OF MACHINE LEARNING)

David Cameron truly opened Pandora's box, and now it's benefitting Boris Johnson and the Brexiteers. In fact, this unleashed a new model of technology abuse, using the people's data in order to bring power to new world leaders. It not only changed the US presidential race by securing the win of President Trump in 2016, it seismically altered the direction of US politics and global politics for generations to come. Moreover, it changed the way Western democracies operate. In essence, it exposed the frailty and the incapability of democracy to actually deliver what is right for its own people.

It is telling that the only time when all of this started to become noticeable and where the regulators and society started talking about it was when Facebook had more than $119 billion (that's the equivalent of £90 billion) wiped from its market value, and more than $17 billion hit the personal fortune of Facebook founder Mark Zuckerberg. This financial loss was a direct result of the Cambridge Analytica scandal, as well as Facebook's complicity. In the end, the consumer data harvested by Cambridge Analytica illegally, involving hundreds of millions of Facebook users, would change the fate and direction of nations forever.

This scandal delivered a cancer scare to democracy, not only in the western hemisphere but anywhere democracy is aspired to and enshrined by law or by constitution. Bear in mind, true democracy operates with a very specific anchor point: citizens are informed and are able to make informed decisions. In the Era of the Unprecedented, partial facts are presented as full facts, and opinions become truths that are treated as gospel.

Citizens need to pay attention to how machine learning and artificial intelligence (etc.) are impacting their day-to-day lives. Machine learning provides the ability for machines to decipher information at the greatest scale possible, determining likes, dislikes, and permutations across hundreds of millions of online users. It reveals how they are interconnected, relating to different methods and topics. And it identifies how people will likely feel or make decisions about certain topics before they even reach a point of consideration.

Today, machine learning is the foundation used in promoting hate and dehumanization for other people, races, and cultures. Because of this, we are seeing a new level of bigotry and racist tendencies in people who they thought would never feel that way. At the core of all this is the utility, the usage of machine learning and artificial intelligence. This is what made Cambridge Analytica so potently devastating in its effectiveness.

When Cambridge Analytica leveraged loopholes in Facebook, it surveyed only the few hundred thousand people who gave consent to participate in those surveys. However, it then garnished the information, habits, likes, and dislikes of participants' friends and family, without permission, which amounted to hundreds of millions of people. Acquiring this nature of intelligence and propensity to think and act in specific ways made Cambridge Analytica lethal in promoting new narratives and mindsets to those who previously would not have gone down that rabbit hole. It also permitted Cambridge Analytica to segment the data of all these users and categorize it in manners that were used to secure votes and decision-making.

Today, referring to fake news purely as "fake news" undervalues the critical aspect of this new development on national and corporate survivability. Today, false or twisted facts are a far greater threat than just mere fake news because they can be used as Purposed Disinformation™ warfare that can bring a nation to its knees. Since 2016, Cambridge Analytica and fake news have successfully ensured Brexit, the 2016 presidential election of Donald Trump, and the election of two African presidents. This development changed the global cyberthreat landscape beyond recognition, and it cannot be fixed by purely addressing only fake news.

Since 2016, we're starting to see the media spreading narratives without full facts or research. Very often, the misinformation of fake news uses partial information or partial truths in the interest of confirmation of bias, so that user opinions become even more strengthened and unwavering. It is no wonder today that those who believe that Trump is America's savior will believe nothing about anything abominable that he may have done, and those who believe that he is the worst thing that ever happened to America will believe nothing about anything good that he may have done.

And the problem goes even deeper. Look at the way search engines operate. Look at the way they seem to know how you tend to lean politically toward certain aspects versus others. If you search for an opinion that you believe was true, you are more likely to receive results that actually match or support what you believe. In fact, reinforcing your perceptions and your opinions (as wrong as they may be) has become the standard operating procedure of search engines. The social divide between one camp and another is unprecedented.

Consider the proposed border wall by President Trump and how it divided America. If you position it as a security feature, to those who believe in security, they are more likely to accept the wall as a solution. If you position the wall as a barrier between humans and civilizations, blocking all interactions, to those who believe in global diplomacy, they are more likely to object to the wall.

The misinformation on COVID-19 has taken this concept to entirely new heights. Although I consider myself probably more informed than the average citizen, I've reached the point where I can no longer tell what is factual and what is a partial fact. I can no longer tell whether COVID-19 was made by China, whether it was made by the US, or if it was made by the US in China (as we should all "remember," Dr. Anthony Fauci funded the money in the Chinese lab). I can no longer tell if it was nature-made, and I have no clue whether the pharmaceuticals were involved in its creation or whether they are now just leveraging the opportunity it's presenting.

So, if the people who are used to researching their information can no longer decipher what is fact from what is fiction, how can anyone become an informed citizen? And when someone acts as a citizen by voting according to their beliefs, is democracy working? I mourn the truth, in that facts have become points of view and points of view have become facts. As I've been saying for years, never in the history of mankind have people had so much information at their fingertips yet never before have they been so misled and misinformed.

Refresh your memory, if you will, on the topic of wearing face masks during the pandemic. As soon as it was up for discussion, there was a multitude of articles on whether they were beneficial or not, followed by thousands, if not millions, of videos on the infamy versus the innocence of pharma. And let us not forget about the conspiracy theories surrounding Bill Gates himself. Of course, it didn't end there.

As 2021 unfolded, look at the way information spread regarding the efficacy of the COVID-19 vaccines. At first, it was focused on results being 90–95% effective. Rejoicing and skepticism alike followed mainstream news as we were told how wonderful everything will be once the vaccines are rolled out and society is saved. It's as if the mainstream believes all we need is a boost of public morale—not relevant facts. There was no room to, say, examine Pfizer.

While Pfizer claimed its vaccine to be more than 90% effective, it also recently admitted to falsifying information surrounding Bextra as well as synthetic heart valves. For this, it paid the largest criminal fine in US history as part of a $2.3 billion settlement for falsely advertising medicines and paying kickbacks to doctors. As it turns out, its rap sheet extends through the last decade. In the face of Pfizer's past settlement and activity, I'm asked to take the efficacy results and percentages provided by them as gospel. I'm sorry, no. I have doubts.

NOTE: Pfizer's criminal fine is not fake news. This is real. You can watch a November 2020 segment on this by clicking the link at the end of the chapter (or scanning the QR code provided).

You might be asking, *But Khaled, what about Moderna?* Let me tell you, Moderna is not a pharmaceutical company; it's an investment vehicle. It pursued pharmaceutical business in 2020 purely due to the funding provided by the Trump administration. This leaves us with an obvious interpretation in which its pursuit is purely opportunistic.

Fundamental to the provision of these vaccines at the request of governments around the world, participating pharmaceutical companies will be given a get-out-of-jail clause. They will not be held responsible if side effects become known at a later stage. They will not be held liable, or suable in a court of law. Much like using Monopoly paper money in Vegas, they just can't lose. Overall, the granting of immunity by governments to these pharmaceutical companies because the vaccine is being rushed is a major concern, and it should be.

Where will this go next? Will we as citizens be mandated? If we are unable to show proof of being vaccinated for COVID, will we be forbidden from catching our flight, renewing our driver's license, or using government services? I'm in a state of alarm, and I'm not alone in that. Continually, media and governments position new narratives as unquestionable facts while they are presenting how governments are succeeding or have succeeded in providing solutions to their citizens.

CAMBRIDGE ANALYTICA AND THE 2016 US ELECTION

The manipulation of citizens through fake news is more than powerful, and I encourage you to reconsider it as 21st-century Purposed Disinformation™ warfare. It adversely impacts opinions, which subsequently affects voting decisions. At worst, it can change the direction of nations politically and economically. And it can be perpetrated by foreign and domestic powers and players.

As mentioned before, after Cambridge Analytica successfully locked down the direction of UK's Brexit vote, officials took it for a victory lap with the 2016 Trump presidential campaign. Against the expectations of many voters and viewers, Trump unexpectedly managed to gain typically Democrat strongholds, such as Michigan, Florida, Iowa, Ohio, Pennsylvania, and Wisconsin. For any swing vote, pivotal states, its targeting was exceptionally effective. The votes that Trump received in Florida, Iowa, Ohio, Pennsylvania, and Wisconsin were more than half. If you haven't smelled the hummus yet, it's maybe about time for you to eat it. Of course, where the votes were Republican, he received full support, such as in Arizona, Georgia, Indiana, and North Carolina.

Cambridge Analytica's approach was so effective because Americans are typically single-issue voters. For example, if a candidate opposes a single point, you vote for that person because of the way they vote (abortion rights, immigration, and the wall, for example). A pro-life voter may like a candidate for most of their platform, but they will vote for another candidate if that platform includes any form of pro-choice agenda. Single-issue voting is unique to US politics, and it was successfully leveraged by Cambridge Analytica and its AI, machine learning algorithm, and protocols.

Voters were targeted and persuaded to vote for or against candidates. For anyone who wants to treat this as just a tactic, I argue that it has changed the modality of American politics for at least a generation. Cambridge Analytica also altered the economic and political welfare of many countries around the world, as well as their citizens, who are paying the ultimate price for it. It also set a new paradigm on global topics like climate change, international concerns (whether it's Russia, China, Syria, or the global war on terror), and even health care.

When the focus is locked on polarizing, single topics—where people are or become passionately for or against it—a lot of the information in the middle gets lost. This has changed American politics forever, creating a new level of discourse between warring political parties to the point where US government shutdowns happened frequently. After Trump's victory, the US pulled out of the Paris Climate Accord, and it adopted new policies on coal and fossil fuel reliance because they brought new jobs, regardless of pollution and environmental concerns.

Manipulation of public opinion changed the course of American history. As far as I'm concerned, Brexit and Trump's election directly illustrate how Purposed Disinformation™ warfare can actually alter the direction of a nation. In Chapter 5 ("A Silent and Undeclared WWIII"), I will address how governments are now more susceptible than ever and why. I also share how a new strategy has emerged whereby neither ally nor adversary is static. We are in the age of Ally-versaries™, where you need to be as cautious with your allies as you are with adversaries or enemies. By the end of Part I, I hope it's clear how the power of cyber can be used to threaten the survivability of nation-states and their citizens through the power of GPCyber™ influence and coercion.

For more information, please visit survivabilitythebook.com/ placeholder (or scan the code below) to see articles referenced as well as my recommended reading list. We have been very lucky to have journalists with integrity on the case. I encourage you to explore how the world received this story.

Don't forget to check out the *Survivability News* segment on Pfizer's rap sheet! I've included it online for your convenience.

5

A Silent and Undeclared WWIII

(Unmitigated GPCyber™ Warfare & the Rise of the Ally-versary™)

TRADITIONALLY, ACTS AND declarations of war take place first, before countries go to combat one another (as seen in WWI, WWII, Vietnam, etc.). After WWII, nuclear weapons marked a new era. Beyond it, in the interest of avoiding the nuclear button being a viable option on the table, countries are resorting to GPCyber™ warfare. Today nations are hacking each other secretly (at times, even openly) until they're blue in the face, and citizens all over the world are paying the price.

In the Era of the Unprecedented, government institutions (congresses, parliaments, etc.) don't need to pass the acts/declarations of old. Any speculation of a war between China and the US—as there most definitely was a conflict in 2020—is misguided. However, these two countries are facing off through modern cyber and economic forms of warfare. As the US administration establishes sanctions, and through COVID-19 speculations, tensions have only continued to mount. We are already in the midst of a silent, undeclared, and ongoing war.

Apart from conflict one might expect, we are seeing relationships change for the worse. On July 15, 2016, a coup d'état was attempted in Turkey against state institutions, including the government and President Recep Tayyip Erdoğan. People woke up to tanks on the streets and fighter jets bombing targets in the capital, Ankara. Turkey named a dissident, Fethullah Gülen, who was residing in Utah, as its mastermind. It also accused the US of supporting both the coup and Gülen directly and demanded his extradition.

Tensions had already been escalating between the two nations. US involvement in the Syrian civil war and its support of the Kurds was a trigger. Turkey views the Kurds as a big threat due to their aspiration of an independent Kurdish state that claims Turkish territory. The challenge is even bigger since both the US and Turkey are NATO founders and allies. But in recent years, they continue behaving like adversaries, more and more. Over time, due to their conflicted geopolitical interest, these allies became not only adversaries but are now on the verge of being enemies. In fact, they are so close to crossing that line that Turkey purchased anti-aircraft missile systems from Russia. This was a clear signal to the US that they were no longer willing to be their "bitch." Tensions increased further in April 2021, when President Joe Biden called the 1915 massacres of Armenians "genocide" as committed by the Ottoman Empire (Turkey's name before WWI).

How did two staunch allies and NATO founders find themselves at each other's throats? How do you mitigate the prospect of your friend becoming your enemy? In fact, not only your enemy, but a party that can destabilize your government, economy, and anything to do with your stability?

If you are an organization operating within the nation-state that is a friend to other nation-states, how do you mitigate not becoming collateral damage when your government falls out of favor with a strong ally? How do you mitigate not becoming targets of your country's newfound enemy?

From government response to basic cyberattacks of the past, and from pandemic responses, we know that we certainly cannot rely on failing governments. From Part I of my book, I imagine it's clear that we are in dangerous times. Extremist groups are becoming more lethal and sophisticated in their methods, while combining their efforts with run-of-the-mill criminals. In this chapter, I want to shine a light on the dynamics and relationships between countries as we carry out similar attacks on ourselves.

In Part II of my book, I will further explain the unprecedented vulnerabilities we face in specific sectors of our infrastructure. And in Part III, I will also share more about the ongoing effects of the systemic corruption and injustice surrounding Western democracy's stage four cancer. However, before we dive into such details, I want to make it clear where we stand internationally (and technologically, as I'll explain in Chapter 6).

I believe this context is important because companies and nation-states acknowledge that they are failing to prepare for conflicts wherein they stand to lose so much, if not everything, due to the status quo. The truth of the matter is that we have plenty to fear and mitigate. We need to be conscientious of our changing threat landscape and surroundings. As our home countries sort out their relationships, our survivability is on the line.

SUPERPOWERS (ALLIANCES FORMED AFTER THE FALL OF THE SOVIET UNION)

When the world had two global superpowers in the US and the USSR (Union of Soviet Socialist Republics), nations found themselves needing to choose one to align with. Since the end of 1991—when Soviet President Mikhail Gorbachev transitioned leadership to Boris Yeltsin and Russia went through its dissolution—the world has had one and only one superpower the US.

For years, America represented 25% of global gross domestic product (GDP) and has dominated economically, politically, and militarily. Meanwhile, the rise of China's economics and military has actually shrunk the gap, as its rise continued on unprecedented scales.

The establishment in the US is strategically focused on keeping China economically at a huge distance. As of 2021, the top three national economies belong to the US ($25 trillion annually), China ($16 trillion annually), and Japan ($5 trillion annually). The rise of China positions it as the new superpower of the 21st century, with the ability to rival the US on GPCyber™ influence. These two nations are dueling with each other to ensure the 21st century is theirs for the taking. As they carry out their conflicts, they are even thinking at least 100 years ahead.

As I'll share in Chapter 17, national security is dependent on economic security, and vice versa. Economic security is also reliant on the competitive and effective survivability of organizations and corporations. Therefore, the survivability of the nation-state requires stable businesses. Let's say there are 1 million organizations in the US during a full throttle GPCyber™ war with another superpower. While a small percentage of organizations might be able to withstand the barrage of cyberattacks for a short time due to their scale and resources, a larger percentage cannot—they will succumb as collateral damage.

The handful of companies in this scenario will survive because of their financial scale, security, and resources. The majority operate without this and have no chance of defending themselves. Their failure will result in job losses and economic impact—meaning, it will damage national and economic stability. And for any companies left unravaged by the devastation of cyberattacks, they will now be vulnerable to the market and its forces.

Organizations need to rely on a government that can efficiently support them in defending themselves through resources, information, and tools. If the majority of them require assistance for their own stability, governments should then step up if they want any hope of their nation-state maintaining stability in the economy.

Agility in adaptability is key to competitive survivability. Effective upgrading of government strategies needs to happen overnight—but it won't, and time is of the essence. For any nation that can accelerate the adoption of a Cyber-Survivability™ strategy model, this will secure competitive advantage over other nation-states and greater independence from possible coercion through GPCyber™ warfare. As shared at the end of Chapter 2, for our clients, this begins with a "Richter scale" measurement in which we analyze the "seismic" activity of nation-states and organizations in order to determine cyber and non-cyber threats specific to them. From there, we then conduct further threat vector analysis to determine priorities as to where they rank on each risk.

Adopting a Cyber-Survivability™ strategy model is not impossible. It's a disruptive concept that's becoming more imperative as this era unfolds. As we live beyond the warnings and the watershed moments I've shared in Part I, there is no longer room for excuses when leaders get caught with their pants down. As the potential for devastation rises, so too do our responsibilities.

ALLY-VERSARIES™ (REDEFINED RELATIONSHIPS IN THE 21ST CENTURY)

At this point, you should be asking yourself these questions:

- Who am I defending myself against?
- Who must I consider as a prospective problem?

The answer is not so simple. Unfortunately, the traditional models of creating alliances between nations based on honor and mutual respect are long gone in the Era of the Unprecedented. In assessing our relationships with enemies, adversaries, and allies, we need to consider the factor of time. Historically speaking, these relationships have been obvious.

In the 70 years or so between the Russian Revolution and the collapse of the Soviet Union, all countries within that union would have been considered allies. The moment that the Soviet Union collapsed, many Eastern Bloc nations began going through changes toward more democratic models and got closer to the West and the US. Today, former allies in the form of Russia and Ukraine are archenemies in a traditional, ongoing war.

Another example, as alluded to at the beginning of this chapter, is the alliance between the US and Turkey. Since the 1950s, the two nations were cofounders of NATO. By today, over the Syrian crisis, the conflicting importance of the Kurds to these allies turned the US and Turkey into arch adversaries in 2019. At the end of this chapter, I will address the 2017 Qatar and Saudi Arabia quarrel in which brothers became archenemies within days. Their conflict is still ongoing.

Our current state of relationships rings true with an old Arabic proverb: "If you see the fangs of the lion shining brightly, don't assume the lion is smiling at you." In the unprecedented era, governments find themselves dealing with many smiling nation-states. Those smiles are not an indication of trusted alliances. For all intents and purposes, in this metaphor, we are either looking at traditional adversaries or the new Ally-versaries™.

Traditional adversaries are enemies that sometimes collaborate within specific issues, contexts, etc. Today, the US has no issues declaring the Chinese Communist Party an enemy. However, the US positions itself as a friend to the people of China. These two countries consume one another's goods and collaborate on entertainment, technology, pandemic response (for what it's worth), etc.

Even with enemies, a nation may want to have trading and economic relationships in order to use this as leverage, such as sanctions, if not coercion. If you have no ties, you have no leverage. For current GPCyber™

tactics used between adversaries, the objective is seldom military imposition; it's predominantly to gain an upper hand in negotiation or conclusion of agreements or treaties. Coercion is accomplished using sensitive data/information to "inspire" the adoption of any desired programs, plans, policies, etc. There was a time when coercion was exclusive to traditional adversaries or enemies.

Since 2011, the Bush Doctrine, as in "You're either with me or against me," and the right for preemptive strikes on perceived threats—the proactive strategy of coercing allies and adversaries into taking a position that is in line with the US—meant that the US was willing and able to accomplish this. This could be executed through aid, collaboration, and so on. The doctrine continued through Barack Obama's presidency. It was heightened under Trump with "America First." And it's essentially thriving with Biden's administration in the White House (more on the war hawks advising him in Chapter 21).

Governments from this day forward must reconsider all established relationships with allies and reconsider each and every one of them as an Ally-versary™. Furthermore, they need to reassess those relationships continuously, be it quarterly/annually/etc. Gone are the days of sticking to your five-year strategic plans like gospel. As we can see from Turkey, relationships can change on a dime. And for anyone who is already aware of the events between Saudi Arabia and Qatar, you know how easily brothers can be turned into adversaries and then enemies within days.

Alliances take different shapes, formats, and structures: diplomatic, economic, educational, security, collaborations, geopolitical interests, etc. Relationships between countries can be strengthened or coerced through such alliances. Geopolitical interests being the root cause of many political and diplomatic earthquakes, regionally and globally, these interests end up becoming the earthquakes that shatter established collaborations.

Within the US, the desire to go to war with China does not exist; however, trade tariffs and financial sanctions on China are tools the US leverages to impose its political and strategic doctrines to slow down China's growth and its ability to become a competing superpower to US supremacy. Where the US has alliances with many different nation-states (like Turkey), it specifically has arrangements with China.

As China is treated as an adversary, there are less vulnerabilities in comparison to countries in alliance with the US (the EU, Mexico, Canada, etc.). A nation-state is more vulnerable being an ally to another country than if it were an adversary or an enemy. The level of vulnerability increases if the relationship between the two nations is not equal in terms of size, power, influence, economics, etc. Therefore, the greater the dependency of one ally on the other, the greater the risk of becoming adversaries—if not enemies. This must be considered in the reassessment of threat vectors for nations and organizations alike. Nevertheless, today, the greater the alliance, the greater the dependency and risk exposure.

Typically, there are preparations in place for situations where adversaries become enemies to the nation-state. However, it is not often that any in-depth preparations are in place for an ally becoming an adversary or enemy. Today's ally leader may become an unwilling collaborator in the future. The factor of time is key to why allies would also be targeted.

Global and regional superpowers often have succession plans in place for one or multiple favorable new leaders that are prepped and ready to take over from incumbent-friendly leaders who might one day decide to no longer kiss the ring—or even start having ideas of their own, God forbid. When PRISM was started in 2007, it began as a US/NSA spying program intended to make us safer from terrorists. It ended up being an unprecedented scandal.

By 2017, after Edward Snowden's infamous leak, it was discovered that the US was spying not only on its citizens, which was illegal, but on the world—which included allies such as Germany's Chancellor Angela Merkel. So, the US government was caught with its hand in the cookie jar, spying on its allies. With PRISM in mind, a superpower like the US has the ability to leverage its capabilities to coerce allies into doing what they would not be willing to do under normal circumstances. It clearly has the tremendous ability to spy and reach parts of the world others cannot reach.

The spying methodology allows an ally to gather pertinent information on national leaders, government officials, and other important stakeholders to twist the arm of an ally to do whatever is asked of them. The US is not the only nation-state with these capabilities, nor is it alone in exercising them. Virtually all governments are engaged in GPCyber™ warfare. Most of them are on a defensive level because that's all they can afford or what their resources allow.

You'll find that most powers utilizing spying offensively often do so in the name of freedom/democracy/etc. This includes the US, Russia, China, Japan, Germany, France, UK, Israel, Saudi Arabia, and newly emerging economic powers like India, Pakistan, North Korea, Brazil, and Mexico. No matter the cause nor the intention, just as the risk exposure increases in alliances, actions of leverage have more power against declared allies than against adversaries or enemies.

Many nations will leverage the cyber capabilities of their allies to defend against or directly perpetrate GPCyber™ attacks, which also makes them more exposed to being coerced by their allies. For example, looking at the Western alliance, the US is the alpha dog. All of the other partners rely on the alpha's scale and strength, and higher capabilities of implementing GPCyber™ methods offensively and defensively.

This means that the US remains uniquely positioned to choose what information to pass to its allies and when, and what information to withhold to serve its own GPCyber™ and strategic interests. Often, the US does not share all of its discoveries or capabilities with its allies, nor should they feel obligated to. The US chooses which information to share at the time based on how it serves their strategic, national, or security interests. This is key.

Looking back at PRISM, the GCHQ in the UK (equivalent of the NSA) was directly and globally involved in the PRISM deployment by the US. That included any spying on Germany's Chancellor Merkel. In other words, the UK was a direct accomplice of the US in perpetrating its spying upon the world, including its own ally.

This goes to the heart of showing that even nation-states in an alliance can be compromised by the best of their allies. And because of this, it is vital that governments reassess their current national strategies vis-à-vis a national survivability strategy to encompass all government ministries, departments, and operations, and the legislative road map necessary to implement this.

TAINTED BROTHERHOOD (SAUDI ARABIA, QATAR, AND UAE)

Until 2017, Saudi Arabia, Qatar, and the United Arab Emirates (UAE) typically considered and treated each other not only as allies but as brothers. This brotherhood was on every level—economic, social, and community.

This was illustrated by the formation of and their membership in the Gulf Cooperation Council (GCC).

If you are an American citizen from California or Oregon, you understand where you fit within the US as a federal government. The GCC is similar to the EU and federal US. There were tremendous benefits for citizens within the council. Moreover, the level of interdependence by these countries is also on unprecedented scales—meaning, a Qatari can establish a new business in Saudi Arabia even though they aren't a Saudi and can operate it with similar rights (and vice versa).

In May 2017, weeks after President Trump visited Saudi Arabia, the Qatar Foreign Ministry of Information was hacked. The hackers posted statements attributed to the Emir of Qatar on its official website in support of known terrorist groups. Before the information ministry had a chance to discover the hack and take corrective actions, social media went through a viral domino effect within hours of the attack, positioning the Emir in support of terrorist groups. And within a few days, UAE and Saudi Arabia issued a boycott of Qatar by land and sea (any transport) and cut all diplomatic ties. Statements released claimed their position was based on the Emir's support and provided conditions Qatar needed to meet in order to rectify the situation.

Overall, this escalated into a pissing contest of sorts. Each of them began engaging in unprecedented deals on weapons acquisitions from the US. In total, this nearly reached $500 billion, and included the "Deal of the Century" (as you may recall from the famous picture), which became the highly controversial subject of the Palestinian/Israeli conflict resolution.

We made a special episode in MLi Group's *Era of the Unprecedented Investigative Program* using this crisis to illustrate what GPCyber™ warfare looks like in the 21st century. I'll further explain modern forms of coercion in the next chapter. Nevertheless, I want you to keep in mind that a single internet posting managed to change the direction of a country, a union, and the status of a long-standing alliance.

By now, I trust it's clear that Western citizens are participating in broken democratic processes with toxic information, nation-state alliances can barely be trusted, and perpetrators are not alone in using GPCyber™ tactics on their targets. Outside of specific regions, the traumatic sounds of warfare are fading into an uncomfortable stillness. As we continue moving forward, we are truly living through a silent and undeclared world war.

For more information, please visit survivabilitythebook.com/ placeholder (or scan the code below) to see articles referenced as well as my recommended reading list. We have been very lucky to have journalists with integrity on the case. I encourage you to explore how the world received this story.

Specific to this chapter, you will also find more regarding MLi Group's Comprehensive Cyber-Survivability and Security Risk Audits & Pen Testing™. You can also watch our official release trailer from 2018 (specifically touching on Qatar and GPCyber™ warfare).

6

Quantum Computing

(The False Narrative of Cyber Supremacy)

ON OCTOBER 23, 2019, Google made a "seismic" announcement. The Silicon Valley giant's research lab in Santa Barbara, California, claimed to have reached a milestone that scientists around the world had been working toward since the 1980s. Its quantum computer performed a task that isn't possible with traditional computers, according to a paper published in the science journal *Nature.*[9]

Could such an announcement be made without clearance by the US government and its national security administration? Absolutely not. And why, might you ask, would that be required? This announcement makes Google a geopolitical target. In fact, it also makes America itself a target by other nations and organizations pursuing quantum supremacy. Within the US, it's no surprise that companies like Microsoft are competing for milestones; competition comes with capitalism and technology. More concerning, outside of our borders, China and Russia are flying under the radar, occasionally announcing their progress.

Competition is inevitable within organizations and nation-states, and competitive advantage often leads to some form of supremacy. In Chapter 4, I explained the use of machine learning (Cambridge Analytica). Implementing artificial intelligence (AI) is a must-have for both corporations and nations alike. In terms of business, scalability drives profit. The use of AI means serving customers at a faster level while further understanding habits and decisions. For political leaders, this means altering and securing votes of the people. And as these same parties work closer to quantum accomplishments, citizens are put in further danger, yet again.

As if it weren't enough that we have machines deciphering at great scale, leaders are always seeking to increase speed-of-thought processing. The "positive" potentially brought by quantum computing would enable companies to further serve their customers in ways never considered before. This pertains to determining user habits, planning for peaks and lows of consumptions, and generally predicting what simply is not predictable today. Acquiring this before competitors delivers a significant competitive advantage for increasing customer base, consumer loyalty, and most especially, profitability.

Companies like Google, Microsoft, Facebook, Samsung, Huawei, and Tencent (etc.) are in the trenches of research and development. These private companies have numerous direct and indirect cooperative roles on cyber and technology with the governments of their nation-states. I am 100% confident that Google's announcement was choreographed with the US government on many levels. Nevertheless, for the corporations and the companies above, quantum gives them a definite competitive advantage. And for the nation-states they belong to, quantum computing can provide cyber supremacy.

When the Wright brothers announced their first flight in 1903, this wasn't just significant because we were flying. It was significant because everyone could now leave their villages and circumnavigate the globe. The advancement of airplane technology generally advanced travel and communication. This meant a competitive advantage for any company improving air travel designs. But for the nation-state, this meant supremacy; airplanes were immediately put to use as a weapon. As soon as WWI was underway, we had soldiers in the sky, immediately followed by legends of airborne skirmishes against the Red Baron.

FOOL'S GOLD RUSH

Quantum computing is the end of encryption as we know it. In traditional computing, the binary coding of 0 and 1, simply put, means *end* and *continue*, respectively. Computers can do this with such speed. For super computing, the same principles apply. And for quantum computing, the reality is a game changer, as it allows for computers to occupy the 0 and 1 simultaneously (and vice versa).

The arrival of quantum computing means the best encryption will become useless, and the data of nation-states, organizations, and individuals can be exposed in a matter of seconds. There are no data that can't be leveraged or exposed. The race for quantum supremacy is not necessarily about developing the "weapon"; it's about being able to defend against it. Ultimately, nobody can afford for others to have it first, be that offensively or defensively.

I'll share more on the following story in Part II (see Sector 4: The Cloud), but in the Marriott/Starwood attack identified in 2018, 500 million guest records were compromised, which included extremely sensitive information like credit card and potentially passport numbers. This included everyday citizens and may have included government representatives (politicians, ministers, etc.) and more. Forensics uncovered that hackers had been in the Starwood system monitoring data of half a billion users for more than two years prior to Marriott's acquisition of Starwood. By doing so, they now have the wealth of data on citizens and important players, which can be leveraged to target whatever plans they desire to compromise (democracy, leadership, etc.).

Marriott was not an anomaly. Yahoo! had 2 billion accounts compromised, in which hackers sat in their system undetected for more than three years. For the hack of Equifax, this involved compromised data of 143 million US, UK, and Canadian citizens. In each of these cases, very little of that data was seen or sold on the Dark Web. In all likelihood, these data are now in the hands of certain perpetrators. Yes, it's still encrypted, but they're waiting for the day the information can be unlocked with quantum computing and leveraged for multitudes of motivations.

You can imagine the wealth of leverage they will have upon the end of encryption. The minute someone has the ability to decipher via quantum technology, their capability to coerce leaders, nation-states, and organizations will increase exponentially. We're looking at a future in which GPCyber™ motivations are acted upon by our Ally-versaries™. Long live democracy ...

Quantum supremacy itself is a fallacy—a pot of gold at the rainbow's end. Any major player with quantum computing at its disposal can compromise the security of others. Assuming Google's breakthroughs lead to tangible secret sauce, the US could use it to expose the Russian military (and vice versa). This would leave opponents defenseless, as all facets of the military would be exposed.

At the end of the day, any sense of supremacy would be temporary euphoria. Due to the nature of weaponized quantum computing, no major world superpower can afford for its competitors to have that weapon without an antidote. Any success in this quest will be a short moment in time at best while it incentivizes competing superpowers to accelerate in attaining said antidote. Their survivability is now on the line.

COLD KILLER COMBINATIONS

As shared in the previous chapter, the story of Qatar involved a successful attack within hours/days/weeks. Part of this included a viral social media movement to discredit the current Emir of Qatar. Even without quantum computing involved, they still accomplished much within a very short time. If someone combined social media strategies with quantum computing and artificial intelligence (AI), the impact itself would not only increase but the targeting could be simultaneously further specified and well spread.

We've seen what machine learning and AI have been able to showcase: (a) leveraging the mass content of consumer data and (b) analyzing in order to determine habits of users (who had no awareness of such habits themselves). Cambridge Analytica was able to accomplish too much through a simple questionnaire. And again, while only 100,000 people participated, insights were gained on hundreds of millions of people. As shared in Chapter 4, this information was used to alter the direction of elections, including both in the US and UK. In the end, our likes and dislikes are truly vulnerabilities for persuasion.

Quantum computing will bring abilities far beyond hacking and destruction. A nation-state that acquires this before another can choose to breach defenses of other competing states and organizations. Through the work of machine learning, they can learn their way around data that have been protected in order to influence not only leaders but the population of target nations through coercion.

The cyberattack on Equifax resulted in citizen data being stolen and compromised. Again, that involved 143 million US, UK, and Canadian citizens. With quantum computing, not only would GPCyber™ hackers have breached these companies instantly, but they would be inside its system with full access to all data on all users/citizens with little to no chance of being discovered until it was too late. At the time of the Equifax hack, the hackers remained unnoticed—like "No evidence of data being leaked exists yet." The damage was implied to be mitigated or minimal: *Wrong.*

Once the information is on hand, and especially once the data can be decrypted, a very powerful strategy enters the realm of possibility. The combination of AI and quantum computing can enable sinister hackers to launch their own fake news or social media campaigns, which can literally change the direction of a nation. This can apply to data stolen from Marriott/Starwood and Yahoo! as well, but Equifax can be seen as a holy grail of sorts to the perpetrators. Ninety percent of its users are in the US and 10% in the UK. Armed with such information, a quantum GPCyber™ attacker would be armed with a plethora of information based on previous employment history, passport information, Social Security data, birth certificates, etc.

Imagine the seismic consequences! Not only would the US government's information and defenses have been compromised, but the hackers involved would now use that information to target 90% of the US's citizens. While the attack remains unnoticed, the people around you would be influenced by misinformation tailored to them on unprecedented levels. So, not only are your national defenses disarmed, but everyone is distracted and overwhelmed by what they're reading/watching online. Checkmate.

When the inner workings of nuclear energy were discovered, there was promise of new infrastructure, high energy, and potentially a "clean source" in comparison to coal. Competitive advantage would be found by the first to gain the ability of providing this to the public, as they would be able to serve a higher percentage of the population. Of course, this inevitably led to the possibility of a super weapon. Once we were able to develop the technology needed to make the concept of a nuclear bomb a reality, it only took two of them to bring the superpower of Japan to its knees (they did not surrender until after the attack on Nagasaki).

Nation-states and players that accomplish the goal of developing quantum computing can use it for GPCyber™ goals to affect opponents. They would be able to infiltrate a nation-state overnight and successfully paralyze it from the inside. As you will soon see in Part II, we are already vulnerable to GPCyber™ attacks, but in this case the scale will increase exponentially.

The day a government or nation-state truly cracks the quantum conundrum, they and their partners/contributors would be highly unlikely to announce their success. Why would they? By not announcing it, they exercise this unique, unprecedented advantage. That nation-state can now implement the exploitation of the current encryption defenses of all its enemies, adversaries, and even allies.

Keep in mind that not all uses for quantum computing fall under military purposes; for example, consider economic, political, and corporate. In the corporate sense, competitors would be using this technology to gain access to sensitive data and intellectual property. In some cases, the home countries of such enterprises might even help and support such activities.

Whether you're an enemy, adversary, or ally, if your national interests do not comply with another nation, prepare for GPCyber™ attacks and coercion. And as a leader, prepare yourself for being replaced. As said Chapter 5, today, nation-states need to assess any relationship outside of full-on enemies as Ally-versaries™. There are many fangs within the smiles surrounding you.

YET ANOTHER FALLACY ...

All major players are engaged in research and development both offensively and defensively. Quantum computing is indeed a dangerous tool, but no country can claim themselves to be white as snow in comparison to others on this topic. Virtually every country will struggle with mitigating this and will become compromisable when facing it. But that's not the only superweapon in focus.

As we can see from the world's COVID-19 response, it should be clear that a virus is more than capable of shutting down an economy to the point of devastation within months/weeks. No nation was immune to its destruction. For a global superpower, biotechnology (biotech) can solidify influence over Ally-versaries™, adversaries, and enemies. In fact, it's already documented as being part of assassinations. If social media wasn't already enough for influence, imagine the coercion made possible with biotech. Therefore, it is understandable why major players are investing heavily in research and development within their economic model.

In the western hemisphere, private sectors are responsible for the research and development through government contracts. In other models, such as China's, it's mostly handled by the government directly. Even for small nations, biotech can be a nuclear weapon to defend yourself from a goliath adversary or enemy. Due to biotech's unmitigable nature, it is an efficient equalizer.

Once quantum computing is officially cracked by a nation-state, all biotech information across the globe will become vulnerable to exploitation for ulterior purposes. Marrying quantum computing, biotech, and AI, you no longer need misinformation. All you need to do is create the first domino of a first super virus mistake in any lab and allow the virus to take its toll.

From Chapter 1, we know that GPCyber™ players are capable of causing malfunctions through conventional hacking. They were able to cause Iran's nuclear reactor to malfunction and cause damage to itself. Imagine the nightmare possibilities if such attackers were able to compromise the inner workings of biotech laboratories.

While today the attack could be investigated and dissected, armed with quantum computing, forensics to determine attribution could be made impossible. Devastating attacks could be made to resemble mistakes and glitches on the lab/government's part. Alternatively, "breadcrumbs" could be falsified by a third party, instigating conflicts between nations. Such a strategy was employed in setting Qatar, Saudi Arabia, and UAE against one another, as I've already shared.

THE LOGISTICS OF TODAY VERSUS TOMORROW

It should be clear that the possibilities of destruction are endless once quantum computing is unlocked by a nation-state. As long as they keep their new tool in the shadows, a new breed of preemptive strike will remain available. In the past, the doomsday scenario has been a battle of nuclear missiles, in which one nation launches and the other retaliates with more launches, and both parties suffer great loss. In the future, the missiles can be taken out of the picture, and enemies/adversaries can be made to tear themselves apart from the inside. All of this is possible while remaining anonymous.

With hawks in every superpower—who believe a preemptive strike is always viable, regardless of the cost or loss of human life—the acquisition of quantum capabilities means that the scenario of a preemptive nuclear strike preceded by a quantum hack, defusing all enemy defenses, is scarily plausible in their eyes. In essence, a quantum attack on a nuclear power could disable its ability to retaliate to a nuclear attack. Quantum computing removes the threat of mutual annihilation.

Meanwhile, there is plenty for us to be concerned with. Within international infrastructures, we are more vulnerable than we might want to believe or be willing to admit. I'm not just addressing weaknesses in a fortified wall but the policies and laws within the fortress itself. As briefly addressed in Chapter 5, national security depends on economic stability, and therefore, corporate stability. Within the last decade alone, consumers have been left with the bill after companies failed to protect their information. Not only are GPCyber™ hackers successful in their methods, but corporate leaders have no incentive to improve the playing field—in fact, they're working hard to keep it that way.

Over the course of Part II, I want to explain where you are most impacted and where your concerns should lie today, in the Era of the Unprecedented. While the future can be horrifying and out of our control, I believe the present remains actionable. You'll soon see that the regulatory regime's mandatory best practices are no longer fit for purpose or up to scratch. Let's name our threats, so that we may mitigate the hazards ahead.

For more information, please visit survivabilitythebook.com/ placeholder (or scan the code below) to see articles referenced as well as my recommended reading list. We have been very lucky to have journalists with integrity on the case. I encourage you to explore how the world received this story.

Specific to this chapter, you will also find more regarding MLi Group's Private Briefings on the topic of Cyber-Survivability™ versus cybersecurity (for both government and corporate).

PART II

Unmitigated Risks, Threats and Vulnerabilities

(Ten Sectors Under Unprecedented Threat)

7

Sector One: CNI (Critical National Infrastructure)

ACCORDING TO WIKIPEDIA, there are nine categories when it comes to defining what categories constitute critical national infrastructure (CNI):

1. Shelter; Heating (e.g., natural gas, fuel oil, district heating)
2. Agriculture, food production and distribution
3. Water supply (drinking water, waste water/sewage, stemming of surface water [e.g., dikes and sluices])
4. Public health (hospitals, ambulances)
5. Transportation systems (fuel supply, railway network, airports, harbors, inland shipping)
6. Security services (police, military)
7. Electricity generation, transmission and distribution; (e.g., natural gas, fuel oil, coal, nuclear power)
    - ❖ Renewable energy, which is naturally replenished on a human timescale, such as sunlight, wind, rain, tides, waves, and geothermal heat.
8. Telecommunication (coordination for successful operations)
9. Economic sector (goods and services and financial services, such as banking, clearing, etc.)

Whereas, in the UK, CNI pertains to 13 categories:[10]

1. Chemicals
2. Civil Nuclear
3. Communications
4. Defense
5. Emergency Services
6. Energy
7. Finance
8. Food
9. Government
10. Health
11. Space
12. Transport
13. Water

It is worth noting that the UK's definition of CNI does not include "information," nor technology, nor dams, nor commercial facilities. Nevertheless, 9 categories expanded to 13. And yet, in the US, since 1996, there are 14 pillars and 16 critical infrastructure categories whose assets, systems, and networks (whether physical or virtual) are considered so vital that their incapacitation or destruction would have a debilitating effect on national security, national economic stability, national public health or safety, or any combination thereof. From the Presidential Policy Directive 21 (PPD-21):[11]

> "Critical Infrastructure Security and Resilience advances a national policy to strengthen and maintain secure, functioning, and resilient critical infrastructure. This directive supersedes Homeland Security Presidential Directive 7."

The US CNI categories are:

1. Chemical
2. Commercial Facilities
3. Communications
4. Critical Manufacturing

5. Dams
6. Defense Industrial Base
7. Emergency
8. Energy
9. Financial Services
10. Food and Agriculture
11. Government Facilities
12. Healthcare and Public Health
13. Information Technology
14. Nuclear Reactors, Materials, and Waste
15. Transportation Systems
16. Water and Wastewater Systems

Talk about consensus ... what consensus? More like complete misfocus! Most governments have forgotten that the primary goal of protecting CNI is not the infrastructures themselves, nor is it the brick and mortar. The primary goal is defending citizens' lives and livelihoods and their economic prosperity en masse", which directly impact national economic growth and prosperity if any of these infrastructures are allowed to be compromised.

Overall, I believe we ought to expand CNI categories today. No singular definition has an overarching element to protect citizens nor any integration of human behaviors, domestic or foreign, to do harm; nor the agendas of the extremist ideologues to hit the West, where it can hurt most. I believe the definition of CNI should include any sector that, if compromised, can lead to a serious impact on the lives, livelihoods, and the economic prosperity of citizens, and the uninterrupted operation of society. For those who live in countries where freedom and democracy are enshrined by law and/or constitution, I would also add to my CNI definition: any sector that, if compromised, can impact the function of a democratic society.

The people should be our top priority, instead of infrastructures (and buildings) as things currently stand. Where are we threatened if an attack brings significant damage/destruction or our nation to its knees for an hour, a day, or (God forbid) longer? For the purposes of this book, over the course of Part II, I will be focusing on the following:

1. General CNI (energy, water, etc.)
2. Miscellaneous (general manufacturing, but specifically IoT)
3. Smart Environments (homes, buildings, and cities)
4. The Cloud
5. Banking and Financial
6. Telecom
7. Transport (which includes marine and shipping, as well as aviation)

ALL THE MAKINGS OF A DOOMSDAY SCENARIO

How many Americans know the significance of December 2019? Nothing will come to mind for most of them. It's not Labor Day, Fourth of July, Presidents' Day, Cinco de Mayo, Martin Luther King (MLK) Day, or Easter—and Christmas happens every year. December 2019 was a month where four US cities were cyber hacked: Pensacola, New Orleans, Galt (California), and St. Lucie (Florida).

And, yes. All this happened to American cities, in the land of plenty, not in Timbuktu, Zimbabwe, or some faraway place. Yes, this happened where supposedly we have the best minds in cyber security in the world and more money than God (the US is 25% of the global economy). How will other nations with less fare? Google search it and find out for yourself if you are willing to get horrified.

The significance is that the vulnerabilities that can allow the compromise of not just one city but many in such a short time is simply unacceptable. And this was made possible by a serious dereliction of duties and responsibilities of our elected officials and CNI operators and experts. Their sleeping at the wheel is putting citizens' lives, livelihoods, and economic prosperity under unprecedented threat.

And before I'm called a doomsday scaremonger, I want to share a report made by Emsisoft.[12] This cyber security company investigated these attacks. What they discovered and published on their website will make your jaw drop. It included the following:

In 2019, the US was hit by an unprecedented and unrelenting barrage of ransomware attacks that impacted at least 966 government agencies, educational establishments, and health care providers at a potential cost in excess of $7.5 billion. The impacted organizations included:

- 113 state and municipal governments and agencies.
- 764 health care providers.
- 89 universities, colleges, and school districts, with operations at up to 1,233 individual schools potentially affected.

The incidents were not simply expensive inconveniences; the disruption they caused put people's health, safety, and lives at risk.

- Emergency patients had to be redirected to other hospitals.
- Medical records were inaccessible and, in some cases, permanently lost.
- Surgical procedures were canceled, tests were postponed, and admissions halted.
- 911 services were interrupted.
- Dispatch centers had to rely on printed maps and paper logs to keep track of emergency responders in the field.
- Police were locked out of background check systems and unable to access details about criminal histories or active warrants.
- Surveillance systems went offline.
- Badge scanners and building access systems ceased to work.
- Jail doors could not be remotely opened.
- Schools could not access data about students' medications or allergies.

Other effects of the incidents included:

- Property transactions were halted.
- Utility bills could not be issued.
- Grants to nonprofits were delayed by months.
- Websites went offline.
- Online payment portals were inaccessible.
- Email and phone systems ceased to work.
- Drivers licenses could not be issued or renewed.
- Payments to vendors were delayed.
- Schools closed.
- Students' grades were lost.

- Tax payment deadlines had to be extended.

Emsisoft's report also said:

> The fact that governments are failing to implement basic and well-established best practices, even when legally required to do so, can only be described as grossly negligent—especially as these entities know fully well that they are likely to be targeted in the ongoing campaign of cyberattacks. There is no excuse for this. They need to do better. They must be made to do better.

Fabian Wosar, CTO of Emsisoft, concluded the post by saying:

> The fact that there were no confirmed ransomware-related deaths in 2019 is simply due to good luck, and that luck may not continue into 2020. Governments and the health and education sectors must do better.

Are you horrified yet at the sheer negligence of our elected officials and the experts they are relying on? Also, Wosar is correct on almost everything, except that it was sheer luck that there was no ransomware. The lack of ransomware was most likely due to the nature of the motivation behind these attacks—it was by design. And there is more. Just consider the many thousands of patients in hospital wards waiting for urgent surgeries. Imagine if that was the child or parent of a politician grandstanding how well they are doing to make America great again. Just imagine ...

A critical question must be asked: How much notice was taken by the city, state, and federal representatives and legislators, and how much change was implemented since to prevent any repeats of these breaches? To the best of my knowledge and research, little or nothing. Are you asleep at the wheel? We were lucky on some level this time.

All these cities were hit by what appeared to be a financially motivated ransomware. Have you considered that the ransom demands may have been decoys to hide more sinister Geo-Poli-Cyber™ motivations? Moreover, in all likelihood they were actually GPCyber™ motivated hacks with the aim of attacking Western core political and economic models to cause unimaginable consequences. Also, this may have been a dry run of where the soft targets are to paralyze the US, along with its economy and democracy.

Just imagine if similar sequences of GPCyber™ attacks were perpetrated, matched with some fake news stories designed to spread through social media like wildfire. Such Purposed Disinformation™ can truly cause devastation. And it all became possible because CNI has so many soft targets and vulnerabilities that are easily compromised. The problem is the strategic focus, the ethos of what the goal is, and what the prioritization and allocation of resources ought to be on.

I believe the CNI focus must become "people survivability focused," not just infrastructure focused. And, as far as I'm concerned, this refocus must take place immediately because after the first test run of December 2019, the next GPCyber™ attacks will be the real deal and more devastating, and society cannot afford the consequences of such high risk. So, if we were lucky the first time around because we were the guinea pigs being tested on, are we going to be as lucky the next time? If not four times in the same month ...

THE STAKEHOLDERS OF CNI

Elected officials are rarely experts in any particular field, be it finance, building regulation, cyber security, and so on. Generally, they go to experts for advice, which can take strategic, operational, or implementational form. Once these experts have devised a solution or a plan and a budget, the officials call it a day and move on to the next concern/agenda. Leaders will only implement what the experts say is doable—and what is sellable or can be spun to their voters. But most critically, the experts will only recommend what they know is doable, and this is often based on what they have done in the past.

Welcome to our bleak future?

Let me explain. When governments and organizations have a major problem they are unprepared to deal with, and they lack internal expertise, they generally seek out experts to help them deal with it. As I tell national and corporate leaders and boardrooms during our private briefings, "These experts are not only experts in their specialized fields, they are also experts in the 'missionary style.'" What the hell is that? you might ask.

In principle, if a husband and a wife want to have a baby, and the husband only knows how to make that baby in the "missionary style," how do you think the next baby will be made? In defense of the husband, he may go online and watch a few video tutorials to improve his baby-making technique, but the principal methodology remains the same despite the few tweaks. Why is this relevant to defending critical national infrastructure and the nation-state?

Experts who have been doing things for the last 10 to 20 years or longer—who have recommended the injection of high-tech solutions into national cyber security mitigation strategies at a cost of tens of billions of dollars per year in taxpayer money—continue to fail to defend nation-states, corporations, and ultimately the people. These are the experts that our elected representatives, who are supposedly sworn to serving, protecting, and defending us, are continuing to rely on.

Politicians rely on such experts for comprehensive advice, which is not their strength. Another major issue is the fact many of these experts are tied to certain solution providers, which they often recommend. Technology aside, they lack not only necessary comprehensive expertise but also the capability to add critically needed new processes, intelligence gathering protocols, and new human brain talent necessary to upgrade their mitigation models for the task needed today and for the 21st century. So how can these experts recommend what they don't understand to figure out how to mitigate it?

Let me be blunt: How many top cyber security experts and strategists are also experts in geopolitics? How is their expertise in the motivation of terrorists, extremists, religious zealots, or other GPCyber™ motivations behind many GPCyber™ attacks, let alone their effective mitigation? The likely answer is a few (I'm being polite, as it's probably zero). Nevertheless, government leaders continue risking their national sovereignty and security as well as putting their citizens' interest on the line by relying on "missionary style" expertise when attempting to secure their critical national infrastructures, especially soft-target CNIs.

Let me put it this way: although the motto of the MLi Group and our subsidiaries for most of the last decade has been "Cybersecurity Is No Longer the Keyword—'Survivability' in a Geo-Poli-Cyber™ Threatened World Is," some mistakenly assume we mean that cybersecurity is not important anymore. Well, to put the record straight, cybersecurity is critical, and it must be done at the highest standards and expectations and not as a checkbox compliance exercise. Moreover, decision makers and people in general need to come to terms with the fact, and fundamentally speaking, cybersecurity alone is incapable of mitigating GPCyber™ threats, defending a nation or a business, let alone securing citizens' lives and livelihoods—not today and not in the 21st century. This applies to all current national or corporate strategies and their accompanying solutions.

Securing CNI is critical to the sovereignty and security of the nation-state. Any vulnerability within any of these segments has grave consequences on society and on the people. In terms of organizations and corporations, in most of Part II, I will be looking at companies that are meant to follow the laws and legislation under the oversight of the government.

In this case, CNI really ultimately comes down to the mandates and requirements governments place. This includes "best practices," which have the effectiveness of a wet lettuce leaf in keeping a building standing. In my humble opinion, these practices are part of the problem, which magnifies the risk exposure many times and only exists because our system is corrupt.

CNI is either operated by private operators or operated by governments themselves. In either case the regulatory oversight and the definitive responsibility of CNI is squarely on the shoulders of the government. It is the ultimate responsible and accountable party.

With regard to private operators, this usually can also mean nuclear power companies. From Emsisoft, we can see that health, education, and justice systems were affected. How many more compromises can we afford on any of the following?

- Energy
- Dams
- Nuclear reactors, materials, and waste
- Communications
- Defense industrial base (White House hack)
- Water and wastewater systems

One compromise? Two? Three? Can we afford the many thousands that have happened in the latter part of 2019?

And in terms of the people, we should start treating them as citizens, not just consumers. Why? Well, a citizen has more rights. And, when a citizen consumes, their consumption includes some of the basic needs for life (like water, heat, shelter, etc.), whereas a consumer consumes items that improve their quality of life, lifestyle, or aspirations, and they might be consumers of a certain service provider (telecom, gas, nuclear, cable, etc.).

We need to treat people as citizens first and as consumers second. In this fashion, we will refocus our strategic priorities toward safeguarding and securing citizen needs first, beyond just being a paying customer. This will help us redefine our civic roles, responsibilities, and accountabilities as well as those of our elected officials and who they rely on to protect us.

As an example, a citizen needs to breathe clean air, eat healthy food, expect their communication is safe, and to drink water that is clean. A gas supplier whose service is interrupted to the "user" would see themself as less responsible if the user is a consumer, rather than a citizen. After all, gas is used for cooking, heating, and other uses. Only if we think of the "user" as a citizen do we elevate our role/responsibility to better serving them. In doing so, we would be elevating the role of the CNI service provider to becoming a more effective player and integral part of the defense of the nation-state and protecting the lives/livelihoods of the citizen. When all CNI providers start following the same modified and upgraded strategy, they actually reduce the vulnerability risk exposures and the likelihood of a weak link compromising the nation-state.

Stakeholder management does not need to be complex. However, all too often, stake holding is driven by priorities that are often based on political narratives and imperatives rather than what is critically needed to be done. Moreover, leadership and management styles tend to derive relationships based on their own existing cultures, often without exploring the ethos of others. This antiquated mode of operation means top national and corporate decision makers and boards seldom ask the right question, such as:

- What are we not considering?
- What new strategies should we consider?
- What new processes should we consider which we currently do not implement?
- Why are they needed?

- How do we integrate them into our existing risk mitigation models?
- How would they elevate our mitigation strategies to the ever-increasing cyber and non-cyber risk exposures?

Overall, leadership and management are missing the understanding as to how geopolitical and external motivation impacts them directly and indirectly:

1. The predominance of human behavior and failure of operation
2. The welter of bad or conflicting advice which overloads the average operator
3. Lack of transparency when dealing with lessons learned

Although many talk about the above vulnerabilities, which are often not addressed or are addressed as secondary issues, it is key to recognize that this is the wrong focus. Without considering and factoring in the motivation and geopolitical factors (with a focus on protecting people first, not the buildings), CNI will continue to be breached. Cyber security, which often relies heavily on leveraging technology, tries to defend the CNI location by treating it as a fortress.

This is a recipe for more disasters waiting to happen—just name me one single fortress that is still standing in the last 2,000 years. By definition, a fortress is a solid, well fortified, and impenetrable location—until it is breached, and it is no longer a fortress. Well, CNIs are doomed to continue to fall victim on unprecedented scales until and unless governments act with a sense of urgency to upgrade their CNI cyber security strategies and regulatory models to what we at MLi Group call National Cyber-Survivability Strategies with a Legislative Road Map™.

If you still feel that what exists today still works and is okay, here are a few real-world examples to wake you up or help you pull your head out of the sand:

Russia, June 20, 2017[13]
Russia's cyberwar on the Ukraine became a blueprint for what's to come. Blackouts therein were just a trial run …

US, September 5, 2019[14]

Rockford Public Schools were cyberattacked via ransomware in Winnebago County, Illinois. Fifty to sixty of the district's 300 servers were completely shut down at the click of a button.

India, October 31, 2019[15]
Upon cyber-security confirmations, the country's newest nuclear power plant was already the victim of a cyberattack.

US, February 19, 2020[16]
An unnamed gas compression facility was also attacked via ransomware. The facility and its pipeline were shut down for 48 hours.

According to a UK House of Commons report,[17] a major cyberattack on the UK is a matter of "when, not if." And in 2018, according to the magazine *InfoSecurity*,[18] "over a third of critical infrastructure (CNI) outages in the UK over the past year were down to cyber-attacks." In fact, Members of Parliament warned that Britain may not be able to fend off a determined cyberattack. And believe it or not, many think that this was a revelation although the MLi Group and I have been warning about this repeatedly in the last ten years.

Britain's critical national infrastructure is vulnerable to hackers, and neither their government nor privatized operators are doing enough to tighten things up, a Parliamentary committee has warned.[19] The Joint Committee on the National Security Strategy has laid into the government for its slapdash approach to IT security, claiming that officials are "not acting with the urgency and forcefulness that the situation demands."

"It appears the government is not delivering on it with a meaningful sense of purpose or urgency. Its efforts so far certainly fail to do justice to its own assessment that major cyber-attacks on the UK and interests are a top-tier threat to national security," said a UK Parliament report.[20]

Another recent report from the UK Joint Committee on the National Security Strategy has raised concerns about the cyber resilience of UK national infrastructure. As the number of cyberthreats targeting CNI continues to grow in both frequency and sophistication, protecting the energy, water, health, and transportation networks we rely on has never been more important. Independent cyber security researcher

Pete Cooper describes protecting CNI against cyberattacks as a "wicked" problem, in that it is "both novel and complex."[21]

The Joint Committee report's recommendations are in line with the EU's Cybersecurity Directive, now transposed into UK law via the NIS Regulations. With government scrutiny likely to increase in the coming years, it is vital that operators of essential services and digital service providers understand their obligations and make every effort to minimize security risk.

It should be shocking. The US and UK have access to more intelligence and resources than most other nations, yet they're struggling. If these two powerhouses are struggling, how well do you think your nation is doing? What do you think would happen to you?

A NEW SURVIVABILITY DOCTRINE

Outcomes work best when technical capability is matched to process but optimized by human interaction. Common sense plays an important part. Success is often driven by enduring cultural change with CNI operators and those involved in the extended supply chains that make up complex national infrastructure. Good political leadership needs to be a starting point. At that, survivability—not cyber security—should be the driving requirement.

The majority of governments still have their heads in the sand. Some are trying but are still far from getting there and will still need a lot of drastic help. On an optimistic note, MLi Group is working with some governments, which I cannot name. But in Scotland, we are working with the Scottish Business Resilience Centre (SBRC) to bring together the necessary component expertise to develop a new "Survivability" doctrine. This requires modifying current procedures in light of experience and promulgating lessons learned in a cohesive and digestible form.

Other countries are also considering the MLi Model, including some EU and African nations with Comprehensive, Common sense, Cohesion of approach, improved Communications, and Cooperation. To this day, the five Cs have proven to be compelling! In fact, and surprisingly, emerging economies are proving far more willing to think outside the box and are more capable of adapting than those in developed ones. I can attribute this to the well-entrenched relationship between service providers and governments. Competing innovative strategies and solutions present an existential threat to incumbent advisory companies and service providers, and existing players present are a threat to their access to power and continued government contracts.

Today, it is not enough for citizens to expect more from their governments; they need to demand more responsibility and accountability. Governments issuing strong warnings without offering a plan or a solution is no longer acceptable. People should demand and expect their governments to have an effective plan and solutions in place in advance of any attack occurring. The days we could concern ourselves with only financially motivated hackers are long gone. Moving forward, we need to be far more concerned about GPCyber™ attacks by other nation-states and rogue states, but above all, the extremists who have no state—they can be the most lethal of all.

BACK TO DECEMBER 2019 (AND MID-2021, AS IF IT WEREN'T ENOUGH)

In terms of timeline, the four-part hack took a mere ten days. It began on December 7, in Pensacola, Florida. Their government telephone and email systems, internet servers, and the online payment system at the sanitation department and Pensacola Energy were rendered inoperable.

In the longest break of the attack, six days later, a state of emergency was declared in New Orleans after ransomware infected city servers and computers on December 13. In Galt, a suburb of Sacramento, city email and telephone systems were knocked offline on December 16. And on December 17, the St. Lucie County Sheriff's office was knocked offline, including the sheriff's office email server and the fingerprinting and background check systems.

Many businesses, like banks, might have many jurisdictions to comply with on national and international levels. The same can be said for a hotel chain, depending on the company. However, these cities need to comply with their own state/federal requirements to ensure that their citizens' day-to-day lives are not impacted. And they are failing miserably at this.

This makes the focus of what these cities must perform much narrower than a multinational corporation; yet they are failing at this too. Furthermore, when a city is breached, the direct responsibility and oversight is in the hands of the city/state/legislature, not a third party or private-sector contractor (such as port authorities in Sector 8: Maritime & Shipping).

If our elected representatives who are mandated to keep us safe are failing to do so, the following is a fair question to ask:

What must be done about this?

The responsibility and accountability must be placed squarely on the shoulders of the elected officials who keep going back to the same "experts" in cyber security. And the "missionary style" expertise continues to be implemented as a solution and relied upon like the gospel. How's that working out?

Are you still speculating? *Khaled, a multi-state hacking in the US? In the same month? Really?* Yes. All this happened to American cities, in the land of plenty, not in a third-world country in which there would be vulnerabilities by default. The significance is that US vulnerabilities can allow the compromise of not just one city but many in such a short time is an unacceptable risk on people's lives and livelihoods. Additionally, all these cities were hit by financially motivated ransomware cyberattacks that shut down many of their basic services.

This is where I was going to ask you to imagine if these hacks were GPCyber™ motivated! But then I realized the error of my thinking. Why ask you to imagine? Silly me. Let me bring to your attention events that actually happened in mid-2021. So, if you thought the 2019 events led to lessons being learned, mitigations strategies getting improved, and regulations being tightened, prepare to be utterly shocked, again.

In June 2021 the Biden administration called on companies to step up their cyber security, saying: "We can't do it alone." The White House warning call came after the US had suffered two major cyberattacks that were a few weeks apart. Corporate executives and business leaders were told to step up security measures to protect against ransomware attacks after the hacks severely disrupted operations at the US's largest meatpacking company and the biggest fuel pipeline in the US.

Anyone willing to claim these targets are not CNIs (that they do not affect people's lives and livelihoods and the US economic prosperity), please stand up and make yourself known so you can be properly discredited forever. And yes, you read correctly. The NSA, the White House, and the US administration simply warned and politely asked leaders to step up. They did *not* provide new mandatory requirements or guidelines on where they needed to step up, nor did they promise to review the weaknesses in the current national cyber security strategy and the effectiveness of the mandatory regulatory requirements.

But to add insult and incompetence to injury, Anne Neuberger, the cyber security advisor at the National Security Council (NSA), said in a White House memo from June 2021:[22] "The threats are serious and they are increasing. We urge you to take these critical steps to protect your organizations and the American public."

White House press secretary Jen Psaki added:[23] "but we can't do it alone. Business leaders have a responsibility to strengthen their cyber defenses to protect the American public and our economy."

Don't forget, Joe Biden made strengthening the country's resilience to cyberattacks one of his presidency's top priorities—and the White House was keen on reminding everyone during the warning call to "step up" (more on this misguided requirement at the end of the book). Before Neuberger shared further useless and unusable advice in her memo, she wrote: "The most important takeaway from the recent spate of ransomware attacks on US Irish, German and other organizations around the world is that companies that view ransomware as a threat to their core business operations rather than a simple risk of data theft will react and recover more effectively."

Wow, what an amazing revelation, Anne! Did you just discover the disruptive motivation of cyberattacks in 2021? Why didn't someone think of this before in order to figure out how to mitigate such unprecedented threats and the US can be better defended and protected?

There is nothing I hate more than "I told you so." But I find myself having to this time. The MLi Group and I have been warning about the difference between financially motivated cyberattacks and those that are disruptive, destructive, extremist, terrorist, political, geopolitical, and "religious," to name a few. We encapsulated these non-financially motivated cyberattacks in the label GPCyber™, as I shared in Part I. But we even went one step further and formulated the MLi Group National Cyber-Survivability™ Strategies, Solutions and Services with Legislative Road Maps. They are especially designed to configure according to the specific needs and priorities of a nation-state to upgrade its out-of-date national cyber security strategies it is currently following.

Such strategic expertise at the NSA, advising President Biden and President Trump before him at the White House and guiding the formulation and implementation of the US national cyber security strategy, represents the epitome of the "missionary style" cyber security expertise. Is it any wonder why the CNIs in the US and all over the world continue to fall victim to "precedented" cyberattacks? How would they fare against upcoming unprecedented GPCyber™ attacks?

The severity of the consequences is getting more dire by the day, and their impact on people's lives is unimaginable. The biggest problem is the wrong strategic focus and ethos that are currently followed. This leads to having the wrong goals and their subsequent prioritizations, and the resource allocations that follow. I believe that CNI focus must shift to become "Citizen Survivability" focused, not consumer or infrastructure cyber security focused.

Over the course of the remaining nine sectors, it will become clearer that vital and new processes and protocols, matched by new strategies and operational responsibilities and accountabilities, are critically needed. This is because they remain missing from the equation. Also, current regulatory regimes and mandatory best practices are no longer up to the task today or in the 21st century.

This means that not only will our systems remain vulnerable on unprecedented scales, but we ourselves are left defenseless to cyberattacks that are far more devastating than just ransomware. National economic and political stability and security can no longer afford the incompetence of failed leadership, dinosaur mindsets, out-of-date strategies, and "missionary style" cyber security leaderships. The price is getting too high for the people who end up paying for it directly and indirectly, in one form or another.

For more information, please visit survivabilitythebook.com/ placeholder (or scan the code below) to see articles referenced as well as my recommended reading list. We have been very lucky to have journalists with integrity on the case. I encourage you to explore how the world received this story.

Specific to this chapter, you will also find more regarding MLi Group's GPCyber™ Vulnerability Risk Assessment, as well as our five-level training.

8
Sector Two: IoT & Miscellaneous

TODAY, MORE THAN 1 billion internet devices are entering the internet every quarter, with little attention to security or patching. We are in the midst of an exponential rise in the use of internet of things (IoT) products. And all IoT vendors pitch their products as the solution to people's everyday problems. Yet, our chances of serious damage or even peril are also increasing with this specific trend. This is a profound new threat vector to the economy, security, and sovereignty of nation-states as well as sectors and their stakeholders all over the world. Nations that pride themselves on being leading hubs of smart cities, smart buildings, and everything within that umbrella are now under never seen before risks of compromise or even devastation by Geo-Poli-Cyber™ (GPCyber™) warfare or a GPCyber™ motivated attack.

In addition to IoT vulnerabilities, we live in an era of unprecedented GPCyber™ events. This is not only in the cyber arena where we have witnessed major governments and companies being cyber breached with damage on unprecedented scales, but also across politics, business, society, and culture. This is not scaremongering; this is a reality check.

These developments are taking place under minimal, almost nonexistent, or failed national regulatory frameworks—let alone any international multilateral treaties or any serious or effective industry-led standards or best practices. Additionally, today, unprecedented trojan horses present themselves through the connectivity challenges and issues in what is known as "sexy products." So, what qualifies as a sexy product?

Well, consider kids' toys, or baby monitors, or even sex toys, printers, fax machines, coffee machines, etc. If the mention of sex toys made you laugh, let me repeat: this is not a comedy. These are products that contain IoT components that are present not only in the public circulation of everyday life of ordinary citizens but also in the infrastructure of many corporate affairs, locally and globally. While dildos are microchipped to connect to the internet, for God knows what, and can be expected to be used in the privacy of the bedroom, coffee machines connected to corporate Wi-Fi can be the weakest links in security posture. Today, it's the little things that have become capable of compromising the entire security apparatus of an organization or government.

INAPPROPRIATE AND HORRIFYING IN TEXAS

It was Monday, December 17, 2018, just before midnight. Houston, Texas, residents Ellen and Nathan Rigney tucked their four-month-old son into bed and went downstairs to their living room. They expected another routine evening. They were wrong, as they were about to get the scare of their lives.

In the middle of the night, something sinister started happening. According to KRPC News,[24] a stranger's voice began mouthing off "sexual expletives," spewed out through the baby monitor—one that was linked to a Nest camera in their infant son's room upstairs. Alarmed, the Rigneys turned on their lights, but the same man's voice came on telling them to turn the lights back off. They heard him say, "I'm going to kidnap your baby."

Ellen Rigney has recalled his claims that he was in the baby's room. This gave the parents the fright of their life. Nathan Rigney dashed upstairs to his son's crib, only to find his four-month-old was fast asleep with no one in the room. The baby was totally oblivious to what was going on. It was at that moment that the Rigneys became aware they had been hacked. Next, they shut down their cameras and Wi-Fi and called the police.

When Ellen Rigney shared their experience on her Facebook page, she called the experience unnerving: "I did not know what to think. It's a voice that I'll never forget." She told KRPC News, "You have something that's supposed to make you feel better and safer, but instead it makes you feel the opposite. It makes you feel invaded and uncomfortable."

Worth the snazz? Unlike the limited range of a walkie-talkie, baby monitors are Wi-Fi enabled to allow parents to keep tabs on a child from anywhere they have a Wi-Fi connection—not just from down the hall. But the Rigneys aren't the only ones who found that these snazzier baby monitors and camera systems are vulnerable to being hacked. Of course, the problem isn't limited to baby monitors. Consider this pants-down question:

Where does that leave governments around the world responsible for ensuring the economy and security of their nation-states, citizens, and all stakeholders are effectively protected?

Reconcile this with the fact that cyber security, resiliency, and continuity strategies and solutions continue to fail organizations and governments on unprecedented scales all over the world. Yet, most governments continue to follow the same traditional templated modalities, which dozens of cyber breaches in recent years have proven to no longer be effective. Alarmingly, what is at stake today is not just the prospect of a ransomware attack, but a GPCyber™ motivated attack that can devastate your nation's economy, security, government, and stakeholders on unprecedented scales.

WORTH THE SNAZZ? (KEY SECTORS UNDER GREATER THREAT BECAUSE OF IOT)

Today, your declared and undeclared enemies, and even your Allyversaries™, can compromise or devastate your nation's economy, security, government, and people to force you to adopt a new economic or political direction. As established in Chapter 5, GPCyber™ motivated coercion is a new template that is being used by many players around the world.

Key sectors require unprecedented legislative framework and roadmaps to reduce or mitigate them being leveraged by others to compromise a nation-state's economy and security for political, ideological, "religious," and other goals. This coercion can force political changes or alter economic direction. Sectors such as consumers and home users, health care, banking and financial, telecom, transport and transport systems, and industrial control systems (ICS) are all under significantly increased threat because of this seismic change in the global threat landscape.

The above sectors are especially vulnerable to the critical threat from insufficiently regulated IoT in countries worldwide, including yours. This presents unprecedented risk to the economy, security, and your nation-state itself—but above all, your citizens' lives and livelihoods. Below, we address at a high level some of the various sectors, industries, and issues and how they can be compromised by lack of adequate, effective, and timely IoT, and smart environment legislation.

IOT AND CONSUMERS AND HOME USERS

Consumers have played a leading role in the uptake of IoT devices, with their use of mobile phones, tablets, toys, sex toys, smart TVs, coffee makers, etc. Smart watches, smart health monitoring devices, smart appliances, and connected home surveillance equipment are all part of everyday human life of people all over the world, especially in developed countries. In fact, you would be hard pressed to find a TV today that is not "smart," ready to be connected to the internet with a multitude of services to offer. But without realizing it, many homes have at least 30 devices connected to the internet compared with only a handful only a few short years ago.

However, the world has witnessed the largest distributed-denial-of-service (DDoS) attacks ever in the form of the Mirai botnet. It used a single brand of a home closed-circuit TV camera to actually perpetrate its attack. Upon arrival, it literally shut down the internet on many service providers around the world, such as BBC, Spotify, and many other banking services as well.

IOT AND HEALTH CARE

Historically, health sectors globally have been heavily targeted by cyber-criminals because they present a great bounty. IoT adoption in health care is on a great exponential rise, which also raises the threat level to the nation-states. The future of health care, be it personal or hospitalized care, provides great optimism in what this could mean for ordinary people. IoT devices are not only used to provide monitoring of vital signs but also for management of drug and personal care. Successful GPCyber™ hackers can lead to anything from drug overdoses to wrong care decisions. These devices allow too many exploitable vulnerabilities to exist, which in turn become huge threats simply by connecting to the internet.

IOT AND BANKING/FINANCES, TELECOM, AND TRANSPORTATION

As 5G becomes the sexy must-have across the world, IoT may prove to be its Achilles' heel. Citizens are ill informed and not ready for its seismic consequences. Is 5G a hacker's paradise in cyber vulnerability? One must ask the question of the 5G network deployers as to how much focus they are putting on the security of their network at multiple levels to ensure that it is not leveraged for cyberattacks of multitudes of motivations. The same thing applies to IoT in the telecom sector, and same as well as IoT in transport systems.

Transport systems today include road haulage, parking ports, freight, airport luggage, rail/underground, buses, coaches, GPS, and traffic systems (etc.), which basically keeps everything moving on any given day. It should not surprise anyone to find out that transport is the most vulnerable sector exposed to cyberattacks, according to Gallagher, one of the world's largest insurance brokers.[25]

IOT AND INDUSTRIAL CONTROL SYSTEMS (ICSS)

This includes energy production, water/energy manufacturing, food production, farming supply, pharmaceuticals, etc. ICSs are critical to the well-being of any country, yet they remain vulnerable to cyberattacks. We have seen ransomware such as WannaCry and NotPetya give notice to ICS owners. The number of internet-accessible ICSs is increasing every year. Simultaneously, so are the publicly known vulnerabilities around the world.

Staying on this course is a recipe for disaster. While IoT is not limited to the areas in this chapter—and it does have tremendous potential to make life for humans all over the world much better—it has an equally daunting capability to compromise humans and humanity on an unprecedented scale. The nature of its vulnerability grows day by day.

MITIGATION MODALITY

Some governments around the world are in the process of considering one form or another of the MLi Group National Cyber-Survivability Strategies with a Legislative Road Map™. To date, government responses around the world to IoT and its threat have ranged from ignoring it to some veneer of a legislation/regulation that is industry-led self-regulation, or best practices. Such approaches often create standards that are neither sufficient nor adequate to protect its citizens, economy, and infrastructure, and which are often voluntary. Most are still tackling the issue with the same old-fashioned, slow-paced approach known of most governments worldwide, relying on their traditional special advisors' antiquated know-how. This also is no longer sustainable today or in the 21st century.

Governments need to commit their efforts twofold: (1) keeping up with the breakneck speed of technological evolution, and (2) staying ahead of the ever-growing sophistication of cybercriminals—as well as GPCyber™ players and domestic/foreign enemies who can bring a nation-state to its knees at the click of a button. Very few governments seriously consider IoT as an essential, 21st-century vulnerability tool that enemies and Ally-versaries™ can leverage as a cyber weapon to compromise key national sectors in political, economic, or other conflicts.

Technologies that support smart buildings have been around for several years on their own. The difference now? They're not only connected to a network but several other systems involved with usage, management, energy, safety, security, surveillance, etc. Such technologies are now installed in public stadiums, event venues, hospitals, shopping centers, public access buildings, museums, stations, etc.

In many cases, their promises of better efficiencies may appear to have been realized—but at what cost? Their security vulnerabilities are being discovered and leveraged much more quickly. A team of researchers discovered many zero-day vulnerabilities in the protocols of individual components used in smart buildings.[26] As I'll explain next in Sector 3, these vulnerabilities need to be addressed in stronger legislation so that companies can be better regulated with more stringent protocols to adhere to and become compliant to enable them to mitigate GPCyber™ attacks.

As I'll continue telling you, the current approach both is and is not working out, which you'll see from the emerging pattern in the rest of Part II. The citizen consumer is the worst impacted and is left to deal with the consequences on their own. This cannot stand!

INDIRECT TARGETS

In 2016, the Dyn attack took place, in which hundreds of popular and well-known websites and services were shut down as a result. Dyn is a domain name system (DNS) service provider. No operation on the internet with any e-commerce or other modality can perform its task without this service; it's a requirement for any online digital presence and is connected to the infrastructure of the internet.

When the Dyn attack happened, hundreds of websites and their services ceased to operate—companies like the *New York Times*, Spotify, PayPal, and the list goes on and on. Interestingly, this was not a ransomware attack, where somebody hacks a system and holds the target hostage until a ransom is paid before they can access their data. Actually, side note, this is very common with hospitals, which pay routinely for such ransomware. Nevertheless, Dyn was different.

So, if the perpetrators demanded no ransom, if they asked for no money, what was their motivation? you should ask. Well, consider that they literally caused a shutdown of the internet and the way it operates on a day-to-day basis. Incidentally, this also included automated teller machines (ATMs), traffic lights, and gas pumps. Instead of attacking companies directly, they decided to go after the source of their power. For at least a few hours, some for almost half a day, many of these organizations were unable to be online—and you can do the math—at the cost of billions of dollars.

MLi Group classifies Dyn as "non-financially motivated"—but more specifically, as a GPCyber™ motivated attack. So why would somebody want to perpetrate such a hack? It's highly likely that they first wanted to simply show that they can. They provided an example of what they are capable of. On a strategic basis, it could be argued that the perpetrators also wanted to show that they could cause the Western socioeconomic model of operation a blow, undermining a key fundamental of that model: trust. Trust in the system. Trust in the ability to operate under that system. Trust that is often taken for granted. And I predicted that it was highly unlikely that this would be the last attack of its kind. And in June 2021, my prediction came true.

For more information, please visit survivabilitythebook.com/ placeholder (or scan the code below) to see articles referenced as well as my recommended reading list. We have been very lucky to have journalists with integrity on the case. I encourage you to explore how the world received this story.

Specifically, you'll find a *Survivability News* article on the Dyn attack mentioned in closing.

9

Sector Three: "Smart" Environments

(Cities, Buildings, and Homes)

THERE IS A very specific genre of Hollywood blockbuster disaster movies involving terrorists taking over mega buildings featuring the latest high tech and architecture. Anyone who watches such films will notice they begin, in some form or other, by showcasing how advanced the building is, before all forms of destruction pounce upon it. In some of them, the filmmakers set the stage by establishing how the building is intended to be an impregnable fortress. These stories are the epitome of breach through design, tech, and lifestyle. Great examples of this genre can be found as recently as 2019 (*Skyscraper,* with Dwayne "The Rock" Johnson), as early as 1974 (*The Towering Inferno*, starring Paul Newman and Steve McQueen), as well as 1988 (*Die Hard*, right in the middle, with Bruce Willis).

Outside of entertainment, and back to reality, thousands of smart buildings around the world are being hacked by GPCyber™ perpetrators without any heroic involvement of John McClane, or even John Wayne for that matter. Using exposed NSC Linear eMerge E3 devices, hackers compromise the building using a specific malware (CVE-2019-7256) to take over devices, download and install further malware, and then launch distributed-denial-of-service (DDoS) attacks on other targets.

While these exploits can indeed be used to compromise the building itself and target its tenants, the pattern typically involves using their information to spread their destruction elsewhere. They hack, gather data, and move on to more targets. The first of these attacks began on January 9, 2020, and was spotted by intelligence firm Bad Packets; the attacks have continued in a steady stream ever since.

Experts described this vulnerability as a command injection flaw. It is one of the two that received a severity score of 10/10, meaning it can be exploited remotely, even by low-skilled attackers without any advanced technical knowledge. SonicWall said in a security alert[27] published over that summer, "This issue is triggered due to insufficient sanitizing of user-supplied inputs to a PHP function allowing arbitrary command execution with root privileges. A remote unauthenticated attacker can exploit this to execute arbitrary commands within the context of the application, via a crafted HTTP request."

DDoS attacks involve perpetrators sending far too many requests/transactions and an abundance of link clicking, causing a tidal wave of activity on a given website. The site becomes incapable of handling the sudden spike in traffic and therefore crashes as a result of this strategy. DDoS attacks can even impact the servers themselves (depending on the magnitude of the service targeted).

Part of the significance of DDoS attacks includes the financial consequences on the target. For a company that trades $100 million in transactions per day, in a matter of hours they will lose hundreds of thousands; in half a day, they will lose millions. Imagine what this means for multi-billion-dollar companies—both the impact on their organization and society at large. That said, this is not about gaining money on the attacker's part. If they compromise the business operations of their enemy, they may be serving a GPCyber™ goal. As established in Part I, their motivation is specifically not financial gain; however, compromising you financially is a means to an end.

The significance of all this to smart environments (buildings and cities) is that the current regulatory requirements on making them secure is not fit for purpose. With technology evolving at breakneck speeds and society running with it toward everything becoming "smart," we are on track for virtually every home, building, and city becoming a vulnerability. Truly, the "smart" of these environments is simply a series of devices comprising a system of systems. Making such things safe and secure for all stakeholders is in itself a monumental challenge that will be impossible to mitigate with the current regulatory/legislative models and processes.

CHALLENGES AND INEFFECTIVENESS OF REGULATORS (EVEN THE BEST OF THEM ...)

Regulators cannot act in time to respond to changes resulting from technology advances. Agreeing on any regulation or legislation takes time. Apart from fitting it into the priority of any government, it still takes several years. At that, draft legislations are often watered down as they move forward because of political compromise to satisfy the business stakeholders and their lobbyists—this is part of the process.

In the EU, the 1994 Directive took four years for the UK to enact (DPA 1998), and the 1994 Directive itself took several years before it was accepted by all member states. From the moment the EU first considered changes to its member states enacting them as law took about 10 years. This serious lag time was the reason why the EU considered changes in 2008–2009 and took the path of using regulation rather than a directive—this meant not only that each member state would be bound by it immediately without separate legislation in each country but that it would be worded in the same way in all their member states' jurisdictions to prevent it being watered down.

When the draft of the General Data Protection Regulation (GDPR) came out in February 2012, it was lobbied on immediately by the big-tech companies (mainly US giants). The amounts of money each one spent was unprecedented, and never before had the EU had so many amendments to a single draft legislation. There were nearly 4,000 amendments. In many instances, the lobbyists provided each member of the European parliament (MEP) they were lobbying the exact wording they wanted to see used.

In contrast, there was relatively little spent by privacy groups. In essence, the eventual GDPR[28] laws the EU enacted were drafted and funded by the big-tech companies. There are still many aspects of data protection that are yet to get addressed appropriately. One is exemplified by the Article 29 Working Group of the 94 Directive, which provided clarification guidance in a paper on IoT devices, such as its guidelines on GDPR.

Before looking at that specifically, we need to understand the guidance on data protection by design and default as set out in Article 25 and Recital 78. This states that the data controller and processor shall "at the time of the determination of the means for processing and at the time of the processing itself, implement appropriate technical and organizational measures."

It adds:

> [T]he controller should adopt internal policies and implement measures which meet in particular the principles of data protection by design and data protection by default ... enabling the controller to create and improve security features.

And ...

> [P]roducers of the products, services and applications ... to take into account the right to data protection ... developing and designing such products, services and applications ... with due regard to the state of the art, to make sure that controllers and processors are able to fulfil their data protection obligations. The principles of data protection by design and by default should also be taken into consideration in the context of public tenders.

In layperson's terms, this informs stakeholders that they are required to implement better security processes and procedures that are ongoing in order to adhere to this requirement. If you have the right design, you should then be able to continuously improve said ongoing security processes/procedures. You would think this means smart cities/buildings should be well defended/protected from Geo-Poli-Cyber attacks or privacy threats.

Well ... evidently not.

Reality says otherwise, as you'll see in Article 29 Working Party Opinion WP223. The following excerpt is from an internal discussion within GDPR by policy experts on how to deal with IoT data collection:

> This Opinion thus does not deal specifically with B2B applications and more global issues like "smart cities," "smart transportations," as well as M2M ("machine to machine") developments.

> Yet, the principles and recommendations in this Opinion may apply outside its strict scope and cover these other developments in the IoT.

The policy formulation was aiming to address IoT in the consumer environment, not in the industrial context (such as smart buildings/cities/infrastructure). This is a key weakness of the regulation, which leaves it to the operator (i.e., the owner of the building) to follow the "best practice" of their choosing. As you'll see over the course of Part II, best practices are themselves a vulnerability. These operators neither comprehend nor understand how to mitigate GPCyber™ attacks that go far beyond privacy threats. Therefore, we must ask ourselves this question:

Why don't GDPR policies and regulation deal with business to business (B2B) apps or smart buildings/cities, etc.?

The answer is as clear as morning sunshine.

Regulators and legislators cannot move fast enough to keep up with the breakneck speed at which technological innovation is moving. The GDPR examples illustrate an inability to legislate laws that serve citizens first and can also adapt as innovation moves forward. To legislate you first need to envisage the solution to the challenge you wish to regulate against, then you must draft it, and then you need to create consensus for it to pass.

The consensus building goes through the politicians' compromise process, where most politicians concern themselves with special interest more than serving their voting citizens and their needs (more on this in Part III). The result is very often a static, watered-down legislation that seldom serves the ultimate goal of serving the public good.

This failure to serve by politicians adds to the continuous lack of "corporate social responsibility" (CSR), which I consider a lip-service masquerade. Regulators and legislators cannot move as fast as tech companies, who in turn attempt to nullify regulation that would impede them from maximizing their financial goals and opportunities, which are seldom governed by any real corporate social responsibility ethos. Many of the abuses by IoT vendors stem from their lack of real CSR or vision, their ability to lobby for watered-down and/or weak data protection laws, and their mechanisms of enforceability.

When GDPR was being written way back in 2008, IoT was not in widespread use. Many devices were only invented for mass production as late as 2012. For example, today, every car manufacturer wants to present themselves as IoT leaders promoting their IoT label as if it were a sexy blond bombshell in a red dress and high heels, branding their products as 21st-century high tech. Meanwhile, they are ignoring the infections and viruses she has under that red dress.

As most corporations in most industries like to promote themselves as tech innovators and leaders, their adoption and use of IoT helps create this branding exercise. But then IoT itself ends up becoming their Achilles' heel. Still, the EU and the UK together with standards bodies have recently worked toward IoT standards. As of 2019, the ETSI standard on Consumer IoT lists 13 requirements:

1. No universal default passwords
2. Implement a means to manage reports of vulnerabilities
3. Keep software updated
4. Securely store credentials and security-sensitive data
5. Communicate securely
6. Minimize exposed attack surfaces
7. Ensure software integrity
8. Ensure that personal data is protected
9. Make systems resilient to outages
10. Examine system telemetry data
11. Make it easy for consumers to delete personal data
12. Make installation and maintenance of devices easy
13. Validate input data

However, both the EU and UK have worked together to legislate only the top 3 of the 13 requirements:

1. No universal default passwords
2. Implement a means to manage reports of vulnerabilities
3. Keep software updated

As important as they might be, they are truly insufficient to really protect consumers. There are two issues to consider:

Why only the top three requirements?

And why are they only regulating consumer devices?

TOP 3 REQUIREMENTS

Western governments, considering themselves to be democratic, tend not to legislate and leave businesses to self-regulate and innovate. They would rather let their own businesses break the rules and be market leaders than foreign competitors do the same. However, vendors do not have the skills, knowledge, or expertise to do much more.

And because most Western governments rely on the private sector to lead through innovation, they do not have the skill or know-how as to drafting regulation, therefore they are rendered incapable of legislating without further private sector input. Vendors have grown accustomed to providing insecure products without worrying about security, to the point that any more than the top three are too big of a step for them. Regulation is limited by a compulsory, baby steps approach, as the remaining ten requirements remain voluntary as a competitive edge over others.

Despite this, competing foreign products are likely to be available at a much lower price point. Consumers are more sensitive about price and may ignore the secure products if they happen to be more expensive. Meaning, the remaining ten requirements are left ignored by the consumer as they look for a good deal.

WHY CONSUMER DEVICES?

Three assumptions seem to be occurring here: (1) Commercial vendors already understand security and (2) how to implement IoT in their systems, and therefore (3) regulating this is unnecessary. Therefore, consumers with little knowledge of security will need protection. And, if consumers are getting more secure products, commercial buyers will also benefit at the same time.

In theory, it is unlikely that vendors will produce secure products for consumers and insecure products for commercial customers. The desired outcome is that both products will be made with at least the same security. The fallacy here would imply there is no need to create GDPR or requirements for companies to protect the privacy of their customers/consumers and penalize them severely because they should already know what they're doing.

To some extent there are benefits for commercial products, in that commercial buyers can purchase such things to advance operational efficiency and scalability and increase profitability; the security involved with the price ensures those benefits. Beyond baby-step requirements, the approach assumes that commercial buyers already have an idea of their security requirements and don't need regulatory protection. Consumers, on the other hand, do not understand security and therefore have a need to be protected.

The eternal alternative for consumers is to buy cheap, subpar knock-offs. Existing consumer IoT regulation is important and needed, but it's incomplete. It is missing critical components such as making subpar and insecure products illegal to import, sell, and distribute (in that country), with severe penalties for failure to comply.

MAIN CHALLENGE (WHO WATCHES THE SYSTEM OF SYSTEMS?)

Today, much of the security of IoT has not effectively been standardized or regulated. Policy makers and regulators need to consider that technology, like smart environments, are in essence systems integrated in many other systems. Specific to buildings and cities, these so-called "smart" environments not only lack a security operations center to respond to attacks, but they also don't have a privacy officer (let alone a Chief Survivability Officer, the necessity of which I'll explain at the end of my book), or mechanisms to oversee and respond to the wide-ranging cyber-threats and privacy issues.

For a single home, your smart system is likely composed of single IoT items such as a printer, refrigerator, air-conditioner, doorbell, washing machine, surround sound, television, and lights throughout the house. The systems of each item are integrated together into one. For a single building, there would essentially be multiple smart home systems connected together, resulting in thousands of interdependent systems becoming one massive system. For any offices that might be in this building, as you can imagine, the amount of IoT items involved could increase tenfold.

For a city, this involves connecting many smart homes and buildings as well as implementing "smart" infrastructure, so to speak, resulting in a system featuring millions of IoT components. For a single home or building, the systems already have wide-ranging privacy, security, and survivability ramifications, but when you connect all of them together, the collection of multiple data points about individuals is a great minefield that has not been considered at all. At that, it only takes one poorly configured IoT device to compromise an entire home; that's one of 10 to 20 items.

Now, imagine a smart building with thousands of systems and millions of devices; or a city with millions of systems and billions of devices. In principle, as addressed in Sector 2, entire empires can crumble purely because someone bought the wrong coffee machine. In the case of smart cities, one compromise can lead to control of traffic lights or elevators, or worse.

No matter the entry point, once a perpetrator is inside the firewall, all bets are off. Unfortunately, while there may be some regulation to force smart buildings or smart cities to deal with either security or privacy issues, none yet are in place to address and mitigate their own survivability. Additionally, since experts advising on the future direction of IoT could not envision how it would be used, it would appear regulators decided to let things play out to see how they can regulate the IoT consumer, commercial, and even critical national infrastructure spaces.

Bear in mind that the members who helped formulate the GDPR draft were not necessarily technologists but primarily policy experts within data protection. Here, we run into the same problem mentioned in Sector 1 (CNI). In this case, both the government leaders involved in the creation of legislation and the corporate leaders charged with maintaining the security of their organizations continue relying on "missionary style" models. A catastrophe waiting to occur will be the result of top management failing to add the correct expertise—or better still, a Critical Incident Survivability Response Center—as the single point of authority and accountability for this system of systems.

As the regulators are not demanding such centers, operators of smart cities and smart buildings don't feel the need to implement them. And many of them remain unaware of how critical they will be. In the meantime, the hands-off approach is no longer enough.

Western governments that consider themselves to be democratic tend to shy away from legislating, opting to leave it to businesses to self-regulate themselves as they innovate. They follow a laissez-faire economic model and would rather see their own businesses break the rules and be market leaders than be beaten by foreign competitors. This type of thinking has enabled the big-tech companies to get away with so much as they grew, and a lot more, once they actually became huge. As explained in Chapter 6, regarding the "race" toward quantum supremacy, with the many benefits involved of enticing these companies to remain in their country, it seems unlikely that Western governments will restrict their own big tech in any significant way.

FACTORING MORE THAN TECH

In recognition of the work MLi Group has been doing in this space, I was invited by the United Arab Emirates (UAE) government to the World Future Energy Summit, which they were hosting in Abu Dhabi in January 2020. There, I delivered a keynote titled "Securing Smart Cities' Survivability in a Geo-Poli-Cyber™ Threatened World."

In my keynote, I addressed the vital need to shift strategic thinking from cyber security and start focusing on survivability. I also advocated for reprioritizing the focus on CNI and IoT from the Cyber-Survivability™ angle; when compromised, they stand to cause the most impact on citizens' lives, livelihoods, and their society's economic welfare. I had the opportunity to observe many interviews with and presentations by a number of government presidents, prime ministers, ministers, and regulators from around the world, as well as top corporate executives.

It was such a shock to see how many top government officials who were invited along with myself were still pressing forward with cyber strategies that continue failing. I could see that they were genuinely attempting to mitigate major challenges their countries were facing; however, even though a lot of tech was being factored in, I could see they were facing the challenges of old mindsets, modalities, and models still in place. Previous to the summit, MLi Group announced that we would be holding board and one-on-one private briefings for senior government and corporate decision makers in parallel to the event itself. I was astounded by the greater-than-expected Expressions of Interest (EOI) requests for private briefings we received, which prompted us to announce the addition of a Dubai week of private briefings from January 19 to 22.

Our briefings opened up some very important high-level awareness and engagements with very senior Middle Eastern, African, and Asian government and corporate officials. The majority of these leaders were keen to understand how the MLi National Cyber-Survivability Strategies with a Legislative Road Map™ differs from the strategies they are currently following. Many were keen to learn two things:

1. How this will help them more effectively defend their nation-states, citizens, and other stakeholders from cyber and non-cyberthreats
2. How they can mitigate these new threats and turn them into national and corporate competitive advantages in the medium to long term

The reality is that we need to admit where we need to refocus and reprioritize before any true progress can take place. Some might think that, over time, the right experts will be in place at the right time, and legislation will catch up and maintain pace with today's technology. That's a wonderful pipe they're smoking. It's worth burning into your brain that the "right" perpetrators can strike at any moment in the interim. Beyond GPCyber™ attackers themselves, time is the other enemy.

Until then, MLi Group is committed to helping leaders and officials do what they can now in order to mitigate crises in the future. Our work extends across many sectors, as you'll see throughout Sectors 4 through 10. Our next sector connects many of the dots and I'm sure you use it quite regularly. Let's see how the cloud itself brings its own vulnerabilities to the table in Sector 4.

For more information, please visit survivabilitythebook.com/ place-holder (or scan the code below) to see articles referenced as well as my recommended reading list. We have been very lucky to have journalists with integrity on the case. I encourage you to explore how the world received this story.

Specific to this chapter, you will also find more regarding MLi Group's Survivability Risk Audit for IoT and Smart Cities and Buildings.

10

Sector Four: The Cloud

THE CLOUD IS often promoted by service providers as the place for individuals, businesses, and governments to store their own data with them. In essence, the cloud is a third party's servers that you can access remotely over the internet. Simply put, when something is in the cloud, it means it's stored on someone else's internet servers, rather than your own computer's hard drive. Threats that could affect cloud computing services include the following:

Cryptojacking: An illegal activity that happens when cybercriminals hack into business and personal computers, laptops, or mobile devices to install malicious software. This software then uses the device's power and resources to mine for cryptocurrencies or even steal cryptocurrency wallets owned by unsuspecting victims.

Data breaches: An illegal act that accesses confidential, sensitive, or protected information without the owner's permission to an unauthorized person. It is also the exposure of such files without consent.

Distributed-denial-of-service (DDoS): An attack in which multiple compromised computer systems attack a target, such as a server, website, or other network resource, and cause a denial-of-service for users of the targeted resource. (The Dyn attack was a DDoS, which I will talk about in this chapter.)

Insider threats: When an insider inadvertently misuses or intentionally abuses access that adversely impacts the confidentiality, integrity, or availability of the organization's critical information systems.

Hijacking accounts: This is where an email, computer account, or any other account associated with a computing device or service is stolen or hijacked by a hacker.

Virtual private network (VPN): A private computer network designed to protect your identity and internet browsing activity from hackers, businesses, government agencies, and other snoopers. Your data and IP address get hidden by virtual tunnel. The reliability of VPN providers is subject to their ethics and reputation.

Application vulnerability or insecure applications: This is a flaw or weakness in the system of an application that allows it to be exploited by third parties to compromise the security of the application and the device or website of a business or government. Hackers typically rely on specific tools and mechanisms to perform application vulnerability discovery and compromise. This is at the heart of many hacked and compromised big names. And it will be focused on in this chapter with a major example.

Inadequate training: Use your own imagination ...

A CLOUD NIGHTMARE

When Paige Thompson broke into the servers of Capital One, America's second largest auto finance company, she gained access to 140,000 Social Security numbers, 1 million Canadian Social Insurance numbers, and 80,000 bank account numbers—in addition to an undisclosed number of people's names, addresses, credit scores, credit limits, balances, and other information. This is according to a press release directly from Capital One.[29]

On or around March 12, 2019, Thompson attempted to access Capital One's data from a TOR endpoint and through IPredator, a VPN company. The code file from her GitHub contained the IP address for a specific server used to steal the credentials of a WAF-Role (or Web Application Firewall). This is an application that protects web applications from common exploits such as SQL Injection and Cross-Site-Scripting. Keep in mind that a classic method for compromising a server's role is by exploiting a Server-Side-Request-Forgery vulnerability. In layperson's terms, this permits the hacker to forge a request by the server and gain access.

On June 26, 2019, Thompson posted a list of files she claimed to possess. This connected the Capital One, WAF-Role, and another role, WAF-Web role, to her. The technical details of the breach are complicated, and The technical details of the breach are complicated, and Thompson's trial concluded with a conviction. But what made the hack possible was quite likely due to Capital One having misconfigured its Amazon server. A cloud server.

In my opinion, the fact that Thompson had worked at Amazon years earlier is inconsequential despite some describing the hack as an "insider threat." But discovering such server misconfiguration is a routine operation for security specialists and service providers. Such misconfigurations are common and fixable, which did not seem to have happened in the case of Capital One.

But the nightmare to follow Capital One and its customers was just about to unfold. The breach of March 22 and 23 affected about 100 million people in the US and about 6 million people in Canada (according to Capital One) and included credit card applications as far back as 2005. The company indicated it fixed the vulnerability and said it is "unlikely that the information was used for fraud or disseminated by this individual" and that it was still investigating.

Capital One CEO Richard Fairbank apologized in their press release,[30] saying, "While I am grateful that the perpetrator has been caught, I am deeply sorry for what has happened . . . I sincerely apologize for the understandable worry this incident must be causing those affected and I am committed to making it right." The press release pointed out that "no credit card account numbers or log-in credentials were compromised and over 99 percent of Social Security numbers were not compromised."

Although Fairbank's apology might sound more sincere than other CEOs in his position, this does not remove the responsibility in Capital One's failure under his leadership.

According to Capital One, it would notify people affected by the breach and would offer them free credit monitoring and identity protection available. The company incurred between $100 million and $150 million in costs related to the hack, including customer notifications, credit monitoring, tech costs, and legal support due to the hack. But above all, Capital One's stock was down 5% in premarket trading. Consumer trust and its brand name were seriously damaged. A similar event took place with a far bigger company, which I'll share at the end of this chapter.

CLOUD STAKEHOLDERS

It is important to identify the stakeholders in the Cloud sector and identify their roles, responsibilities, accountabilities, and their interlinked relationships with each other, domestically and internationally. We need to better understand how they interlink and interact with each other in order to identify what's working and what is not, and what is critically missing.

So, who are the cloud stakeholders?

1. You (as a citizen and consumer)
2. Service providers (business to consumers and business to business)
3. Government (regulatory agencies)

You, as an individual, use the cloud such as OneDrive or Google Docs, etc. You take photos or videos and have them automatically uploaded to such servers after giving your consent on your phone or device once. The service is often free, but you should expect them to be safe and secure. Also, the dozens or hundreds of apps on your phone or device are continuously monitoring, collecting, and sending back data about what you are doing to app providers—often labeled as "to improve customer experience." All this is legal but highly intrusive.

Businesses as well as governments around the world use the cloud. Service providers offer them specialist services. Large corporations often subscribe to Amazon, Microsoft, Google, IBM, or other cloud servers. And while this ongoing arrangement between businesses, governments, and service providers might tempt a financially motivated hacker, breaching servers therein for geopolitical, ideological, terrorist, and extremist motivations would deliver other strategic rewards and goals beyond money.

The web and app service providers collect this consumer and business data. Such data can include highly sensitive legal corporate secrets and ultra-sensitive data such as banking details. Service providers are expected to handle this data in conformity with the domestic laws of the country you live in—often by international laws as well, such as the European Union's GDPR—which govern how they are expected to process, use, and keep your data safe. But these laws are often years out of date and seldom reflect the breakneck speed at which technology is evolving.

You can start imagining the challenges to governments whose legislation can never act and effectively regulate fast enough. Also, imagine the leeway or ambiguity this gives service providers who wish to "innovate" or, in other words, push the legal boundaries to offer a service and be first to market without falling foul of the law à la Cambridge Analytica, or fail to meet the regulatory minimums.

This brings me to the government regulators who have the unenviable role and responsibility of enforcing the laws on the books and ensuring that sector stakeholders operate safely. In fact, sometime in 2019, I was talking to the head of a telecom regulatory agency in an EU country, who happens to be a very good friend of mine. We were discussing recent unprecedented cyberattacks.

We hypothesized what would happen if his regulatory agency were to adopt/upgrade certain specifics in their current cyber security regulatory policies to Cyber-Survivability™ ones. This would upgrade their current mandatory cyber security requirements, elevating the national cyber hygiene poster of all sector stakeholders, also elevating the entire national Cyber-Survivability™ and security defense posture, making his country more attractive to foreign investment. Ultimately, this would also boost the economy.

We then discussed how the result could deliver a National Cyber-Survivability™ strategy that would give his country a competitive advantage over other nations. His eyes opened wide at such implementation and positive prospect, and he said with pain in his voice, "I would love to see this implemented. But as a regulator and authorized regulatory body, I am not allowed to demand of stakeholders to encrypt passwords they store."

In case you missed it, this is in an EU country, meaning, it adheres to the GDPR privacy laws, which are the most advanced in the world, setting a maximum fine of €20 million or 5% of annual global turnover (whichever is greater) for infringements. And not all GDPR infringements lead to data protection fines.

Let's take a moment and focus on the current practice for fines. When a company is breached and fines are levied by regulator, fines go to the government, but little or no help is provided to compromised citizens. In fact, citizens/consumers are last in consideration of being served. So ...

- What happens when your identity has been stolen/misused or your sensitive data is compromised?
- Who really jumps to help you?
- Who is helping you recover your information?
- Who is compensating you for the time involved and damage caused?
- Who is helping you stop the abuse of your identity?
- Who is helping you in the recovery of your identity?

The answer to all the above is: *no one*. In fact, adding insult to injury, some of these breached companies created new revenue streams and business models out of failing to secure their customers' data being hacked by offering help and recovery services to compromised clients. Capital One specifically offered its clients free credit monitoring subscriptions. Can you imagine the audacity of the sales pitch?

"Has your identity and personal data been compromised by us? Subscribe to our Silver Service and get 50% off the first year—just our way of saying Oops!"

Or ...

"If you want the premium package, subscribe to our Gold Service and get 25% off for being a loyal customer."

Does the law and regulation mandate them to help you? No. So, when you've been compromised, the law is not mandating they help you adequately or speedily. But if you thought writing to your democratically elected representative would help—I say, don't waste your breath. A legislation bill that never saw the light of day under the Trump administration was the Data Breach Prevention and Compensation (DBPC) Act of 2018. It was proposed by Democratic senators Elizabeth Warren and Mark Warner in January 2018.

The DBPC Act proposed making data breaches affect the bottom line. If passed, companies that are hacked would be required to pay a fine and compensation to users. Not only did it never see the light of day, it actually died before birth.[31]

VULNERABILITIES WITHIN THE CLOUD

You may be shocked to discover that 90% of cloud cyberattacks are due to application and web vulnerabilities that are not discovered and patched fast enough. Worse still, lessons are seldom, if ever, learned. Too often it boils down to money and not enough budgeted resources being dedicated to this particular task.

It is important to explain to my readers that what may not be a vulnerability today may become one next week. Therefore, continuously looking for new vulnerabilities and speedily patching them 24/7 is a critical component of a national or corporate Cyber-Survivability™ strategy. There is no app, shortcut, or download for this. There is no aspirin pill. By not adopting this as a 24/7 protocol and standard operating procedure, your risks of being devastated by a cyber breach remain significantly high. In fact, delaying your decision to implement such a process is as good as volunteering your organization or government to be the next prospective victim of targeted GPCyber™ attacks, just like Capital One. And it was not alone. Many other major brand names were victims to similar unprecedented cloud cyber compromises.

From Chapter 2, please recall France's TV5 Monde. It was the victim of a highly sophisticated cloud vulnerability. The cyberattack exploited this vulnerability, shutting down its 11 TV channels and causing its websites to go dark in the middle of a new channel launch. The timing is further proof of the sophistication and determination of a motivated GPC attacker.

And do you remember Yahoo! (also from Chapter 2), the internet company with the best technology and brains around? They were compromised by the largest data breach on record—*twice*!

Yahoo!'s first reported attack was in September 2016. It had occurred in late 2014. That hack impacted over 500 million Yahoo! user accounts.

A second data compromise occurred around August 2013. This one was reported in December 2016, and it was initially believed that 1 billion user accounts were impacted. The total later turned out to be 2 billion. Adding insult to injury, it was later discovered that the hackers had been present in the system for a number of years, monitoring and gathering intelligence unbeknown to Yahoo! and its cyber experts.

Most readers may not be aware of this fact about Africa. For years, a very common practice existed whereby top government officials such as ministers, prime ministers, and even presidents used Yahoo! email addresses for official and nonofficial communication. It is highly conceivable that the hackers may have acted on behalf of a foreign nation or superpower that was surveilling Yahoo! email communications to gain relevant intelligence. Advantages can be gained by learning what negotiation tactics officials were considering. This would certainly help them gain better negotiated outcomes or secure improved trade and business deals.

From Chapter 6, Equifax, a US company and one of the world's largest custodians of highly sensitive citizen data, such as Social Security and passport numbers, addresses, and dates of birth (etc.), was also cyber hit. Between May and July 2017, the private citizen records of 147.9 million Americans, 15.2 million British, and about 19,000 Canadians were compromised. The US government and its legal system pointed the fingers of blame at China. In February 2020, they issued indictments in US courts against four Chinese military personnel. China denied these claims.

This watershed breach will be taught as a GPC case study at universities for years to come.

But what is undeniable is that the evidence points to no financial motivation. However, the sensitive data of citizens, which included those of top officials, getting in the hands of enemies or a foreign nation's security agency or even a terrorist group provides the ability to exert political, economic, or coercive leverage on these compromised officials, and subsequently, their governments and nations. It can help such groups undertake GPCyber™ attacks or warfare against the US, UK, or Canada (as in, the nations of the hacked Equifax officials).

As I shared in Chapter 2 and will explain further in Sector 5, Marriott was also breached twice. In 2014, Starwood Hotels was hacked, which Marriott acquired in 2016 not knowing of the hack. Marriott moved forward with the $13.6 billion acquisition, also not knowing that the hackers had been in the system for years, monitoring guests records and habits for long after the acquisition. Then it was hacked again in October 2020. What was the bounty?

- 383 million guest records
- 18.5 million encrypted passport numbers
- 5.25 million unencrypted passport numbers (650,000 US citizens)
- 9.1 million encrypted payment card numbers
- Many thousands of unencrypted payment card numbers

Stolen information also included travel arrangements of VIPs (where they're going, where they've been, likes and dislikes, etc.). All of this data can be a great tool for a GPCyber™ motivated hacker who wants to target high-value organizations and government installations or entities. Just imagine if the Equifax hackers were to collaborate with the hackers of the Marriott breach, or even worse, were the same perpetrators ...

- Can you imagine the aggregated intelligence that would be assembled? Can you imagine the devastating GPC attacks they would be able to perpetrate to advance their cause?
- Can you identify any defense or mitigation strategy or service today that can protect us against this?

Isn't it plain to see that current regulatory regimes' mandatory or best practices are no longer up to scratch ... and must be overhauled? The defense of nations, organizations, and therefore the citizen continues to fail. Fines are levied, excuses given, but blame is always laid at "factors"—never at the failed system itself. If you wonder why this continues to happen, I will answer this question later in greater depth in Part III.

Take GDPR, for example. It was originally conceived because the EU wanted to instigate the adoption of a better cyber security hygiene ethos by organizations. On May 25, 2018, GDPR became EU regulation. Its framework was instituted as a mandatory requirement for all member states—and anyone operating in the EU or anyone who serves a user within the EU. It meant that if your user data is compromised, you must follow the protocol. If you are found not compliant, as shared previously, you could be fined up to 20 million euros or 5% of your global turnover (again, whichever is greater).

But as stringent as this might sound, the law has many loopholes that organizations can leverage. Not convinced yet? Consider what I was sharing in Sector 3. The first GDPR draft came out in February 2012 but was immediately and heavily lobbied against by big-tech firms (mostly American). Nearly 4,000 amendments were proposed. In fact, never before had the EU faced and had to consider so many amendments to a single proposed legislation. Just imagine the money spent by the tech firms on lobbyists/specialists between 2012 and 2018 when GDPR became law.

Lobbyists "helped" by providing each member of the European Parliament (MEP) exact wording they "suggested" would better serve the regulation. The result of such lobbying assault means that one can make the argument that the final GDPR regulation was so watered down from its original plan. This is all thanks to the "support" of tech firms' funding and lobbying.

Having observed the GDPR journey and some of its subsequent implementation by organizations, I can tell you with confidence that more than 95% of companies who rushed to become compliant with GDPR before the deadline did so by following checkbox processes that would give them a plausible defense in case they were fined by the regulator after a breach that resulted in user data being compromised. They most certainly were *not* rushing to adopt a higher cyber security hygiene posture or ethos.

Worth noting is that California is ushering in its own version of GDPR. The California Consumer Privacy Act (CCPA) was passed as law on June 28, 2018, but it didn't go into effect until January 2020. It is supposedly meant to be one of the most comprehensive data privacy regulations in the US. But this is where I go on the record to say that this will also fail to live up to its goal, and it will fall into the same trap as GDPR did by becoming a tick-box exercise instead of elevating organizations' holistic cyber security risk and mitigation preparedness.

The bottom line is both GDPR and CCPA are touted as breakthrough regulations but are already out of date. They will fail to command what is needed to be implemented by all parties involved, today and tomorrow. To become more effective, regulations need to be transformed from cyber security to Cyber-Survivability™ strategies.

THE GOOD NEWS OF OWASP

The Open Web Application Security Project® (OWASP) is a nonprofit foundation that works to improve the security of software. It operates through community-led open-source software projects, hundreds of local chapters worldwide, tens of thousands of members, and educational and training conferences. The OWASP Foundation is a respected source for developers and technologists to secure the web. Its work has been critical for cloud and application vulnerabilities. It publishes the "Top 10 Web Application Security Risks," which is followed by cyber security industry professionals to prioritize their risk focus (owasp.org/www-project-top-ten).

In late 2016, OWASP organizers invited me to deliver a keynote presentation at one of their London events to their highly skilled expert members. My talk was titled, "Can Your Organization Survive a Poli-Cyber™ Breach?" Some of these experts were cyber security leaders for major banks, tech firms, and others. The talk can be seen at YouTube; the link is provided at the end of the chapter (my talk starts at 11:20).

In my interactive talk, I focused on non-financial GPCyber™ motivations of hackers, the unheeded warnings by top experts, the magnitude of damage they cause, and how this requires additional expertise above and beyond cyber security, which cannot mitigate it. Overall, I addressed how the additional but necessary processes can help them do their work even better. The feedback was very positive.

Many attendees wanted their company leaders and boards to become aware of this unmitigated threat vector. Some went back to their companies and shared what they had learned about factoring survivability strategically. This resulted in private briefings being scheduled with their company's senior executives, as well as with external execs they made introductions to MLi Group (as per style guide) and myself.

ANOTHER CLOUD NIGHTMARE (THE BIGGER THEY ARE, THE HARDER THEY FALL)

Deloitte, one of the world's "big four" accountancy and consultancy firms, was the target of a sophisticated cyber security attack that went unnoticed for months according to many international news outlets. The hack compromised the confidential emails and plans of some of its high-profile business and government blue-chip clients. Usernames, passwords, IP addresses, sensitive business data, and health information may have been compromised. Although the hack was reported in March 2017, it appears the hackers had accessed and remained in its systems as early as October 2016. The hack also compromised the firm's global email server through an "administrator's account" that provided them privileged, unrestricted "access to all areas."

In 2016, the year before the breach, Deloitte's revenues were in excess of $37 billion. They jumped to $47.6 billion in 2020. Deloitte was a client and user of the Microsoft Azure cloud service. Emails to and from almost a quarter of a million of its staff had been stored on Azure. How would a global provider of auditing, tax consultancy, and high-end and especially cyber security advice and services to some of the world's biggest banks, multinational companies, media enterprises, pharmaceutical firms, and government agencies get compromised the way it has? Does this tell you anything yet?

The usual PR and protocols followed. A Deloitte spokesman announced:[32]

> In response to a cyber incident, Deloitte implemented its comprehensive security protocol and began an intensive and thorough review including mobilizing a team of cybersecurity and confidentiality experts inside and outside of Deloitte . . . As part of the review, Deloitte has been in contact with the very few clients impacted and notified governmental authorities and regulators.

It worries me to learn that Deloitte also estimated that only 5 million of the emails that were on the cloud could have been accessed by the hackers. But I find their insistence that only a small number of its clients' emails had been "impacted" is even more alarming. I wonder how they came to that conclusion. Were they simply underplaying the risk exposure of their clients' data associated with these compromised emails? Or was it because the compromised email data did not surface for sale on the Dark Web?

Can one claim zero or minimal impact just because the data did not resurface on the Dark Web? Such conclusion would be highly inaccurate and irresponsible. In fact, GPCyber™ hackers who acquire such high-value data and intelligence can leverage such information for a multitude of future activities, including GPCyber™ target hacks against Deloitte's corporate and government clients directly for political, ideological, or coercive goals.

The spokesman concluded by saying,

> We remain deeply committed to ensuring that our cybersecurity defenses are best in class, to investing heavily in protecting confidential information and to continually reviewing and enhancing cybersecurity. We will continue to evaluate this matter and take additional steps as required. Our review enabled us to determine what the hacker did and what information was at risk as a result. That amount is a very small fraction of the amount that has been suggested.

Contrary to Deloitte's claims, its "cybersecurity" was not best in class. Not even close. Don't you also wonder, as I do, how Deloitte came to the certainty that only a small number of its clients' emails had been "impacted"? Or how did they reach the conclusion that enabled them to have "demonstrated that no disruption has occurred to client businesses"? Was it because the compromised information did not appear to surface for sale on the Dark Web?

They and many cyber security specialists make this grave and erroneous conclusion to the detriment of their clients who are being wrongly advised. In fact, GPCyber™ hackers are proving to be very creative in leveraging high-value data and intelligence they acquire to perpetrate future activities.

So, what went wrong? Why did a global leader and "best of class" in cyber security fall victim to hackers it guides governments and blue-chip clients worldwide to defend against? What made it get caught with its trousers down? Is it possible that the cyber security and defense strategies and services it cuts, pastes, and implements for clients—and the regulatory models it recommends, operates under, and advises on—is no longer fit for purpose?

The unprecedented hack of Deloitte is a testament to models that continue being followed like gospel that are incapable of mitigating today's global cyber and non-cyberthreat landscape. We are only four sectors into a total of ten, and I pray you are seeing the pattern that haunts me every day. But it doesn't end here. Now that we've established infrastructure, IoT, "smart" environments, and the cloud, let's continue with the vulnerabilities of Sector 5 (Banking & Financial).

For more information, please visit survivabilitythebook.com/ placeholder (or scan the code below) to see articles referenced as well as my recommended reading list. We have been very lucky to have journalists with integrity on the case. I encourage you to explore how the world received this story.

Specific to this chapter, you will also find more regarding MLi Group's GPCyber™ Incident Response and Communication Audits, as well as my OWASP Keynote (my talk starts at 11:20).

11

Sector Five: Banking & Financial

READERS OF THIS chapter might expect me to talk about incidents in which banks were the direct victims of cyberattacks. Well, while I will touch on that—and there are too many examples of such breaches—I will instead focus on two world-renowned victims of major cyberattacks that were not exactly banking sector players. Are you wondering why I am doing this and who they are? Well, I briefly talked about them earlier in the book: Marriott (Starwood) and Yahoo!

Banking and financial sector cyberattacks have become as frequent as the common cold, despite bigger budgets and some of the strictest mandatory regulatory requirements among all sectors. Some lessons are being learned, but many remain unlearned, as remains the case with cyberattacks and vulnerabilities in other sectors relating directly to this one. This sector must adapt ASAP.

It is a known fact that this sector is regulated to much higher requirements than other sectors when it comes to cyber security and compliance. And yet, almost on a daily basis, we hear of new events of breached banks and financial service players around the world. I find it fascinating that not enough people are asking what and why that's not working. Is it the regulatory framework? How about the "best practices" followed? Or is it the leadership that's not focusing on new mechanisms to make them less vulnerable?

NO CROSSES AND NO DOTS

It is my hope that by looking at the two cyberattacks mentioned above, I might be able to share with you not only why current cyber security, resiliency, and continuity formats are not working but why more needs to be done ASAP. Let me begin with Marriott, which bought Starwood Hotels & Resorts for $13.6 billion, as I wrote earlier. You would expect that the best of the best due diligence processes and experts were involved and top legal and financial advisors and firms would have been engaged. This would have been standard operating procedure for acquisitions, takeovers, and similar undertakings, more so with a deal of this scale. In fact, they are critical to making sure that all Ts are crossed and all Is are dotted.

Well, your expectations would be accurate, but this is not what happened in this case. Starwood was a hotel chain that came with a huge database. Marriott wanted to buy Starwood, and part of that motivation was to acquire its database to expand its outreach on a global scale. One key failure by these top experts was not to demand, at a minimum, a cyber security audit as a condition of the acquisition. I will explain what "at a minimum" means a bit later in this chapter.

In 2018, as I shared in Part I, it was discovered that 500 million guest records were compromised, which included extremely sensitive information (credit card information, passport numbers, etc.). Impacted users included many people who can be assumed to be VIPs (such as government officials from around the world). A day late and a megabyte short, forensics of the cyberattack uncovered that the hackers had already been in Starwood's servers for at least a couple of years. Unfortunately for Marriott, that means they were engaging with an acquisition of a company that was already infected. So, unknown to the owners of Starwood, the information had already been accessed, observed, and taken.

Marriott was first aware that it had been hacked when a security tool flagged an unusual database query. The tool was actually monitored by Accenture, which had been running IT as well as info security for Starwood before the merger and continued doing so for the legacy network afterward. The query was made by a user with administrative privileges. In a strange turn of events, analysis quickly revealed whomever the account was assigned to did not actually make the query. This means that someone else had the ability to manage or take control of the account.

As investigators secured the system for clues, beginning their investigation, they discovered a remote access trojan, RAT, as well as Mimikatz, a tool for sniffing out username and password combos in system memory. Together, these could have given attackers control of the administrative account. It is not clear how the RAT was placed into the Starwood server, but such trojans are often downloaded from phishing emails. Similar to the attack on Iran's power plant, it's very reasonable to guess that this might have been the way the hack was perpetrated.

What the forensics revealed is alarming. Had Marriott conducted a cyber security audit, which may or may not have exposed this—let alone a Cyber-Survivability™ audit—it would have most likely been able to determine that the company had already been infected. As a result, the final acquisition price would have been lower than $13.6 billion. Beyond a lower price, at the point of conclusion of the acquisition, Marriott would have received a company free from infection.

In principle, the flawed due diligence process meant that Marriott ended up acquiring an infected company, at an overpriced price. But to add insult to injury, not only did this faulty due diligence end up compromising its operation and brand, it also compromised the value of the Marriott share price itself. As I will share at the end of the chapter, Yahoo! experienced its own unfortunate acquisition due to following the same faulty due diligence process. I pray their stories are fair warning.

BANKING & FINANCE STAKEHOLDERS

As with every sector, we have key stakeholders that determine the way the relationships and the effectiveness of this one operates: the government, organizations, and, of course, the citizens and consumers. Well, the governments provide the compliance and regulatory regime, but they also provide the enforcement tool that the banking and financial institutions need to operate under. It also imposes how users/customers apply these regulations, follow them, and at the same time, be compliant with them.

Organizations, more often than not, make their primary task to comply with these regulatory requirements in order not to be caught and be fined. Anyone who wants to debate that point is more than welcome to. Very few companies actually implement a holistic approach to cyber security. In fact, the board governance is often predicated on ensuring their compliance agenda is to minimize being fined or being on the wrong side of the law. At that, many financial sector players already allocate reserve funds that are recognized to cover the cost of the damage of such activity as part of the day-to-day operation of their institutions.

These rules and the regulatory framework are meant to protect the citizen and their stakeholders. However, the reality here is that they hardly do. In fact, I would claim that the sector is a prime candidate for Geo-Poli-Cyber™ motivated hacks for a fundamental reason: opportunity cost (as established in Chapter 1). Mechanisms and cyber security implementations meant to defend the institution are designed *not* to prevent the attack but to make the hacker find that it is far more rewarding for them to go somewhere else where it will take less time to hack the target. Bad news: this premise no longer applies when you have a hacker with a political ideological, religious, or destruction-motivated agenda.

UNPRECEDENTED BANKING & FINANCE VULNERABILITIES

More often, GPCyber™ players are willing to stick to the target in breaching it for days, weeks, maybe even months, due to the magnitude of their agenda. Unfortunately, they do not place opportunity cost value on their time. Therefore, any vulnerability exposed or identified that could lead to the breach of an institution will be leveraged to further their cause. And their reasoning has little to do with financial gain. This makes the sector even far more susceptible to Geo-Poli-Cyber™ motivation. It's not about what the institutions protect—it's about proving their capabilities to the world and to like-minded groups and individuals.

And to add to that, virtually all banking sector players continue to implement due diligence processes from the dinosaur era. In fact, the due diligence processes followed by these banking and financial sector players are often missing GPCyber™ and other geopolitical risk calculations and processes, without which these final calculations on risk, yield, and return on investment are all wrong. They impact conclusions on decisions to buy, sell, invest, lend, or borrow, which can all now be proven to be faulty. Let me repeat myself: Their risk calculations end up being faulty. Their return on investment (ROI) and yields end up being faulty. And this will compromise not only the value of the company you're acquiring or lending against but the value of the financial institution's portfolio, or that of the fund that may own the institution.

To put it in perspective, risk and return on capital for investing, selling, or freezing are all erroneous. Modern threats add an entirely new threat vector to the mothership investment portfolio. By way of example, if you have 100 investments and you invest poorly in five assets—whereby you did not follow a Survivability Due Diligence model—the impact on those five investments and the ramification of their performance will contaminate your remaining 95 good investments. In essence, it contaminates the entire vehicle that is driving your 100 investments and it renders the risk and return on investment on your overall portfolio invalid; the performance of the entire portfolio would be poorer than what you projected.

Without a doubt, this must be changed. Financial sector players need to modify and adapt their due diligence processes to make them viable. In the 21st century, without this, they are no further than a blink of a technology-eye away from such compromises and devastating impact. But this is a great risk not only to these institutions; this is a great risk to the citizens and the consumers of these financial and banking institutions. Today, as citizens, as consumers, we depend 100% on their uptime of operations for our daily lives and livelihoods. Any disruption can be very serious or worse—especially for those living paycheck to paycheck. In fact, too many cyberattacks in the sector are the result of application security vulnerabilities that remain unaddressed and unpatched for longer than is acceptable.

From South Korea's bank hack of 2013 to JPMorgan's in 2014, to the 2016 SWIFT hack, and so on (the list goes on), I continue drawing the ongoing conclusion of Part II. The regulatory regime's mandatory framework, as well as the best practices followed in regulating this sector have proven to be ineffective in dealing with the threat landscape. This is proven more today than ever before; but we seem to have discovered this from sources outside of the regulatory framework.

When Mossack Fonseca, the Panamanian law firm, was hacked, the attack exposed corruption on a global scale, directly involving top politicians all over the world (more on this in Part III). At that, it exposed their ability to hide money through the banking system that they are supposedly overseeing and regulating. Similar to this is the Deloitte hack. Deloitte is a top firm around the globe that advises governments and organizations on multilevel strategies, which includes cyber security. They were hacked. Caught with their pants down, the same organization provides leadership and services to governments and organizations all over the world.

And if we were to focus on the defense of nation-states and of organizations in the 21st century, we can conclude that these modalities are no longer fit for purpose and must be adapted. Fundamentally, there are not enough responsibilities (legal and financial), nor are their enough penalties placed on directors and decision makers when they fail. Adding insult to injury, there is not enough legal and financial responsibility placed on these decision makers to offer recourse for consumers who are affected. And this is where the strategic mindset needs to shift from a traditional cyber security, resiliency, or continuity focus to survivability. Only then can we avoid or prevent a sector Pearl Harbor event.

LESS THAN SEVEN MINUTES

In hacks such as the Dyn attack mentioned in Sector 2 (IoT & Miscellaneous), horrendous effects are all the result of GPCyber™ players showcasing their capabilities. This type of impact is capable of affecting virtually every single business or government stakeholder and their operation—their bottom line, value, and ability to function. This brings me back to the way many mergers and acquisitions are being done.

Using a flawed due diligence process, as well as flawed risk and return on investment calculations, impacts the overall performance of the company and the entire portfolio. In fact, acquisitions of companies or stock of companies need a new mechanism that assesses the direct/indirect GPCyber™ and general cyber terrorism risk exposure. Very few companies are capable of this.

Lucky for all stakeholders, we are unique in offering such a service for nearly a decade.

As established in Chapters 2 and 5, many companies may not think they are an ideal target; however, companies need to acquire the expertise of experts who can then advise them of the risk exposure as to these issues. Far too many companies are exposed but fail to realize it. And that makes the risk exposure and the nation-states they operate out of even greater.

Application security vulnerabilities are 70–80% of the reason why cyberattacks are executed successfully today. Many of these vulnerabilities are never identified in time. In fact, there's often time when a vulnerability may not be a vulnerability right now; but in in one or two weeks' time it becomes one because of exposure from new developments in application security. The trick here is that exposure is often unknown until the worst time for internal experts to identify and patch it before it becomes exploited by either a financially motivated or a GPCyber™ hacker.

Consider funds, whether they are sovereign, investment, or even hedge funds. Consider billions' or even trillions' worth of investments taking place by these funds annually, whereby they invest in stocks or acquisitions of other companies. Consider the mechanism they implement today and the due diligence process they're following and how it's erroneous as I previously stated.

MLi Group's uniqueness relates to the upscaling and adapting of the existing due diligence processes of funds, investment and mergers, and acquisitions firms to a Survivability Due Diligence model(s). And these are services that we neither publicized, advertised, nor promoted; however, we often get recommendations via previous customers or partner companies. In October 2021, the MLi Group launched Survivability Wealth Management™.

One day, a few years before the launch of Survivability Wealth Management, I was introduced to a CEO of a major fund. The recommending party stated that they thought MLi Group could be instrumental in helping them and suggested we meet to explore if and how our services could be of value to them.

Well, due to both of our busy schedules, it took us more than six weeks to arrange a mutually convenient 30-minute time slot. We elected to sacrifice meeting in person and went with a simple phone call as our schedules were so conflicted. And in that call, we spent maybe the first minute or so on pleasantries before diving straight into the subject matter.

I started describing how the current due diligence process of investing, acquiring, and selling was exposing investors to erroneous risk and return on investment calculations. As I then explained how this was impacting the valuation and the performance of their portfolios, I began making the case that critical processes are missing from due diligence processes, which are not being currently administered or followed. I told him, "If they were to be implemented and added, I believe they would prove the overall calculation, therefore improving the final return on investment and reducing risk on your investments." And then I gave him examples.

Of course, we had already signed NDAs, and the conversation was very, very confidential. Within three to four minutes, he stopped me. "Khaled, don't say any more. I see it. I totally see the value. And if you and your organization can actually help us in delivering these additional processes and calculations, then this would be very valuable to us in the way we decide on investing or divesting." And he concluded, "Let me set up a follow-up meeting in person with my senior executive team and your people. We'll sit down and figure out how we can make this implementable and figure out the processes."

So, in essence, a 30-minute scheduled call was concluded in less than seven minutes. He told me, "Leave it with me," and he got us scheduled within 10 days. It went very, very well. And in fact, we learned more about how they operate by way of investing and methodologies used, and how we could make the process even better.

Our improvements crystallized a systematic approach to investment that can cover the 500+ stocks they maintain, which they are constantly reviewing as to whether they should keep or sell, or any additional stock they want to consider adding to their portfolio. The process that we added included not only cybersecurity, but Cyber-Survivability™ and GPCyber™ risk exposure on individual stocks. Our process flagged every stock bought/sold in advance so that either a deep dive or a high-level audit could be administered to determine its viability to proceed forward or not.

NO ANOMALY

On March 7, 2019, Marriott's President and CEO at the time, Arne Sorenson, testified before the Senate Committee on Homeland Security and Governmental Affairs.[33] In this, he covered the official details of the Starwood cyberattack and its impact. With regards to any fraudulent activity with the stolen data, he said:

> Thus far, we have not received any substantiated claims of loss from fraud attributable to the incident. Moreover, none of the security firms we engaged to monitor the dark web have found evidence that information contained in the affected tables has been or is being offered for sale. We have not been notified by any banks or card networks that Starwood has been identified as a common point of purchase in any fraudulent transactions, which typically identifies the merchant location where cardholder data was stolen or where a data security breach may have occurred. We will continue to be vigilant for fraudulent use of guest information or attempts by anyone to profit from the incident.

Of course, there was a chance the hackers had financial motivation—that their purpose was stealing data in order to sell it on the Dark Web for financial rewards. I believe it is much more likely that their intention was using the data to compromise senior executives of major companies, or even government ministers or regulators of many countries. In essence, the hack exposed a serious flaw in the operations of the Banking & Financial sector—one that impacts players globally.

The addition of a Cyber-Survivability™ audit would conclude a more accurate risk versus return-on-investment calculation, leading to a more informed purchasing acquisition. But, as I told you at the beginning of the chapter, Marriott was not an anomaly. The Yahoo! breach was very similar.

In essence, Yahoo! was being acquired by Verizon. It was discovered after the purchase that Yahoo! already had one billion accounts compromised. In other words, the hackers had been sitting in the Yahoo! system for numerous years with the ability to screen and observe emails and communications of all users. Readers are recommended to go and do some searches on the Yahoo! acquisitions and the subsequent price, which ended up being negotiated to be lower. At the time of the purchase, no due diligence process included doing a cyber security or Cyber-Survivability™ audit of Yahoo! As it was for Marriott, this meant Verizon was about to purchase an infected property, which actually impacted its own value.

With 2 billion accounts compromised, Yahoo! had hackers sit in the system undetected for more than three years. And guess what? Many government officials (ministers, even prime ministers, and presidents in countries like that of Africa) today use Yahoo! email accounts for their own private or other communications. I leave it to your imagination what could be a good purpose to actually access the data of such accounts and the rewards it could amass to those who can have access to them.

What's even more interesting, from a GPCyber™ angle, most hackers who steal for money or hack for money end up trying to sell the acquired data on the Dark Web for profit. I encourage you to confirm this for yourself, but I believe you'll notice there were no attempts to sell these data. You must ask yourself, *What motivated these hackers?*

The perpetrators went to the trouble of sitting in the service for two and a half years without any financial motivation. If that's not a red flag worth raising, I don't know what is. Business and national leaders like the CEO of Marriott are the dinosaurs I continue referring to. Their mindset is an existential threat to national and corporate survivability and security today in the 21st century.

For more information, please visit survivabilitythebook.com/ placeholder (or scan the code below) to see articles referenced as well as my recommended reading list. We have been very lucky to have journalists with integrity on the case. I encourage you to explore how the world received this story.

Specific to this chapter, you will also find more regarding MLi Group's Financial Institutions Due Diligence Processes Audit, as well as our new Survivability Wealth Management™.

12
Sector Six: Telecommunications

WITH MORE THAN 8 billion mobile phones already in use around the world and rising—out of which more than 3.6 billion are smartphone subscriptions as of 2020—lives and livelihoods of citizens across the world have never been so dependent on being connected. This sector has never been so critical as it is today; as it will be tomorrow.

Mobile and network operators serve unique roles that go beyond helping us consume goods and services. They are also key to weather, tsunami, and storm advance warnings, the capabilities of which can truly save lives. In fact, 2020 brought an unprecedented use of telecom by national governments and other stakeholders during the COVID-19 pandemic. Some of them were leveraging many of the telecom tools and technologies to disseminate important pandemic-related information. Some were Purposed Disinformation™, in the form of fake news, false narratives, and propaganda pertaining to either facts or fiction, all of which was subject to one side's point of view or position on the pandemic and vaccination.

Much of this disinformation was pertaining to the virus, whether it was nature made, man-made, China or US made, and whether pharmaceutical companies were masterminds of all this or just lucky benefactors from the vaccines—as well as Big Pharma's successes and failures in the development of the latter. This illustrates the critical role and power of telecommunication to impact society. It is a medium that can be leveraged to bring society together or create societal divide greater than the Grand Canyon, as we have seen.

SHADOW IT

In June 2019, stories of major coordinated cyberattacks on many telecom operators around Europe, Africa, the Middle East, and Asia started surfacing. Dubbed Operation Soft Cell, the hacking campaign compromised the IT infrastructure of many telecom network operators. This enabled the hackers to function inside the networks like a shadow IT department, complete with administrative privileges. Once inside the network, Soft Cell operated in stealth mode as it collected information about the network and compromised usernames and passwords. A modified version of Mimikatz helped the hackers do this, and it also allowed them lateral movement around the targeted network, including access on demand.

The perpetrators were able to set up their own VPN and at least ten different accounts with administrator privileges, providing them access to vast swathes of data. They were able to gain access to call records and geolocations of hundreds of millions of people. Worse over, they had the capability to shut off the networks altogether.

What I find particularly fascinating about this highly successful and globally coordinated attack on major telecommunications provider networks around the globe was that while Geo-Poli-Cyber™ (GPC) perpetrators had the entire fate of these networks in their hands, out of nearly a billion users, the attackers seemed to be only interested in gaining information about 20 or so individuals who can only be described as "high-value targets." The names of these targets were not disclosed publicly.

Moreover, the gained intelligence was metadata relating to who these users were calling—such as the time and duration and frequency of calls. It also included information about who they were texting and when. This metadata provided attackers with the ability to track users as their geolocation was compromised by the cellular towers they were connected to.

TELECOM STAKEHOLDERS

As with every sector, it's important to identify the stakeholders in the Telecom sector, as well as their roles, responsibilities, accountabilities, and their interlinked relationships with each other, domestically and internationally. Equally important is how they interact and communicate with each other to help, as well as how they are regulated domestically and internationally to identify what's working and what is not, why, and what is critically missing.

So, who are the Telecommunication sector stakeholders?

We'll start from the opposite side of the spectrum. In this sector, I'll begin with you—as a citizen and consumer. Second, we have service providers that provide business to consumers and business-to-business services. And last, government and regulatory agencies.

Citizens and consumers use or subscribe to telecom networks such as AT&T and Verizon (in the US), Vodafone (in the UK), or Etisalat (in Egypt or Saudi Arabia). Your services are calling, texting, and internet access or home broadband. In the process, you give numerous authorizations to your network to enable them to give you these services. In return, telecom operators store and analyze your data supposedly in order to provide you a "better user experience." Of course, both you and the regulator expect telecom companies to keep your data safe and secure. All of their storage and analysis is legal—until their network is hacked, your data is compromised, and you are left all alone to reclaim your stolen identity.

Businesses as well as governments around the world also use the telecom networks as subscribers to their business, be it corporate or government services. This makes successful targeting of telecom operators a potential treasure trove of intelligence worth compromising. As alluded to in previous stories of cyberattacks, in many cases, telecoms are conduits to exploiting vulnerabilities of nation-states. GPCyber™ hackers target high-value government officials who are users of the targeted network. Geopolitical advantages gained go far beyond any sought by financially motivated hackers. Breaching telecom networks for GPCyber™ purposes will deliver numerous strategic rewards including intelligence, very similar to the very goals seemingly behind the Soft Cell Telecom compromises in 2019 that saw telecoms worldwide lose over 100GB of call record data. In fact, the hackers had the ability to shut down entire cell networks had they wanted to.

Now ask yourself this question: How important is the role of telecom operations and operators for the superpowers of today? Do you realize how important this is for them to attain and maintain "empire" status, with political and economic dominance and continuity today and in the 21st century?

Not only is it critical; in fact, the very empire status becomes unachievable without dominating telecom today and tomorrow.

This brings me to key players such as Google and Apple (both US companies). I'm confident that most of my readers are aware of the conflict between Android and iOS operating systems. This issue forced Huawei to launch its very own operating system.

We cannot address the Telecom sector without addressing the 5G narrative in the US and around the world. The forty-fifth US president, Donald Trump, was fixated on blocking Huawei not just in the US, but globally—even to the point of issuing an ultimatum to US allies to force them to reconsider their use of the Chinese company's 5G technology in their country. The successive US administration recognized that whichever nation's 5G technology is adopted around the world will give it the upper hand in telecom, which also means becoming, or remaining, the primary economic power of the 21st century.

By way of further context, whichever 5G technology is deployed will enable its technology provider to incorporate mechanisms that allow snooping. This could be put in place instantly via initial infrastructure or a backdoor could be added via future updates. The concern spreading across the US was that if Huawei was adopted in a particular country, they would be able to match or replace the snooping capabilities of competing US 5G technology providers. Additionally, the Chinese have become stronger technology competitors to the US 5G. They were able to begin offering the deployment of advanced 5G offerings to governments around the world while the US players were still in testing mode.

Chinese technology players of course have strong ties with the Chinese government. While US carriers are private enterprises, they also have "relationships" with the US government. 5G carrier relationships may not appear to look as direct or intrusive as that of China and its own carriers, but it is no less "highly coordinated." I already shed some light on this in Chapter 6 ("Quantum Computing"). Meanwhile, I encourage you to not forget the ongoing pattern of special-interest lobbying keeping regulation and taxes at a minimum—a typical method that the government leverages to get operators to do what is necessary to accomplish their own interests labeled at times as "national security."

The US government's strategic concern is that if a Chinese carrier's 5G technology is adopted in a country, the Chinese government will gain strategic competitive advantage and have the upper hand in matching or challenging the US empire in dominating the 21st century. This is why the Trump administration promoted the narrative that Huawei is "unsafe." It would gain China backdoor access to the technology. This is because the dominance and economic power and influence of the US around the world is put at stake.

The fact is bright as day. National leaders and decision makers around the world—who will make the decision as to which technology to adopt—already recognize that whichever one they choose, it will have backdoors to snoop on them, along with their nation, businesses, and people. So, if you are buying from the US, the US is listening to you. If you are buying from China, China will be listening to you.

This makes a key point that must not be missed. All telecom providers play critical and intricate roles in their respective nation-states' governments. They often serve as the extended arm in their governments' global and regional, geopolitical chess games as well as their GPCyber™ warfare defense, offense, and chess gamesmanship. Many stakeholders participate willingly and actively, others tacitly. In my humble opinion, no stakeholder can afford to say a blanket "no" to their respective government. So, in light of the above, what can we say about the existing telecom regulatory model that oversees this sector? What about its current mandatory requirements and much revered "best practice"? Are they adequate or capable of defending the nation-state, securing stakeholders, or protecting users and citizens (as with previous sectors)? I strongly believe they are *not*, and I'll tell you why ...

VULNERABILITIES WITHIN TELECOM

As it should be clear by now, current regulatory regimes' mandatory frameworks and "best practice" touted as "world leading" and "best of class" are failing systemically on unprecedented levels; they are specifically failing to defend nation-states, critical national infrastructures, and government facilities. They are also failing to secure organizations and protect users and citizens today. In fact, defending the nation-state in the 21st century will require a different mindset, whereby critical national infrastructure (such as telecom) needs to become regulated very differently.

The evidence of such failure is blinding. Just look at the cyber hacks compromising some of the who's who of the global telecom sector, such as T-Mobile, Deutsche Telekom, AT&T, Verizon, Bell Canada, Cox Communication, MTS, and Vodafone, to name a few. Many of these breached telecom operators also happen to be critical national infrastructures of nuclear superpowers.

The failure of their mitigation strategies elevates their continued compromisability on not only themselves but also on users and citizens—whose lives and livelihoods have become so dependent on services provided. Even the regulator of one of these nuclear powers (which just so happens to be a permanent UN member with veto power), UK's Ofcom, was hacked and compromised. These startling reality checks are conclusive evidence that our current regulatory requirements are not adequate to defend the nation-state, especially when critical national infrastructures like telecom operators can be so routinely compromised.

So why and how are regulatory regimes' mandatory and best practices no longer up to scratch? This is partly because of key fundamental elements, some of which include the following:

- Checkbox exercises
- Breakneck speed of technological and threat landscape change
- Regulation's lack of agility and its inability to respond to speed of change
- Business and special-interest lobbying of government

Checkbox exercises are often followed in order to have documentation that can satisfy the regulator in order not to get fined when a breach happens. It is *not* focused on elevating the cyber security preparedness and hygiene of the organization nor is it tasked with upscaling its mitigation strategies and solutions. This approach became very prevalent since the General Data Protection Regulation (EU) 2016/679 (GDPR), which is a regulation in EU law on data protection and privacy in the European Union (EU) and the European Economic Area (EEA).

GDPR regulation was adopted on April 14, 2016, and became enforceable as law on May 25, 2018. Worth noting, GDPR is a regulation, not a directive, meaning it is directly binding and applicable. However, it does provide flexibility for certain aspects of the regulation to be adjusted by individual member states. GDPR ushered in the toughest penalties ever seen in the world on organizations that are breached and their user data being compromised. But, regardless of the new laws and the severe penalties being levied as punishments, telecom operators and other companies are still getting breached. Clearly, one of the key goals of GDPR is yet to be achieved. This is despite having to pay the higher of either 20 million euros or 4% of the company's global revenues as a fine.

As a result, neither the defense of the nation-state, nor securing organizations, or protecting the individuals is rendered better. The breakneck speed of technological and threat landscape change is a major challenge to any regulation. It continuously opens up loopholes that can be leveraged. Additionally, the current process of creating regulation and their lack of agility and inability to respond to technological speed of change compounds the problem. This is due to the lengthy time government processes take, which can last a decade or longer before becoming passed and made enforceable laws.

When you add business and special-interest lobbying of government in advance of any legislation being considered or passed, you realize why many laws end up becoming watered down—and forced to include improved "best practices" that are recommended but not made mandatory. This renders resulting laws less effective for the required task.

So, what is needed? What is missing?

First and foremost, we need an audit to improve and upgrade existing national security strategies to National Survivability & Security Mitigation Strategies—with a legislative road map. This would add and integrate needed new processes and solutions that are not currently factored in. Then we need to create a collaboration framework to serve as a Multilateral Survivability Regulatory & Cooperative Framework (MSRCF).

This new national and multilateral regulatory model is needed ASAP and must be created and collaborated on yesterday. They can be formulated as part of a nation-state's own National Cyber-Survivability™ and Security Strategy with its own Legislative Road Map. Having a specially designed legislative road map is critical to any nation-state, as many may not have the necessary laws in place to be able to lawfully and effectively defend their nation.

So, if you are a national leader, minister, or regulator, you might think your country is doing fine and will be okay. Well, just wait until you discover that your national sovereignty is under unprecedented threat from outer space. Just wait until you further discover that none of your government's existing laws, strategies, expertise, and know-how can do anything about it.

GPCYBER™ THREAT FROM OUTER SPACE—AND IT IS NOT ALIENS

In the last few years, multiple companies have been in a race to provide internet broadband and other services from outer space. The key players are Starlink (a SpaceX company) and Facebook's OneWeb—both of which are US companies. Starlink has already launched hundreds of their low-orbit satellites. The company also claimed that it would be ready to offer broadband services to users and companies all over the world by the end of 2021—which they accomplished. And aside from seeking regulatory approval from the US telecom regulator, Starlink can offer its services to stakeholders in any country around the world without first seeking the approval of local national government, telecom ministries, or regulators.

These private companies suddenly have the potential to access hundreds of millions (if not billions) of users in the first year of operation under/over the noses of national governments and regulators. This can impact or compromise national security like never before. Without any direct oversight to regulate, or the ability to penalize for improper practices, national regulators are rendered impotent, or even obsolete when it comes to internet service providers deployed from outer space. In fact, this new phenomenon of exploiting poor, ambiguous, or nonexistent international telecom regulatory frameworks has created a new and unmitigated national survivability, sovereignty, and security threat vector.

Let me add some proper context. Their ability to offer unhindered and unregulated internet access and services to billions of people all over the world and across national land and space boundaries, in one go, means that the cyber and space landscape will become impossible to regulate/police domestically and internationally—especially by sovereign nations. It also means that GPCyber™ motivated attackers and Cambridge Analytica–like activities will become routine practices. It will allow space-based network operators and GPCyber™ perpetrators the ability to operate more freely and successfully than from the deeper shadows of space, at that.

It has created never seen before opportunities for existing superpowers, and other wannabes, giving them new abilities to exercise or facilitate GPCyber™ coercion, influence, and to deliver Purposed Disinformation™ campaigns for multitudes of goals. GPCyber™ targeted attacks on officials/facilities of organizations and governments to gain access to highly valuable user data will increase significantly. They will be used for sinister goals, such as compromising national and corporate leaders to coerce them into adopting different political and economic directions than those that serve their national interest. This would make the unprecedented Soft Cell coordinated attacks that compromised dozens of telecom operators around the world, just to gain data on 20 or so high-value individuals, look like child's play (or pale in comparison).

And let me not forget to predict a new space genie that will be unleashed—one that is far worse but not too dissimilar from the genie that Cambridge Analytica (CA) released out of the bottle. For ease of labeling and future referencing I will call this new genie "Space-CA." Remember how CA took social media users and their data, sprinkled them with a harvesting mix, and then infused the results with AI? They developed techniques that UK regulators later found to be illegal, forcing CA to shut down. But not before CA had successfully altered the direction and fate of nations, such as the UK Brexit vote, Trump's 2016 presidential election, and a couple of Africans becoming presidents in their own countries.

Although advances in science and technology throughout history have always led to the good, the bad, and the ugly outcomes and directions, I believe that the bad and the ugly have always found a way to rise faster than the good. This is especially so when innovation is infused by modern, unhindered laissez-faire and supply-side capitalism's "greed is good" creed, which was made famous by the '80s movie *Wall Street*.

Therefore, I will go on the record and predict with certainty that a lack of any regulatory oversight at the national and international levels will remain absent for the next five years. It is highly likely this absence may last ten years. And if any international regulatory framework is born to regulate this space, it will be a highly inept and ineffective regulation. This will give Starlink, OneWeb, and Space-CA unfettered access and free rein for the next decade to establish unshakable first-to-market advantages and privileges. While some might claim that this will inspire new innovation, they they often neglect to mention the damage of such advances operating like the wild, wild west and which will also be capable of altering human habits, values, and discourse in ways and on scales humanity has never witnessed before, and ones which are capable of further widening the north–south, and rich–poor divides.

You might ask, "Khaled, why are you so pessimistic?"

You need to realize that a single provider will have control over billions of consumers and their data at any one time. That control comes with no clarity on their governance model or the regulatory, privacy, or legal framework that will govern them, nor their code of practice for their global consumers. With such a scale of users at any one time—knowing that we'll always have the good, bad, and the very ugly—the ugly out of billions could be millions of GPCyber™ attackers. This in itself is an unprecedented new threat to defending the nation-state or organization, but above all, it is a threat to those same businesses and citizens now consuming these services. And I have not yet addressed the possible abuses by that single provider in the style of Cambridge Analytica.

The ability to keep pushing the envelope is human nature, even with rules in place. How about when you can push as far and fast as you want, with only one regulator to answer to out of more than 200 around the world? What if that sole regulator is the US Federal Communications Commission (FCC) you need to keep happy? Keep in mind that the FCC's mandate is serving American stakeholders and US national interests first and foremost. I can see serious harm to society coming through space-based cyber services being deployed, and this manifests in the way governments and organizations and citizens will be impacted. Sadly, it will be a continuation of the failures of our current regulatory regimes at national/regional/international levels.

This phenomenon overrides national/regional/etc. frameworks that will make the ability to police these threatening activities virtually impossible, especially because of the scale. There are many questions that Starlink, OneWeb, and future others must answer. Some pertain to where and how their user data will be stored and used by these providers.

- Will the data of their global users be managed according to only US regulatory jurisdiction (as SpaceX is a US company)?
- Will they conform to the EU GDPR?

- How about the laws of small nations? Will they adhere to them too or totally ignore them, simply because they can?
- What are the enforcement mechanisms on this?
- How and where are the data stored?

As of the time of finalizing my book, where their user data will be stored and the regulatory jurisdiction they will comply with remains a mystery. Hackers will be able to leverage regulatory accountability loopholes in perpetrating acts with grave consequences and little or no oversight, enforceability, fear of penalties, or other consequences. They could be anywhere in the world, using Starlink to hack any target on the globe. Local governments would be even less able to stop, track, or mitigate than they are today—which is already poor at best.

This is a new Pandora's box of ways to perpetrate GPCyber™ attacks that would shatter previous unprecedented scales. These new threats cannot be mitigated by cyber security, resiliency, and continuity strategies and solutions that continue to fail. They could be mitigatable by survivability strategies, only after being considered and adapted to the specific needs of the nation-state making this request. Again, on this note, agility in adaptability is key to competitive survivability.

ANSWERS IN ESCALATION

In late October 2019, I was attending GSMA (Mobile World Congress) in Los Angeles as a guest of the organizer (along with VIPs like GSMA Director General Mats Granryd). I seldom get fazed by new revelations, but a couple did strike me during the opening ceremony when keynote speeches were being delivered by Los Angeles Mayor Eric Garcetti and FCC Chairman Ajit Pai.

Mayor Garcetti said LA was the sixth-largest city economy in the world ($1.2 trillion a year). I did not realize that; therefore, it was surprising. However, the next and more surprising insight was raised by Chairman Pai. He said that the US wants to be the number one 5G leader and technology provider around the world.[34] Pai was actually describing the US strategic goal and position on 5G. So, I started wondering how the US would be able to achieve this goal. Huawei has already secured gains in many parts of the world on 5G. My thought was that it seems to have successfully outcompeted US 5G technology providers on many fronts.

Huawei was already implementing full deployments in major cities in China and other parts of the world. Meanwhile, US 5G players were still in deployment testing mode in US cities and had serious grounds still to cover before any of them could effectively compete with Huawei. My questions were answered when the US–China Trade War started escalating. In essence, 5G is the new frontline to determine which of the two empires will win and claim the 21st century for themselves, which I established in Chapter 5.

The empire that is able to dominate with its 5G technology improves its chances of capturing the century for its nation/government economically, politically, and quite possibly militarily. At the heart of the 5G value is access to unprecedented data and information. Such knowledge means power. And such power will give the government behind the technology the ability to exercise tremendous GPCyber™ influence, coercion, and attacks on enemies and adversaries, but most crucially on friends and allies.

When you add the element of time to changing geopolitical interests, at a particular time or corresponding political event, adversaries and allies will be placed in the same box and converted into Ally-versaries™ to be coerced in the same manner. And they will be treated and subjected to similar GPCyber™ motivated attacks and influence. The stakes are so high for this outcome to be allowed to happen unchallenged by lovers and true believers of freedom and democracy as forces for real good.

The need for changes in our understanding of the ineffectiveness of cyber security alone is imperative to survive the Era of the Unprecedented. Many of my readers may find it of interest to read a published post I wrote in 2019, which was featured in SAMENA Council's *Trends* magazine[35] (the official magazine of telecom operators of the South Asia, Middle East, and Africa regions, which includes a third or more of the world's telecom operators). The featured post was titled "Cybersecurity Is No Longer the Keyword, 'Survivability' in a Geo-Poli-Cyber™ Threatened World Is."

Trends magazine is aimed at the top telecom decision makers. The post served as a great thought leadership conduit to make telecom leaders become better aware of critical game changing trends that will adversely impact them and their business models. Also, it helps them to identify solutions to remain profitable as new challenges materialize in the very near future. At that, it enables news strategies and solutions to be considered, adapted, and implemented.

I also addressed possible remedial strategies to consider before such fates become real. Moreover, the post was a stark warning to regulators that they will soon face becoming obsolete in their own countries. A key factor is how decision makers can put themselves in a position to turn these unprecedented threats into 21st-century competitive national and corporate advantages and opportunities. Overall, I communicated that it was not too late to turn the tide by reaching out. I encouraged readers to ask MLi Group to help by submitting an expression of interest to start the engagement.

ONGOING TARGETS

When financially motivated hackers go through extensive effort, patience, planning, and time to perpetrate attacks, they are always seeking a profitable payday. The process normally includes selling stolen data (such as dumping it for sale on the Dark Web). But the strangest thing about Operation Soft Cell, much like other stories in Part II of my book, is that this did not happen.

Who would embark on such a hugely detailed task and journey that requires high skills and expertise, and be able to absorb the costs? Who would do this with no return from the sale? It clearly means the perpetrators were compensated by other means, and their motivation was to serve different goals. Conclusion: the attacks were not financially motivated.

With their ability to directly gather highly valuable data of 20 or so VIPs—without the need to compromise personal phones with malware—nation-states could enhance intelligence and surveillance operations to advance geopolitical interests, both Purposed Disinformation™ and propaganda narratives, and cyber ops warfare to influence domestic and foreign public opinion for their narratives. In other words, the compressibility of telecom's strategic assets permits hackers to gain access to a never-ending stream of vital data, information, and intelligence of users and VIPs without even needing to compromise the users' phones.

What adds insult to injury is the fact that many global telecommunications providers had already been targeted and compromised for a number of years without knowing about it (which may or may not be a continuing trend, as you read more). Hackers were inside their systems with access to call data records, geolocation, habits, and other information about hundreds of millions of their subscribers. In the case of Soft Cell, the hackers were in the networks since at least 2017, if not before. They were going from computer to computer, stealing credentials and stealing an unusually high amount of data.

If you're wondering what you can do about this, you're asking the right question. As you keep reading, my hope is that some of the answers will provide a way forward. And if you're wondering if any of our models are up to scratch, you're getting ahead of my punchline. Let's take a look at Sector 7: Transportation.

For more information, please visit survivabilitythebook.com/ placeholder (or scan the code below) to see articles referenced as well as my recommended reading list. We have been very lucky to have journalists with integrity on the case. I encourage you to explore how the world received this story.

Don't forget to check out the article I wrote for SAMENA Council's *Trends* magazine!

13

Sector Seven: Transportation

TO ADDRESS THE many issues in the Transportation sector, nationally and internationally, it is important to identify the key segments within it, which are so interdependent. It is also important to assess the critical importance for these segments not to be allowed to be disrupted in any way, shape, or form. Transportation is not only vital to our economic prosperity but it is critical for our stability—it impacts people's lives and livelihoods both directly and indirectly.

Key Transportation sector segments include airlines (and their national/international operations such as air traffic control), public transport (trains, cars, and buses), maritime and shipping, and the smart grids used to manage this sector domestically and internationally. Some of these are considered critical national infrastructure. Aviation as well as maritime and shipping technically fall under this sector, but I chose to give them their own dedicated chapter in this book because of their critical importance to society's day-to-day operation and survivability.

When you recognize that so much IoT and AI are being added to the above functions within transport, and the additional and exponential vulnerabilities they add, you can start to imagine how the prospect of a major compromise within this sector is only a matter of when, not if. Imagine the grave consequences. But before I dig deeper, let me start by throwing a couple of questions to get us thinking together:

- Did you know that Transportation is now the third most vulnerable and exposed sector to cyberattacks?
- Did you know that this is only a small part of this sector's big picture?
- How likely and how soon do you think we will see a car manufacturer closing or filing for bankruptcy protection due to a class action lawsuit over negligence for scores of car owner and passenger deaths—victims of a cyberattack that leveraged installed IoT technologies/devices in which the car maker executives failed to mitigate the threat?
- Worse over, how likely do you think it is that they knew of the potential risks and did nothing?

NOT SO IMPOSSIBLE NUMBERS

Chrysler issued a safety recall in July 2015 for 1.4 million Jeeps in the US after hundreds of thousands of them were discovered to be hackable. This was allowing hackers to not only take control of braking or steering but to even remotely shut Jeeps down on the highway. It's excusable if people thought that would be the end of that problem.

When researchers and ethical hackers Chris Valasek and Charlie Miller tried to hack the multimedia system of Jeep through Wi-Fi connection, they were able to show conference viewers how easily it could be done. This was because the car Wi-Fi password is generated automatically, based on the time when the car, its multimedia system, and the head unit were all turned on for the very first time.

Their approach was simple but very clever. It was based on the thinking that if you know the year when the car in question was manufactured, and if you can successfully guess the exact month, (that's just 1–12), you can bring the count down to just 15 million combinations. You might be thinking, *Wow, that's crazy and impossible to crack.* Well, not quite, because if you then assume a.m. or p.m. of the day, you can drop it to just 7 million combinations. And if you add the exact hour, you can bring this down even more. And surprise, surprise ... for a hacker, this number was easy to figure out. Not only that, believe it or not, they could crack it within an hour.

Since then, car manufacturers have made connected cars even more connected than ever. And the more connected they are, the greater the number of vulnerabilities that can exist and be exposed by not just bad actors but also very sinister people too. Even the best of the best, Mercedes-Benz, was the victim in early 2019. Hackers stole more than 100 of their vehicles in Chicago by hacking the Car2Go carsharing app.

Lucky for Mercedes and Chrysler, the hackers were thieves who were just after money. Can you imagine if a Geo-Poli-Cyber™ (GPCyber)™ motivated hacker identified this vulnerability? I won't give new ideas to bad people; instead, I will leave it to your imagination as to what the dire consequences could have been.

TRANSPORTATION STAKEHOLDERS

We are all involved parties and stakeholders within transport. We use it for everyday commutes. We are consumers of resources (food and other goods) and fuels that need to be transported. We and our economies cannot function or thrive without it. The military cannot exist nor defend us without it. Simply put, transport is used across the board and we need it just like we need oxygen.

Governments are users but predominantly regulators of the sector. However, sector transport hacks can be used to target government officials, facilities, and installations, which illustrates how poorly they are regulating the sector. Remember the Equifax breach from Chapter 6. The perpetrators—likely direct foreign government operatives or their associates—would have gained specific data of high-ranking government officials. Such intelligence would enable them to undertake GPCyber™ activities by reverse engineering how to target that official.

From the events I've shared, GPCyber™ players are now looking at a treasure trove of infamous opportunity. First, it would not be that difficult to identify whether an important official had made a purchase of a new car, and the following details could easily be determined: make and model, where that car was at the moment, its vulnerabilities, and how to directly hack that car. Second, using relevant data from both the Equifax and the Marriott breaches (or Yahoo! and Operation Soft Cell, or Capital One and Facebook, etc.), the Valasek-Miller method of hacking an automobile would become much simpler than ever before.

If that car can be accessed and compromised, so can the official and their highly sensitive data. If GPCyber™ perpetrators can compromise the official, they can gather new intelligence. And this new intelligence could then be used to perpetrate an array of nation- compromising and sinister GPCyber™ activities. This would then put government entities, critical infrastructure, transport grids, and so on at further risk.

Unlike *Live Free or Die Hard*, this is not a Hollywood script. This is real, and it happens. Government officials are falling victim to such practices routinely all over the world, including in the most advanced Western capitals.

I now feel the need to quickly return to a core topic of the lack of more effective legislation. This is especially needed to govern the manufacturing and import of IoT devices and the use of AI in connected cars. I believe our legislative models are inept. They need a major overhaul if society and our way of life are to be better protected in order to survive.

Nevertheless, the next stakeholder in focus is organizations, which includes both users and providers of transport. Auto manufacturers rely on many of the components of their cars to be manufactured by third-party vendors. While they all claim to follow the regulation and stringent "best practices" as requirements for their suppliers, the continuous stories of cyberattacks that exploit supply chain weaknesses are too many to list here. This reoccurring phenomenon ought to lead us to the conclusion that such regulation and practices are not good enough, based on what's at stake.

The vulnerability in the supply chain is how the problem manifests and magnifies itself, but this is a result of an inadequate strategic and operating policy position adopted by car manufacturers despite what they claim. As my broken record continues to relay, many strategies and policies are based on a weak and inadequate regulatory regime. Remember GDPR?

As I mentioned in previous chapters, the creation of GDPR by the EU was to promote a holistic approach to creating a comprehensive cyber security hygiene posture and preparedness by organizations and to better protect users/citizens. But this is not what ended up being delivered by what is considered the most advanced consumer protection regulations on the planet when it became law in 2018.

Again, GDPR became a checkbox exercise that companies go through in order to successfully defend themselves from being fined the higher of 20 million euros or 4% of their global revenues, after being breached, and their user data being compromised. It created a process to document that they've done what is required per the regulation, not what is necessary to secure the organization or its users' data, to escape being fined.

So, did GDPR elevate the holistic or comprehensive cyber security hygiene and preparedness of organizations? Not even close.

This brings us to the final stakeholder, citizens and consumers. Although GDPR has somewhat improved consumer privacy protections for EU citizens, and those whose data passes through the EU, many countries around the world remain very poorly protected. As a result, citizens/consumers remain the worst impacted, and they are the least looked after prior and after breaches. Regulatory models do not hold executives and their companies accountable enough for the impact of breaches that compromise them and their users'/citizens' data. This needs to change ASAP.

Regulation needs to make the personal accountability of senior executives more stringent for professional failures. This is more so when they knew of the risks and could have acted but chose not to—which makes them negligent. The fines need to include prison sentences, going beyond a slap on the wrist and a few hours of community service.

Fundamentally, the severity of the punishment needs to act as a strong personal and corporate deterrent to make the cyber defense and survivability of the organization and protecting user/citizen data, and looking after them after a compromise become the top corporate priority. Today, consumers/citizens are not appropriately and directly helped and compensated to a level befitting the level of impact they suffer. Upgraded regulation needs to force companies to have funds specifically appropriated to helping compromised users remedy damages they suffered and reclaim their compromised identities.

Moreover, penalties go to the government, not the impacted people. This also needs to be changed so that a significant portion of the penalties go to help those affected. Currently, the only serious route that does act as somewhat of a deterrent are class-action lawsuits. But we all know how much coordination this requires to get off the ground, how long the process can take, how infrequently it happens or reaches success, and how ineffective it is in bringing needed change in the laws that would improve security practices. And let's not forget that organizations have budgets for lawyers—most consumers/citizens do not.

TRANSPORTATION VULNERABILITIES

In 2018, Gallagher, the international insurance company, published a white paper concluding that transport was the third most vulnerable sector to cyberattacks.[36] And yet, the white paper hardly touched on extremists, terrorists, national security agencies doing their bit to coerce, and other relevant ideologies. It also did not cover how geopolitical events factor into these cyberthreats as new motivations, nor did it explain how many cyberattackers have sinister motivations other than financial gain. Gallagher was content to have its white paper focus on just financially motivated breaches.

This is understandable. Companies selling services would only talk about the risks for which they have solutions that they can sell. They won't talk about risks for which they have no solutions. Can you imagine any of them explaining a problem lacking a remedy they can provide?

As a global industry leader, Gallagher said it published the white paper in order to help focus this sector's added risks coming from the operational technology side. This is a valid and valuable angle that deserves credit and should demand our attention. The sector is deploying many additional technologies. How these technologies end up being infused, along with the daily operations of their players, makes the Transport sector more dependent than ever on these new technologies. More important, the advent of these new technologies, which come with their own vulnerabilities, increases the overall risk of the sector and its players being hacked. Obviously, Gallagher is offering insurance coverage against operational technologies being hacked.

Gallagher's concern is valid, but it is not comprehensive. I will say that their motivation behind the white paper, in my opinion, can justify raising an eyebrow. It is a fact that critical processes can become vulnerable to attacks that can lead to business interruption, cyber ransomware, and potentially data being compromised and needing protection. Although this is a valid point, it is hardly a comprehensive look at threat mitigation in today's new non-cyberthreat landscape and which has direct impact on the cyberthreat landscape. Furthermore, many decision makers are mistakenly buying cyber insurance thinking they are protecting themselves against cyberthreats.

The white paper focuses on how to mitigate only the risks they chose to focus on and identify. This is so because they are risks for which

Gallagher has cyber insurance policies it wants to sell—policies that could help mitigate some of these threats (not most, and certainly not all of them). In other words, the white paper was a sales lead generator masked as a thought leadership exercise.

What worries me about this very common business practice is that it actually leads decision makers to think that following the advice of such a world leader and buying their cyber insurance means sleeping well at night, thinking they are protected by having cyber insurance that covers them. If only they knew how mistaken they are. (Later, I will dig deeper into why this is the case in Sector 10).

But what worries me even more is that at no time did their white paper get into the non-financial or geopolitical motivations. Of course, I do not expect them to talk about GPCyber™ motivations because it is a label and definition I created under the MLi Group in 2012–2013 (one of our trademarks). Nor do I expect them to offer cyber insurance policies that automatically cover against GPCyber™ risks by default—like the ones we helped create with key international insurance partners, one that is unlike most cyber insurance policies being offered today.

GPCyber™ attacks are not reported by the news on a daily basis and labeled as GPCyber™ hacks. But that doesn't mean they aren't happening a lot more frequently than you think. It is very common for news and media outlets not to know what GPCyber™ attacks are, or of their compromises, which makes reporting on them very rare. However, this is even more true when the target is a critical national infrastructure, stakeholder, or facility. Any disclosure of them being compromised can have a detrimental impact on national security—hence news of them being compromised can often be blacked out. The result means the public seldom hears of them. This most certainly does not mean they are not happening, and at high rate.

In fact, in Sector 9, on the Aviation sector, I will be disclosing never-before-revealed information about an internationally coordinated GPCyber™ attack that happened only a few years ago. It was never disclosed publicly nor reported by the press. It involved multiple airliners being taken over at the same time by hackers, with the goal of crashing them in the ocean. I will also address why I chose to reveal this critical info now and not back when I learned of it.

Gallagher's white paper put at an average cost of $3.25 million per cyber breach. Suffice it to say, the worst cyberattacks are the ones that are targeted and which have GPCyber™ agendas. When they do happen, they cause far graver damage and cost consequences than the financially motivated ones. So, let's get real: $3.25 million often does not get the attention of many chairmen, CEOs, or boards of multinationals and multi-billion-dollar companies after a hack. In fact, in private briefings that I conduct with such parties (and as I said in Chapter 2), I often say: "Many department heads won't dare interrupt their CEO's golf game to alert them of a mere couple of million-dollar ransomware. They just handle it and often add it to the weekly memo."

Sadly, such a cost level of attacks has become accepted and implemented in the model of the cost of doing business. Somehow, it does not serve as a deterrent to do things better. However, what do they do when a breach starts costing them tens to hundreds of millions, or even billions of dollars in actual costs, reputational damage, and loss of future business and revenues due to compromised competitiveness (just to name a few)?

For those who doubt such a damage scale, I suggest you dig deeper into the Equifax and Marriott's Starwood breaches as mere examples. Decision makers and other stakeholders need to start asking themselves these questions:

- What am I not considering?
- What should I do differently?
- How would I do it differently?
- What must I implement that we are not yet implementing?
- If abiding by the current regulation is not enough to protect my company, shareholders, me, and my job, what must I do next?

In 2016, hackers hit San Francisco's Muni transport system, demanding ransom.[37] The Municipal Transportation Agency that monitors public transportation in San Francisco, such as trains, trams, and buses around the city, reported that the attack led to customers being able to travel for free. They did not report that Robin Hood was a suspect ...

It was revealed that 2,000 machines were hacked. Computers across the city's transport network were compromised, including those at stations that were disabled, with screens displaying a message from the attackers:

You Hacked, ALL Data Encrypted. Contact For Key(cryptom27@yandex.com)ID:681 ,Enter

Hackers provided a list of machines they claimed to have infected in Muni's network. However, the trains themselves were not affected. A ransom of 100 Bitcoin was demanded. This amounted to approximately $43,400 back in 2016, but it would have been about $2.22 billion in 2021. In response to the attack and ransom, and as a precaution, staff were told to shut off all ticketing machines on the network. This also included many employee terminals as well as machines that were used to look after payroll and employees' personal information.

Although the hackers demanded payment in the form of Bitcoin, and their motivation appeared to have been money, it is also likely that similar hackers who appear to have similar financial motivation are doing so to fund other sinister plans or to make the hack appear to be financially motivated in order to distract from their real goal. In reality, hackers may do these acts as a dry run to see how the system and decision makers are designed to respond to such a cyberattack.

Nevertheless, vital public transport was vulnerable, and one person was able to impact it for a significant period of time. And if you dig deeper, you may discover that most, if not all, regulatory requirements may have been appropriately complied with. Clearly, they were not up to the task.

Following in the footsteps of the EU (GDPR), California claimed to be taking the lead for a new era in American digital regulation, in passing the California Consumer Protection Act (CCPA). The law came into force on January 1, 2020. It is also dubbed as California's GDPR. But it came nearly four years after the attack on San Francisco. And the lessons learned from GDPR, to my disappointment, were not factored into CCPA. I am not confident it will change the mindsets of senior leaderships and boardrooms to deliver comprehensive cyber security hygiene. I fear CCPA will sadly become yet another checkbox exercise to alleviate the threat of being penalized.

Is this sufficient in defending California or any nation-state? I strongly doubt it. Why? you might ask. Well, let's look at how GDPR relates to an actual event. For a 2018 cyber breach, British Airways was hit with a record fine of £183 million by the EU regulators and £20m ($26m) by the

UK Information Commissioners Office (ICO). I'll explain in the chapter on Sector 9 how this was essentially a slap on the wrist.

Many countries and regions around the world do not have similar deterrents in their laws. Even the latest models of regulation, and the harshest in fines like GDPR and CCPA, are insufficient and out of date, in my humble opinion. As ground breaking as these laws, fines, and deterrents are, they remain insufficient and incapable of mitigating threats facing nation-states and their stakeholders today and in the 21st century.

CRUNCHED WITH PAINE

Readers would be justified if they thought that the 2015 Jeep hack was critical back then. They would be doubly justified to expect all manufacturers and the transportation industry to have learned from that huge mistake and stepped up to the plate to fix holes so big that elephants could walk through them. Well, once again, you would be very sadly mistaken.

I now bring you to July 2019. A professional security researcher, Justin Paine, discovered that the car manufacturer Honda's database had been exposed. After alerting the company, he wrote his findings and shared them exclusively with *TechCrunch*, which then published it as a feature story.

Honda was super lucky because Paine made direct contact to warn them of this exposed vulnerability. As a result, the database was shut down hours after. Alarmingly, Paine had thought he'd discovered a vulnerability in just a single Honda dealership. He was wrong.

It turned out that there was a database containing information related to the entire global network of Honda's employee machines. The database contained records on multiple offices around the world, including locations in Mexico, the UK, and the US. He even found Honda's CEO's computer in the logs, including which operating system he used, the patches installed, and a lot more—such as the CEO's email address and even the last time he'd actually logged on.

This was a global vulnerability that was discovered and fixed/patched early but only because a good guy found it first and acted in a socially responsible and timely manner. In his findings, Paine said:[38]

> What makes this data particularly dangerous in the hands of an attacker is that it shows you exactly where the soft spots are ... This data contained enough identifiable information to make it extremely simple to locate specific high-value employees, and in the hands of an attacker this leaked data could be used to silently monitor for ways to launch very targeted attacks on those executives.

Imagine if this or similar vulnerabilities were discovered first not by a good Samaritan, like Paine, but by a GPCyber™ motivated hacker or "hacktivist." How about an organized or lone wolf ISIS cyber terrorist who wanted revenge against the West and its war on terror that had led to his family being drone-bombed to smithereens?

Just imagine a foreign enemy or rival nation-state that wanted to harm or force your organization or nations to alter their political or economic plan. Better still, why not start thinking about the enemy within? Have you considered what extremist white supremacists, determined to undermine or overthrow the US government, would do? If you have not seriously considered them as a threat, you ought to. Key findings came out two weeks after an annual assessment by the Department of Homeland Security[39] that warned that violent white supremacy was the "most persistent and lethal threat in the homeland" and that white supremacists were the most deadly among domestic terrorists in recent years.

This is important to document for my fellow Americans who may not have been as aware of this. This US domestic threat is fully capable of escalating to an unprecedented domestic US cyber conflict. In fact, a report in 2021, published by the Center for Strategic and International Studies, found that white supremacist groups were responsible for 41 of 61 "terrorist plots and attacks" in the first eight months of that year, or 67%.[40]

As mentioned at the beginning of this chapter, the Transportation sector is a wide umbrella. I've only covered cars and some public transport. We still need to explore the vulnerabilities of Maritime & Shipping, as well as Aviation. As the cyber events grow in numbers, compromised data compounds into horrendous opportunities for infamy. Let's see what that looks like on the high seas.

For more information, please visit survivabilitythebook.com/ placeholder (or scan the code below) to see articles referenced as well as my recommended reading list. We have been very lucky to have journalists with integrity on the case. I encourage you to explore how the world received this story.

14

Sector Eight: Maritime & Shipping

MARITIME & SHIPPING is one of the most technologically outdated sectors across the board. This is even more so when you compare it with other sectors, such as Telecom. Many stakeholders/players, including shipping companies, continue to use technologies that would feel at home in the era of Queen Victoria in the late 19th century. Many company owners who made their fortunes in the billions of dollars, decades ago, appear to think that, if it ain't broke, why fix it? In essence, *Why change what has served us very well in the past?*

Some of the technologies that are still being relied upon in many vessels are so out of date that they are unable to be upgraded or patched. This renders these vessels, fleets, and their owners highly vulnerable and far too exposed to cyberattacks of all motivations. Moreover, the regulatory regimes that regulate and oversee these sector stakeholders are seriously antiquated. In fact, to date, it is a miracle that the sector has not been the victim of a targeted major Geo-Poli-Cyber™ (GPCyber™) "Pearl Harbor," which would not be so difficult a task to perpetrate.

I believe there are specific and fundamental reasons why this has not happened yet. And it most certainly is not because sector players and regulators are doing an outstanding job in cyber security. But in remaining socially responsible, I cannot fully and publicly disclose why a cyber Pearl Harbor has not hit the Maritime & Shipping sector yet (I will share some insights on this later in this chapter). However, I dig a lot deeper during private and confidential briefings with qualified national and sector leaders and other attendees who send in an expression of interest (EOI).

And if you haven't already seen in previous sectors, just wait until you read about the regulatory "best practices." I can already feel the cringe awaiting you.

NOT SO COMPLETE

In June 2017, Moller-Maersk (known simply as Maersk) fell victim to malware known as NotPetya. The cyberattack affected organizations worldwide. You would need to have been living under a rock if you had not heard about the impact of NotPetya on the world that year. But in case you haven't, and were in fact living under a boulder, let's go through some background and what happened.

First, you might ask what's the difference between Petya and NotPetya. The "Petya" malware is not new; it has been around for some time. However, the June 2017 cyberattack unleashed a new variant of it. This variant became known as "NotPetya" due to alterations in the malware's behavior. Although Petya and NotPetya use different encryption keys, they have unique reboot styles, displays, and notes. Nonetheless, both are equally devastating and destructive and can be leveraged for all kinds of cyberattackers' motivations.

The 2017 NotPetya malware started when an employee in the Ukraine responded to an email they should not have. This malware is an excellent example of the typical life cycle, starting with a misunderstanding of the threats. It was followed by

1. missing and/or poor mitigation plans and procedure dynamics;
2. overreaction by some, and underreaction by others; and
3. a massive injection of resources and money to restore operational and business capabilities, trust, confidence, and revenues.

Recovery was tough for most, and hailed by some, but it came with enormous reputational and operating cost, which could have been significantly lower had all parts of Maersk been better prepared and rehearsed to enable it to work together better when the attack happened. Speaking on a panel at the World Economic Forum in 2018, Maersk chairman Jim Hagemann Snabe detailed what his company had to do to bring the company back to full function.[41] He said they had to reinstall "4,000 new servers, 45,000 new PCs, and 2,500 applications." He described it as "a complete infrastructure." He later added, "That was done in a heroic effort over ten days."

If this proves anything to me, it confirms that Maersk was poorly prepared. And while Maersk was being celebrated for its heroic action, no one asked its celebrated leader what was missing from their risk mitigation preparedness strategies and plans that could have saved them all this damage limitation effort and costs. Keep in mind, this is hailed as a success story in postattack response. Just imagine what happened to the other companies who were slower to act.

The great challenge for the sector is that interconnectivity between IT systems and operational technology (OT) has increased so much in recent years, as did shipping companies' reliance on them for their ships. However, the increase in the number of systems connected to the internet also meant a greater increase in their risks and vulnerabilities to cyberattacks of all motivations.

Maersk, which is considered as a great example and/or success story by the industry for its postattack mitigation action, was devastated by the ransomware attack, which reportedly is estimated to have cost it more than $300 million.[42] A 2017 study by *Futurenautics* concluded that 44% of ship operators believe their company's current IT defenses are not effective at repelling cyberattacks, and 39% had experienced a cyberattack in the last 12 months.[43] Many companies are adding digital systems to do a job on a vessel that had not been built with security in mind. This is what makes many of them too old to be kept up-to-date and what I called earlier unupgradable and/or unpatchable.

Today, almost everything is becoming "connected." Ships are no exception, with IT and OT infusing together in daily operations. This is becoming the new norm. Meanwhile, ships continue being managed with dinosaur mindsets instead of recognizing that Cyber-Survivability™ is as critical to their operation as fuel is to their engines and non-interruption to their profitability. Effective Cyber-Survivability™ cannot become as effective as a bolt-on unless existing ship owners recognize that they and their systems need a new set of strategic and operational expertise they currently do not possess in-house. However, to render them even more effective, Cyber-Survivability™ needs to become incorporated by design (meaning built in from the beginning and into the blueprint design of the architecture).

The mindset must change. You can no longer build a ship and expect it to last a number of years, amortize it and get the tax deduction, then scrap it or sell it off—which means you don't feel the need to upgrade it. Whereas from technology, IT, security, and survivability perspectives, all these have to work like a Swiss watch from day one and every day after.

This should explain why, despite the 2017 regulation, and it being reconsidered in 2021, cyber compromises of ships kept increasing and have become the norm, not the exception. Moreover, and despite stories of these hacks hitting the headlines, shipping companies' attention to the ineffectiveness of the cyber security on their vessels appears to continue falling on deaf ears, with reactions more akin to putting a Band-Aid on a cancer patient. In fact, *Ship Technology Global* magazine published a report[44] on November 8, 2017, titled "Did the Maersk Cyber-Attack Reveal an Industry Dangerously Unprepared?"

But since then, little has changed in mindsets or mitigation strategies or, plans. The same goes for the antiquated regulatory regimes and their recommended "best practices" and cyber security standards, leaving the sector exposed to another disaster waiting to happen, unless a serious and unprecedented international intervention takes place. God willing.

MARITIME & SHIPPING STAKEHOLDERS

This sector is more dependent on multilateral treaties, agreements, conventions, and oversight than perhaps the other sectors. Where a regulator (such as the US, UK, or EU) creates a new set of mandatory requirements that can act as a serious deterrent to incentivize stakeholders to do more to comply or expect to be heavily fined, the international maritime sector is seriously lacking such teeth, not just to compel ship owners/operators to do more, but to force them into doing so or levy serious penalties for no action.

The reason is obvious. There is no singular authority that can mandate new requirements. And local and regional authorities are inept. Local and global economies are placed under increased risk from GPCyber™ motivated hacks that could manifest themselves in empty shelves (food) and shortages (gas, resources, etc.). Factors such as these feed directly into the nine meals concept from Chapter 3.

We are lacking oversight that is up-to-date and has teeth. Many port authorities have been breached. Many of these ports are managed by governments, but some are managed by private companies contracted by governments. This means that governments have the ultimate responsibility to keep the ports and their stakeholders secure and safe. Therefore, they must place new demands on port authorities. The pieces are in place for regulation to be implemented—action must be taken.

In terms of organization stakeholders, this includes exporters and importers, shipping companies, private port authorities, and so on. The nature of shipping cargo (crude oil, food, medical supplies, cars, etc.) causes such interdependency of economies around the world on each other whereby any disruption to the flow of supply in one economy can have dire consequences on other economies and their people's livelihoods. Port authorities must also up their game. There's a high probability that many may have already been hacked, allowing manifests as well as cargo to be accessed by hackers, much like Yahoo! and Starwood/ Marriott. Hackers then use this info for themselves or sell it to pirates who ambush these ships. Stolen cyber data is of great value to GPCyber™ motivated perpetrators wanting to perhaps cause food or oil shortages in the destination country to achieve a more sinister strategic geopolitical objective.

What is plain to see is that many industry players are still operating in the 19th-century mentality with 20th-century systems still in operation. This is leaving huge gaps of vulnerabilities in maritime technical equipment. Senior management attitudes need to change in order for them to be capable of adapting to the unprecedented threat landscape, today and tomorrow, or be ready for dire consequences.

For the final stakeholders, the people, they need to consider that anything and everything shipped from one port to another will predominantly be consumed or used by a citizen somewhere around the world. Therefore, this industry serves citizens worldwide. Any disruption to maritime stability and operation has a direct impact on their lives and livelihoods, which directly impacts national sovereignty and security.

Sudden shortages in oil, food, cars, new technology, or raw materials (etc.) can have dire consequences on the nation and its people as we have become more dependent on the regularity of the flow of these products. Economies are built on the routine supply of these products; therefore, disruption could make for a disaster. And this is where the GPCyber™

hackers and actors can strike to bring a nation's economy to its knees and force its leaders and people to accept a political direction that serves the perpetrators' strategic interest.

General tourism and luxury cruises bring massive business to small towns and regions. If those ships are shut down, as they have been during the coronavirus scare, business owners of all kinds may be on the brink of bankruptcy. In order for our daily lives to continue uninterrupted, the Maritime & Shipping sector needs a major overhaul, today before tomorrow.

National and regional regulatory Maritime & Shipping survivability and security regulations need to be brought in. They would form the new regulation and oversight requirements, risk mitigation strategies, and plans that will better ensure local and global operations can continue undisrupted. Today, cyberattacks of all motivations are presenting the threat of a century, especially GPCyber™ attacks. That threat applies to everyone, not just business and government.

VULNERABILITIES WITHIN MARITIME & SHIPPING

To better explain how the sector is regulated nationally and internationally, it is important to first identify the players, their roles, responsibilities, and accountabilities in order to zero in on where the failures are. Maritime regulations are developed and overseen by very specific parties, such as these:

- Port State Control (PSC)
- Classification society
- International Association of Classification Societies (IACS)
- United Nations' International Maritime Organization (IMO)

The Port State Control (PSC) is an inspection regime whereby port authorities of a country inspect foreign-registered ships arriving in their ports. They can take action against noncompliant ships (such as fines, prevention to sail, etc.). Inspectors are PSC officers (PSCOs). They are required to investigate compliance based on the requirements of international conventions, such as SOLAS, MARPOL, STCW, and the MLC.

The inspections can involve checking that the vessel is manned and operated in compliance with existing international law, and verifying the competency of the ship's captain, officers, and personnel as well as determining if the ship's condition and equipment are also compliant (you can find more information in my resource page online).

A classification society is a nongovernmental organization that sets and maintains technical standards for the construction and operation of ships and offshore structures. Classification societies certify that the construction of a vessel complies with relevant standards and carry out regular surveys in service to ensure that compliance with the standards is maintained. Currently, more than 50 organizations describe their activities as including marine classification, 12 of which are members of the International Association of Classification Societies (IACS).

The International Association of Classification Societies (IACS) is a technically based nongovernmental organization that currently consists of 12-member marine classification societies. More than 90% of the world's cargo-carrying ships' tonnage is covered by the classification standards set by member societies of IACS. Marine classification is a system focused on promoting the safety of life, property, and the environment primarily through the establishment and verification of compliance with technical and engineering standards for the design, construction, and life-cycle maintenance of ships, offshore units, and other marine-related facilities.

These standards are contained in rules established by each society. IACS provides a forum within which the member societies can discuss, research, and adopt technical criteria that enhance maritime safety. For further reference, see https://en.wikipedia.org/wiki/International_Association_of_Classification_Societies

The UN International Maritime Organization (IMO) is a United Nations agency and one of the many UN family members. It is

> mandated with setting the standards for maritime, just like its UN sister agencies such as the World Health Organization (WHO) is for health, and the International Telecommunication Union (ITU) is for telecommunications. IMO is the United Nations' specialized agency with responsibility for the safety and security of shipping and the prevention of marine and atmospheric pollution by ships. IMO's work supports the United Nations Sustainable Development Goals (SDGs).

Before I start giving you my assessments on the above, let me address another key piece in the puzzle—the maritime flag. According to Wikipedia, this is "a flag designated for use on ships, boats, and other watercraft. Naval flags are considered important at sea and the rules and regulations for the flying of flags are strictly enforced. The flag flown is related to the country of registration: so much so that the word 'flag' is often used symbolically as a synonym for 'country of registration.'" You will see later in this chapter why this is one of the big problems of the sector that needs to be addressed sooner rather than later. In the meantime, let us now address and put the above organizations, definitions, and classifications in their proper context.

As of 2017, and in terms of the local and international cyber security regulation, the requirements that govern the sector have been limited to seriously outdated "best practices." When a regulation says that their best practices must be followed, they are recommending—not mandating—these best practices to be followed. They are not setting specific mandatory requirements that must be implemented. It means that vessel owners themselves decide on what to implement or ignore and can still justify that they followed "best practices" not to be fined.

Bear in mind, compliance does not mean that your ship's cyber security, let alone Cyber-Survivability™, are up to scratch. Even worse, the penalties for noncompliance are so weak they are softer than baby teeth. In fact, it is often cheaper to take a chance to not comply because the risk of getting caught is so low.

The approved guidelines on maritime cyber risk management came into effect in 2017 and were supposed to provide high-level recommendations. I believe they failed stakeholders and society miserably. Many cyberattacks have occurred since that date and devasted the sector and provided no significant improvements to vessels' cyber security risk preparedness or mitigation strategies and plans (Petya and NotPetya are some of the many examples that attest to this).

And yet, there are no indications that best practices will be replaced anytime soon by solid and specific national and international mandatory regulatory requirements that can elevate vessels' Cyber-Survivability™ to a minimal level of effectiveness. Leaders of this sector are still relying on the same best practice model and ethos in risk and vulnerabilities defense and mitigation.

More than most other sectors in Part II, this sector is in desperate need of a timely regional and international collaboration and regulation treaty befitting the ever-rising and unprecedented magnitudes of the threats. In fact, I hate to repeat it, but the sector is ripe and highly vulnerable for a cyber Pearl Harbor by non-financially motivated GPCyber™ hackers with the goal of destabilizing Western economies and political systems that are highly vulnerable.

I touched on this in Chapter 1. Nevertheless, I want you to imagine a new ISIS splinter group (after the terrorist group was soundly defeated on the ground in Iraq and Syria in recent years), and the putting to death of their lifelong dream—seeing their "Caliphate baby" born and their dream turn to reality in 2013, only for the hand of Western allies to play a huge role in the "murder" of their baby.

Well, now imagine the level of motivation in seeking vengeance for their murdered child. Imagine the ease offered by unpatched cyber vulnerabilities in facilitating a high destruction/devastation motivated cyberattack. Can you imagine them perpetrating cyber revenge on the "murderers and all their stakeholders" in all the countries that had a hand in the killing of their realized dream, their "Caliphate baby"?

Can you now imagine the level of maximum pain and suffering they want to cause to the citizens and stakeholders' economies and their ways of life in these countries? How difficult do you think their task of perpetrating their GPCyber™ revenge will be with all the huge vulnerabilities that continue to exist and plague this sector?[45]

And I have not yet started talking about what some national security agencies can do to impact this sector to advance their ideological, political, or geopolitical goals and ambitions around the world.

Well, all this is already happening. Moreover, it is growing, unhinged and unabated. If this does not compel you to see just how vulnerable this sector and society are to sinister GPCyber™ motivated compromises and the devastation they can cause in people's lives and national economies, then you are choosing to continue living under a rock.

The tracking and hacking of ships through satellite communications happens routinely and regularly. Many satcom terminals on ships are available on the public internet. Many still have default credentials—such as "admin" and "1234" for passwords—which are found on ships too frequently. But even strong passwords are not enough due to the fact that vessels have far too many vulnerabilities that can be exploited by hackers. In fact, a good hacker can exploit one of these vulnerabilities in less than a few minutes to then be able to order the ship to take a new course.

Hackers have even taken control of ships and made changes to the onboard computers to convince the system that more weight was on one side of the vessel than the other. Simple prank? No. This causes the computer to make an adjustment to balance the ship's weight, resulting in tilting the ship, drastically increasing the threat of it sinking.

How about sending a ship the wrong way? This can be accomplished by hacking the electronic chart display and information system (ECDIS). If you find a way to hack the satcom terminal, you're now on the vessel network. The ECDIS is needed to navigate, but when hackers get inside, they can save directly to the autopilot—most modern vessels are in "track control" mode most of the time, where they follow the ECDIS course. Gaining access means they could be able to crash the ship, particularly in fog; younger crews get "screen fixated" all too often, believing the electronic screens instead of looking out of the window.

An MLi Group associate penetration (pen) testing company tested over 20 different ECDIS units and found all sorts of crazy security flaws. Most ran old operating systems, including one popular in the military that still runs on Windows NT! Can you imagine? A military ship still operating Windows NT. And I can tell you, it was *not* a banana republic. Nevertheless, poorly protected configuration interfaces were all too common.

At that, the pen tester was able to "jump" the boat by spoofing the position of the GPS receiver on the ship. This is not GPS spoofing; this is telling the ECDIS that the GPS receiver is in a different position on the ship. It's similar to introducing a GPS offset. These sector vulnerabilities continue to exist on a mass scale.

While most of these types of issues may have been fixed years ago in mainstream IT systems (which are still failing today), current ship security is a pubescent teenager competing in the Hunger Games against NFL-caliber or world-class football professionals. Lives are on the line! And the advent of always-on satellite connections has exposed shipping to not only the usual financially motivated hacking attacks but also devastating GPCyber™ motivated and targeted hacks.

Vessel owners and operators cannot address these new strategic risks by simply hiring more IT people. They must brace themselves and come to terms with the New Era of the Unprecedented. Only then will they be able to better prepare for serious cyberattacks that damage their effective and Competitive Survivability, not just their profitability. The potential maritime cyber Pearl Harbor is becoming a more imminent and daunting reality by the day.

FALSE GOOD NEWS (BUT NOT ALL DOOM AND GLOOM ...)

Here is what appears to be a positive story moving forward, to then realizing upon a deeper dive that it is causing disservice, misguidance, and misinformation.

As of March 6, 2020, the Korean Register (KR) announced it has certified the very first ship to achieve cyber security certification.[46]

KR said it completed a comprehensive cyber security survey of the chemical/oil tanker *Songa Hawk* and has certified the ship to be fully cyber security compliant in all areas. On face value, the news appears to be a positive new story and direction; however, it falls under misguidance and misinformation.

Upon closer inspection of the small print, my eyes started popping out. International cybersecurity requirements have been arranged by the International Maritime Organization (IMO), Tanker Management and Self-Assessment (TMSA), and Ship Inspection Report Programme (SIRE), and KR would align itself with those requirements. This looks to me like a case of self-anointment to certify as a regulatory body by setting your own standard then certifying compliance against it. I would welcome this if it created an improved and effective cybersecurity framework that actually elevates the preparedness before, and responses after, any breach of the vessels—but it does not. In fact, it makes it worse by creating a false sense of security, which is more dangerous, in my humble opinion.

As far as I am aware, there are no definitive standards operating in the Marine sector. This is because BIMCO and CLIA (etc.) have published guidelines that are aligned with IMO Resolution MSC 428(98), but they are just guidelines. IMO has also stated that it "encourages" maritime administrations to ensure cyber risks are appropriately addressed in safety management systems no later than the first annual verification of a company's Document of Compliance (after January 1, 2021). But again, this is an advisory.

When hearing/reading the word "compliant," one assumes this implies measurement against a standard of sorts being met or satisfied. By stating that you are compliant, it means you have attained a higher level of cyber security standard, under which you are now operating. This implies you are more capable to deal with cyberattacks. In the case of this sector, this is not true.

IMO's "standard" is a best practice and is only advisory, not mandatory. This brings us to another problem. Standards must be tightened and improved, and they must become mandatory requirements. Ship owners and operators must then comply with these requirements. We don't have the luxury of time nor decades for new multilateral treaties to be configured, agreed to, and then adopted. Believe me, I have been involved in some of them over the years and decades. They make watching paint dry a 100-meter sprint sport in comparison.

However, it is not all gloom and doom. There is a way forward!

What if a local government and its port authority instituted a new law/regulation whereby making it a mandatory requirement for all ships wishing to dock in its ports to have complied and been certified with a minimum standard of Cyber-Survivability™ requirements? And what if this certification is awarded after a Cyber-Survivability™ audit had been conducted and passed?

In fact, the country/countries to take such a global leadership role would offer a 12-month period for ships who visit its ports to comply. And they would offer advice and solutions, and assist them in upgrading their systems to meet this new mandatory standard in order to become certified. Not only will this instigate many ship owners to start making this a priority, but the country itself would be elevating its role to being a global leader and creating new expertise it can now export—generating unanticipated new economic wealth and prosperity to their nation-state and their stakeholders.

You may have already started visualizing this positive domino effect of other countries considering and adopting a similar Cyber-Survivability™ maritime regime and certification model with better protocols to govern the ports within their national sovereign jurisdictions. And, as more countries start exploring adoption and requiring this model, it becomes very foreseeable for an international treaty and format to take shape to make international governance of the Maritime & Shipping sector more effective in addressing today's and tomorrow's threats and challenges society and the world are up against.

I can share with you that the MLi Group and I are already in deep exploration with a number of countries that are eager to be the first in the world or in their own continent to launch this model. In essence, I am told I have created unprecedented opportunities for leaders of countries and their small nation-states to showcase themselves as 21st-century global difference makers and leaders. Timed with the launch of this survivability book, I am thrilled to inform you that MLi Group has launched Survivability Maritime & Shipping Cyber-Survivability & Security™, with unique and never before offered critically needed services by this sector.

As a reader, by now you are very aware of two glaring and daunting realities facing this sector, both nationally and internationally, which this chapter has brought to light. And these new realities are at the core of why we launched the new business and services and why I am so excited about them. These realities are as follows:

1. **Too many vessel owners continue to live in dinosaur times!**
   Some knowingly. Many unknowingly. The real or effective Competitive Survivability of many of them in the next three to five years is highly questionable if their strategic and operational focuses remain unchanged. This is due in large part to the lack of honest comprehensive guidance and thought leadership about the reality of the new risks they are facing today. And by the way, talking about or focusing on ransomware to sell services is most definitely not it.

   Additionally, service vendors who are above all interested in selling services are not offering nor can they offer comprehensive risk and mitigation advice or solutions. Today, these vessel owners need to become better informed and aware of the comprehensive and potentially catastrophic risk exposures facing their ships, operations, profitability, and survivability, as well as their continued existence in order to come to terms with what is critically and specifically needed to be done in order to mitigate them more effectively.

2. **Maritime & Shipping national regulatory regimes must get overhauled—ASAP.**
   Time is not an ally of all nations, governments, or their regulations. They must improve their ability to mitigate the risk arising from today's GPCyber™ threatened world in order to be able to better defend their national Competitive Survivability and sovereignty.

UNFORTUNATE AND IRRESPONSIBLE INABILITY

On September 25, 2018, the San Diego Port's Information Technology Department received reports that port employees were locked out of their files and messages were popping up, demanding Bitcoin as ransom to unlock them. As a result, all staff members were told to turn off computers as an investigation was launched. It was revealed that the port of San Diego (US) and the port of Barcelona (Spain) were the targets of ransomware attacks within five days of each other.

A spokesman for the SD Port Authority confirmed via email that the cyberattack was a ransomware infection. The type of ransomware used was called SamSam. The FBI issued a statement that the hack was attributed to state-sponsored hackers operating inside the Islamic Republic of Iran but provided no evidence and that the port was the final victim in an international computer hacking and extortion scheme involving the deployment of sophisticated ransomware. The scheme began in December 2015 and targeted more than 200 public agencies and hospitals.

Although the hackers who breached SD Port demanded a ransom, it is not always conclusive that a ransom demand means the hack was only financially motivated. As I shared before, GPCyber™ hackers may often demand a ransom to camouflage their motivation or to fund their true sinister goals. A great example of this is WannaCry. However, when hackers do not demand a ransom, are not selling stolen data on the Dark Web, and appear to have "no direct payday," it would be safe to conclude that their motivation is GPC and is far more sinister than making money from Bitcoin demands: they are carrying out one or more GPCyber™ motivations.

Think about it. Even hackers do not work or cannot afford to work for free. If they are not expecting a payday, it means someone is paying for their efforts directly, indirectly, or subsidizing them in stealth for seriously more sinister goals that dwarf financial gain.

Why is the SD Port Authority hack so significant? you might ask.Well, its proximity to the US Navy, its importance to the state of California's economy, and therefore its importance to the prosperity of Californian and American stakeholders make it of great value to a GPCyber™ nation-state or motivated lone wolf attacker. In fact, I am able to make the expert and professional conclusion that the SD Port Authority hack must be considered as a GPCyber™ attack despite the perpetrators demanding a ransom.

This leads me to the next point about our incompetence to protect public installations and the failure to defend them by our public officials. After 1962, the SD Port Authority became a self-supporting, public-benefit corporation (SS, PBC). This means that the state of California and the US government own and operate it. In principle, the Port of San Diego, being an SS, PBC, derives its legitimacy to operate from a California State legislative act in 1962. Therefore, the state of California is the final overseer/operator of the Port of San Diego, with the ultimate responsibility to ensure it operates in the public benefit.

With that in mind, the inability of the port and its management to secure it against cyberattacks is dereliction of duty by California officials—and a failure to protect California, its citizens, its stakeholders, and its critical national infrastructure. However, when you consider that the US Navy is its neighbor, this failure's responsibility falls also on the shoulders of the US federal government and its leaders.

California, if considered a country, would be the fifth-largest economy in the world by GDP. It had already surpassed the UK in 2019. To have mechanisms that fail to defend what is a key public operation, and one that has such proximity to a naval base, while having all the economic wealth, prosperity, and brain power the state commands, means that the strategies and solutions they are following like gospel are no longer fit for purpose. Californians and Americans cannot afford this to remain unchanged for much longer.

In the next sector, I will trade water for air as I turn your attention to the skies. If our ships are in danger of being manipulated with such ease, in a post-9/11 world, you can imagine the dangers and vulnerabilities of interconnectivity and technology within airplanes. Perhaps you can't imagine yet. And if you're thinking to yourself that, surely, the Aviation sector must be significantly better safeguarded, I challenge you to question yourself and ask why I included it in the first place, as you read through.

For more information, please visit survivabilitythebook.com/ placeholder (or scan the code below) to see articles referenced as well as my recommended reading list. We have been very lucky to have journalists on the case with integrity. I encourage you to explore how the world received this story.

Specific to this chapter, you will also find more regarding MLi Group's Maritime & Shipping Cyber-Survivability™ & Security

15

Sector Nine: Aviation

AVIATION IS A sector that requires more than just local or national regulatory compliance and enforcement. In fact, international agreements and collaboration among nation-states, international regulatory bodies, and the cooperation between their stakeholders is critical. It is worth noting that many governments around the world take lead and follow the US model of governance and compliance.

For example, when Richard Colvin Reid, infamously known as the Shoe Bomber, attempted to detonate a shoe bomb while on American Airlines Flight 63 from Paris to Miami in 2001, it was the US that introduced new regulation on shoes being taken off and being scanned before boarding. Also, it was the US that initiated the prohibition of liquids over 100 mL, including water, to pass security points. Shortly after, these protocols started getting followed by almost all international airports around the world even though they were under different national jurisdictions and laws. In essence, when the Federal Aviation Administration (FAA) establishes a new rule, virtually the rest of the world follows by implementing it.

One can say that in aviation regulation, the US has shown it can take real and effective leadership, when it chooses to. This is possible in my opinion because special-interest groups have no competing political or financial skin in the game to undermine it. Sadly, not all attempts on the Aviation sector fail to deliver on the horror the perpetrators hoped for. Some do succeed, as you will discover later in this chapter.

THE WEAKEST LINK

One particular such event happened in 2015 to a Russian airliner.[47] The flight took off on October 31 from Egypt's Sharm el-Sheikh resort airport at 03:58 GMT. And it fell off the radar before making contact with air traffic control in Larnaca, Cyprus. Authorities later located the wreckage in the Hassana area of the Sinai Desert.

By November 17, Russian authorities investigating the crash determined the cause was a "terror act" after finding "traces of foreign explosives" on debris of the Airbus plane. UK security service investigators suspected that someone with airport security access had placed an explosive device in the baggage compartment. The US also claimed it had preliminary evidence suggesting this was planted by a local affiliate of the jihadist group Islamic State (IS).

Shortly after the crash, the militants of Sinai Province claimed responsibility, saying it was "in response to Russian air strikes that killed hundreds of Muslims on Syrian land." They provided no evidence to validate their claim and their spokesperson stated that they were not obliged to disclose any mechanism behind the attack.

A reliable source of mine in Egyptian security, with direct access to the investigation, told me that "the explosives and device may have been hidden inside a branded soda can." Regardless of how the terrorists perpetrated their act, it is abundantly clear the safety of the Aviation sector and its stakeholders is as good as its weakest link.

AVIATION STAKEHOLDERS

The responsibility falls on government(s) to legislate and oversee with appropriate and adequate regulation to ensure that citizens are safe when they fly an airline. Airlines often push back on what they perceive as heavy-handed regulation, and they often succeed in watering it down. I am not talking about creating 100% safety; this cannot be achieved in practice. But the result of this watering down means that incoming regulation would not be as strong as it needs to be, nor are the highest possible levels of safety ever achieved.

The evidence to prove what I am stating is blinding. Look at how many airlines were cyber breached in the last few years. And look at how many of them this happened to despite being compliant with the EU GDPR regulation, such as British Airways (BA) and easyJet. In fact, BA was facing a record $230 million fine by EU regulators after its website failure compromised the personal details of about 500,000 customers. BA was also fined £20m ($26 million) by the British Information Commissioner's Office (ICO) for the same data breach. And the sad irony is that BA had gone through the GDPR compliance process. Clearly while they thought their tick-box exercise made them compliant, it most certainly failed to elevate their cyber security posture to enable them to fend off the cyberattack that breached them.

In terms of government stakeholders, aside from being legislators and regulators, they are also users and consumers of the sector. They happen to be passengers on diplomatic missions, meetings, appearances, trade delegations (ascertaining or solidifying economic ties), and the transportation of military personnel, soldiers, equipment, and resources in wartime.

But when it comes to responsibilities, different layers of these roles need to be recognized by all stakeholders. Governments regulate how an airliner (be it commercial or private) interacts within its airspace. It also has a regulatory regime as to compliance, in which standards are established, and they must be met in order for a plane to be permitted to operate.

For airlines and their manufacturers, each component is expected to meet multiple regulatory standards that would be set (tightly or loosely) by governments across the globe. The same applies to the security regulatory regimes that are followed, be that for passengers, information, traffic control, and so on.

And citizens should be able to expect all this to be well performed to make them safe. It is reasonable for people to expect this—and that the regulation/legislation in place is sufficient to ensure any and all bad actors would fail during any attempts.

If you doubt what I am saying, how then would you explain why hundreds of millions of people board airplanes and fly if they did not feel it was safe and they can expect to get to their destination safely? In fact, how often are we told that it is safer to fly than to drive?

Mechanically speaking, airlines are expected to continually fulfill the highest safety expectations in order for us to maintain having high confidence to fly with them. But when it comes to allowing technical and cyber vulnerabilities to exist, and remain—which can be leveraged by cyberattackers of all motivations to happen—the sector is performing at serious subpar levels and still has a long way to go. And for a sinister hacker, they only need to succeed once to accomplish their devastating GPCyber™ motivated goals.

MULTILATERAL RESPONSIBILITIES

You may recall from Sector 8 where I wrote that many stakeholders of the Maritime & Shipping sector would feel at home during the era of Queen Victoria. Well, Aviation may not be less of a dinosaur. At least, when considering the mindset of some of its regulatory and business leaders, I would argue this to be the case.

Airline responsibility and accountability often shift depending on the airspace an airplane is flying through. Air traffic control (ATC) technically falls under the responsibility of the airspace belonging to the nation-state below the airplane; however, it's also coordinated internationally with other governments for seamless operation by airlines. For example, when a plane flies from the US to Mexico, and it enters Mexican airspace, the ATC of Mexico picks it up, which moves it technically under Mexican control/guidance. This is well defined and coordinated internationally.

Based out of a Chicago Convention, the Air Transport Agreement, also referred to as Air Service Agreement, allows air travel between signatories. Other agreements have been made, such as EU-US Open Skies Agreement, Bermuda Agreement, and so on. This sector has seriously unique challenges to overcome that other sectors don't have.

Let me explain it this way: If a bank gets cyber hacked and the bank accounts of its customers are compromised, none of the account owners will plunge 30,000 feet to their deaths.

The problem is that none of these conventions—which took decades to negotiate and get ratified by world governments—are capable of formulating, with any sense of urgency, a much-needed new convention. So, formulating and ratifying and integrating and updating a new international treaty, let alone a Cyber-Survivability™ Aviation Regulatory Model with solutions and mitigation plans against GPCyber™ motivated attacks, may take years, even decades. Infusing this into an international aviation regulatory framework that can make the sector and its fliers safer may take decades more.

Think of it this way: When was the last time you had an emergency and felt you had the luxury of time? Never? Clearly, we need something that can make change now.

CORPORATE RESPONSIBILITIES

Many other sectors and industries rely on Aviation being able to function reliably and seamlessly for them to be able to prosper. For example, air travel provides speedy shipments in comparison to maritime shipping. This has created new industries in the last 30 years for exotic foods, fruits, and fresh fish, due to short shelf life.

Sectors such as transport of sensitive consumer goods, hospitality, and tourism are all dependent on Aviation. Shut down Aviation for any significant time and many industries and sectors would suffocate, wither away, or simply die. We all witnessed this with our own eyes early on and during the COVID-19 pandemic when airlines were shut down for months.

This is to make the case that the interdependence of all sectors on each other is critical. The same applies to how they must be regulated and overseen to ensure that sectors are individually and collectively made safer by a more effective regulatory model that can ensure the lives and livelihoods of stakeholders and people around the world are better protected than they are today.

For example, the UK is famous for its strawberries, and the Wimbledon tennis championship made this a globally known fact. Well, strawberry picking got ravaged in 2020 during the COVID-19 pandemic; pickers from all over the European Union usually fly in to help the growers do the picking, which needs to be done within a very tight period of time for optimum flavor, production, and maximum revenue on the market. The shutdown of the airline industry due to COVID-19 precautions meant that pickers could not travel into the UK and much of that fruit ended up perishing before it could be picked.

The Aviation sector (and the airlines that operate in it) serves and contributes significantly to national economies while adding value to the global economy on multiple levels. This is integral to the prosperity of lives and livelihoods of citizens worldwide. Any disruption can have dire ripple effects from supply shortages to fear of flying, which could devastate the tourism industry.

With the added pressure of expectations for airlines to get things perfectly right 100% of the time, this makes for an ongoing tremor and leaves us all waiting for an earthquake. No airline or manufacturer wants to witness an airplane crash due to a mechanical failure or pilot fatigue. Unfortunately, such things do happen.

And of course, none of them wants to be compromised by a cyberattack, but cyberattacks also continue to happen, routinely, and at a greater rate than ever before. This is unsustainable by the Aviation sector. And waiting for a major disaster to force urgent corrective modifications to the way it is regulated nationally and internationally is not an option, nor is it acceptable.

A GREATER ROLE FOR THE PEOPLE

People, as citizens and consumers, do play a role in the Aviation sector, but they have a greater role that they can play. As people, what do we use the sector for? What are our uses, needs, and wants? Aside from overnight shipping, business travel, going on vacations, family emergencies, and the many other uses we have, there is one key fact we hardly take notice of.

What is that? you might ask.

The effects!

Similar to other sectors, we the citizens and consumers are the most impacted when bad things happen. Think beyond plane crashes. The people are dependent on airlines, and airlines often do not step up to the plate. If you are an American citizen who hardly travels overseas—especially to any country in the European union—you most likely would not know the following fact.

Let me now compare EU and US consumer protection in the Aviation sector. In the EU, if any flight originating from an EU country is canceled or delayed by its airline, by EU law you are automatically entitled to compensation regardless of the airline's reason for the delay or cancellation. The law makes the compensation larger depending on the length of the delay or the shortness of the cancellation alert to the consumer. It includes stipulations on flight distance as well. The longer the flight, the bigger the compensation.

Meanwhile, in the US, if a flight is late or canceled, there are hoops left for the consumer to leap through. For fellow American readers living in the land where customers are supposedly "king," I have a question: Do US flying consumers have any laws that are anything remotely similar to EU laws, protecting us from the systemic flight delays and the cattle-class quality of service most domestic US carriers operate under?

This goes to the heart of how the Aviation sector players and lobbyists in the US have been very successful in making sure that governments only adopt regulatory requirements that are toothless when it comes to consumer protection. Many times, you've likely heard politicians justify not passing consumer protection legislation (to protect their election donors) by saying lines like ...

- "The proposed law will stifle innovation ..."
- "We are a country that is 'market driven' ..."
- "We believe in competition ..."
- "The American people are best served with less, not more government ..."

I'll share more of my thoughts on this topic in Part III. Well before that, let's look at how this sector's regulatory regime's mandatory/best practices are no longer up to scratch.

VULNERABILITIES WITHIN AVIATION

Due to the 2018 cyber breach of British Airways' (BA) security systems, the company got hit with a "record" fine by EU regulators and the UK Information Commissioners Office (ICO). As shared in Sector 7 (Transportation), that totaled £183 million.

Here are some basic facts you should know that led to BA being fined.

- First, hundreds of thousands of payment card details of customers were stolen in a hack of the BA website.
- The compromise went undetected for months.
- BA only discovered the breach while investigating another breach of its website that took place prior to the one they were investigating.
- BA owner, International Airlines Group (IAG), said both attacks seemed to have been carried out by the same group or gang.

- About 500,000 customers' data were harvested by the attackers, the UK ICO said.

When Information Commissioner Elizabeth Denham fined BA £183 million, she said,[48] "People's personal data is just that—personal. When an organization fails to protect it from loss, damage or theft, it is more than an inconvenience." BA did announce that it would contact the impacted customers to let them know that their information had gone astray.

Although the EU GDPR law and its fine of up to 4% of global turnover or 20 million euros can at times act as a hammer deterrent, many countries and regions have nothing similar to the EU laws. So, it is highly likely that many African, Middle Eastern, Eastern European, and Asian airliners may have been cyber hacked without any public report or disclosure.

Such news blackout becomes a certainty when you consider that many of these airlines in the above-mentioned regions are state owned, sponsored, or subsidized. You can hardly expect the government to tell its people or the world that an airline it owns was a victim of a cyberattack. This means that a daunting reality exists, wherein the actual number of Aviation sector cyberattacks may be significantly higher than what is being publicly reported.[49]

To add insult to injury—and despite GDPR being one of the most advanced regulatory regimes around the world to date—events have proven that GDPR has simply failed to instigate corporate leadership and management to elevate their cyber security posture, as it was originally envisaged to do. As I mentioned before, it became a checklist exercise organizations go through in order to have a plausible defense from being fined by the regulator in the EU and/or the ICO in the UK. Specific to this scenario, airline companies continue being compromised and their internal security processes are not being elevated enough to mitigate threats or defend themselves despite becoming GDPR compliant.

Coming back to the thought of mechanical safety and that airlines need to be 100% successful on flights, 100% of the time, I have a dark and simple truth for you: a GPCyber™ attacker only needs to be successful once.

Often, the action of adding more beeping machines to existing ones is believed to create a safer environment. Despite all of the bling/high-tech added to airlines, operators, governments, and aviation systems globally, the threat from GPCyber™ motivation can come in any shape or form—even in the most unsophisticated manner. Case and point, the downed Russian flight in 2015 (from the beginning of the chapter), in which, allegedly, a soda can was sufficient in causing the destruction and devastating outcome.

A STRATEGIC RESET

After implementing a GPCyber™ risk audit as well as a cyber insurance audit (see Sector 10) for an airline company, I was having a conversation with the CEO who requested it. I asked him, "When people ask you what industry your company operates in, what do you answer?"

He replied, "It's obvious. We are an airline. We operate in the airline sector."

I then followed his answer with another question. "As a percentage of your yearly revenues, what's the percentage of your revenues and/or sales made online rather than directly at physical shops?"

He answered, "92% is online."

And then I asked, "Wouldn't it be more appropriate for you to reconsider that you are not an airline company but an internet company that operates in the airline sector?"

I could see his eyes rolling back and reflecting. Nevertheless, I continued, "This is so because your revenues are so heavily dependent on the internet operating seamlessly for you to generate 92% of your annual revenue. If the internet is shut down for a few hours, like what happened with Dyn in 2015, and a similar one that happened early June 2021 that shut down sites all over the world for a good part of a day, some for even longer, how could that impact your yearly revenues? What if your airline internet operation is down for one day, two days, or longer? What if the internet overall is down for one day, two days, or longer?"

He replied, "That's interesting, I never thought of it this way."

And I concluded, "Only when you think of it this way would you realize your revenue's true risk exposures, and only then would you realize that you are not allocating the necessary budgets and acquiring the executive expertise and resources to protect the 92% of your revenue from being cyber compromised by not only run-of-the-mill financially motivated hackers but the GPCyber™ ones who want to cause devastation, destruction, and mayhem to the country you belong to, and you become collateral damage." I added, "Only then would you start asking the questions, what am I not considering? What must I do in addition to what I am currently doing? And how soon can I implement this?"

Decision makers and readers alike need to take away that Aviation sector players whose revenues are heavily dependent on the internet need to reconsider what type of business they are. They need to question what they are today beyond how they have been labeled during their early dinosaur days. This strategic reset is priceless. It is key to initiate a rethink to help them better understand the challenges their businesses are facing now and tomorrow, so that they can better identify what would be effective solutions before wasting their limited budgets on what is not.

Ensuring their survivability and security, not just their cyber security, is not a luxury. In turn, a model is needed whereby a percentage of the yearly revenues generated from online activity gets appropriated to ensuring uninterrupted, effective, and Competitive Survivability and security. This is becoming more critically needed by the day.

Survivability strategies and solutions for Aviation stakeholders address these issues in board and decision-maker briefings and subsequent audits conducted for them to support their navigation of these unprecedented times. Part of our process is assessing strategic operational elements vis-à-vis the threat landscape they are currently exposed to. This involves identifying weaknesses that could be strengthened, which can be implemented through specific solutions or new processes, protocols, and governance models that the company never had before.

Ultimately, the strategic and operational expertise we provide is often highly unlikely to have existed internally before. Many companies, even outside of airlines, don't realize they have significant deficiencies in specialist skills at senior management and top leadership levels to help them mitigate GPCyber™ threats capable of compromising them with great ease. However, as with the previous chapters where I address the lack of awareness of the significant new types of threats they are facing and which manifest themselves through cyber, the Aviation sector is no better. In fact, it could perhaps be even worse.

MUCH, MUCH WORSE (THE FIRST TIME I REVEAL THIS PUBLICLY)

In early 2016, hackers were close to succeeding in gaining access and taking control of more than half a dozen commercial airliners while in the air. Their goal was to force multiple airline crashes into a particular ocean. This information has never been publicly disclosed before by anyone, until now.

Take a moment and think how sinister and bold the plan was. Also, think about how many lives and what else was at stake. Let's do the math together.

Bear in mind, in the September 11, 2001, attacks, 3,000 people had their lives taken. If the number of planes hacked was half a dozen, and let's say there are at least 500–700 flights per day over that ocean, with half a dozen planes and an average of 400 people on board per plane, we're looking at 2,400 passengers killed in one move.

Now, add the devastation this would cause to public confidence in flying; the damage to aviation, tourism, and other industries and sectors; and the overall national and global economy. According to History.com's "September 11 Attacks: Facts, Background & Impact," if we purely look within the boundaries of New York, the cost of that tragedy was more than $60 billion.[50] That's one state, and we aren't even looking at the global repercussions.

Thousands dead and billions of dollars lost (if not more), all caused by a single sinister act because vulnerabilities are not identified in time and are allowed to remain unpatched for too long. GPCyber™ hackers are constantly looking to find these vulnerabilities to exploit them. These sinister hackers were very close to succeeding, and their efforts are often relentless. And in this scenario, they found six compromisable airplanes within their reach.

This time we were very lucky. And I'm not saying that because the security and defense models were so strong and effective. The fact remains the perpetrators were successful to compromise the systems; they should not have been able to. And while international security agencies thwarted them at the 11th hour, luck played a vital role in this. We cannot afford to rely on luck. This is not a soccer match.

And although the plan and execution were bold and highly sophisticated, the attack most certainly was not unpredictable. Moreover, these hackers almost succeeded and the catastrophe almost happened. What's worse, while nearly 2,500 lives were saved, no lessons were learned and nothing in the system was significantly or appropriately improved. The world continued as if nothing had happened.

For those wondering how I learned of this incident, all I can say while protecting my source—a highly qualified person in the national security service of a major country—is that this event came to my attention shortly after it happened. Suffice it to say, it was classified internally as a GPCyber™ motivated attack.

Understanding the specific driving forces behind the motivations of the perpetrators is important to me. And I believe it ought to be to others. Also, what was of grave concern to me was how little or no change to improve the system happened thereafter.

Worth noting, because of the nature and scale of the act, I truly felt that any public or private disclosure of it would have been socially irresponsible at that time, regardless of the public credibility and increased business it would have generated for me and my group.

As shared in Chapter 3, MLi Group was the organization that uncovered the hack of more than half a dozen UK NHS trusts by ISIS affiliates. You will also recall we passed the intelligence we uncovered to *The Independent* newspaper in the UK, which ran the story as an exclusive in which I was featured as a key expert. I gave the intel to *The Guardian* for zero financial return and without conditions.

While we may have been able to do the same thing with the Aviation cyber hack, I chose not to. Here are the reasons I'm choosing to disclose it now.

- Again, lessons were not learned, and little or no change to improve the system has happened.
- The public needs to know that such an event did happen.
- I will only talk about generalities; I will not talk about specifics, such as how they did it.
- I will not name airlines, routes, national security agencies involved, dates, or people involved.
- I want to see real or systemic change in the protocols that are being followed that permitted the hack to happen in the first place.

- My primary motivation is to see an improved system and to make it safer for us all.
- I decided that we need to turn this sinister plot into an unprecedented learning opportunity that could instigate better safety systems being implemented.

I'm fine if some wish to accuse me of being an eternal optimist. If people stop believing that a better way is possible, none of us will ever attempt to improve anything around us. After all, when was the last time you saw hopelessness deliver a change or a solution?

Let me be blunt: we can no longer afford to wait for another brick to hit us on the head to wake us up to start demanding real change or force us to change the way we do things—or how to better approach defending and protecting nation-states, businesses, and stakeholders domestically and internationally. Decision makers out there, such as CEOs, chairmen, ministers, prime ministers, and presidents, who still think that time is on their side are delusional. Many of them and their mindsets will eventually meet the fate of the dinosaur, like their predecessors did before them in eras gone by.

A better future awaits those who ask:

- How can I turn these unprecedented threats into national or corporate competitive advantages?
- What must I consider implementing that I have not before?
- How can a Survivability Strategy help me deliver this to my nation, organization, fellow citizens, and consumers to excel now and in the future?
- What must I reprioritize?

Only those who get those questions answered and follow through stand a real chance of ensuring their effective and Competitive Survivability today and in the 21st century. Some of you might have a little voice in the back of your head thinking there's always some form of cyber insurance to use for a longer survivability. I can't imagine that's too many of you, but for the ones who do have that thought, Sector 10 is just for you. For the rest of my readers, you will appreciate, as you continue reading, the practice most cyber insurance players follow and how conflicting clauses are used as loopholes to give legal ground to deny claims and how they fail to protect.

For more information, please visit survivabilitythebook.com/ placeholder (or scan the code below) to see articles referenced as well as my recommended reading list. We have been very lucky to have journalists with integrity on the case. I encourage you to explore how the world received this story.

16
Sector Ten: Cyber Insurance

WE ARE ALREADY in the midst of a global paradigm change. At the beginning of Part I, I shared how MI6 chief Alex Younger informed everyone in attendance that cyber terror threats from ISIS/Daesh to the UK and its allies was "unprecedented," and how damage could be done without the attackers leaving their borders.

Younger's words were spoken at the end of 2016. Two months later, on February 8, 2017, *The Independent* reported ISIS hacks that damaged, defaced, and destroyed many NHS Trusts in the UK. Again, the forensics of these NHS hacks by ISIS were uncovered by the MLi Group and shared exclusively with *The Independent*. Overall, I hope the proximity of the event to Younger's conference serves as a stark reminder that "Survivability" is an unprecedented threat, that no one is immune, and that immediate action is inescapable if dire consequences are to be prevented.

By this point in the book, it should be clear that cyberthreats are evolving at breakneck speed. Geo-Poli-Cyber™ (GPCyber™) attacks, perpetrated or inspired by extremist groups like ISIS/Daesh, rogue states, as well as national security agencies and their proxies have caused a global paradigm change in the cyberthreat landscape.

GPCyber™ hackers are far worse than conventional hackers. They will ransomware you; steal, damage, destroy, and expose your data; and DDoS attack you—but they won't stop there. They will only stop when there is nothing more they can gain, either in publicity, fame, or intelligence.

Overall, they gain the most by causing the maximum damage possible and showcasing to the public how effective they can be in devastating or destroying their targets. They are motivated not just by profit but by political, ideological, terrorist, or so-called religious agendas:

- Showing their followers "victories" against their superior enemy
- Boosting morale and bolstering their recruitment drives are their goals
- Changing the course of another nation's economic and/or political direction

In this chapter, I want to explain how your current cyber insurance policy, or the one(s) you are considering buying, may no longer be fit for the purpose of protecting you against cyber breaches. What your insurance company often neglects to mention is that while you or your company might be covered in a typical ransomware attack, anything considered a GPCyber™ attack technically falls under the definition of an act of terrorism.

Go ahead. Read the small print. If your insurance company's policies resemble the majority, if your GPCyber™ attackers reveal anything to the world regarding why they targeted you, you will not be covered by your cyber insurance. If you don't believe me already, well, I hope you don't have a sweet tooth ...

TWISTED DAMAGE

In 2017, Cadbury, the chocolate manufacturer, was attacked in a NotPetya cyber strike, among dozens of other well-known food brands owned by Mondelēz International. Employees were shocked when computers stopped working. Their email was no longer functioning, nor were they able to access any files on their network. Much to their surprise, the crash impacted the very software behind their deliveries and invoicing tracking. Not only that, they were struck for a second time.

When Mondelēz filed with its insurance company, it declared that nearly 2,000 servers and 25,000 laptops were rendered "permanently dysfunctional." Its policy was intended to cover "physical loss or damage to electronic data, programs, or software, including physical loss or damage caused by the malicious introduction of a machine code or instruction." Cut-and-dried case, right?

Swiss-based insurance company Zurich was working with Mondelēz at the time of the hack. As it happened, in March 2018 NotPetya was classified by Zurich as ransomware. Ironically, Zurich was even mentioning it specifically to encourage companies to take out cyber insurance. You can imagine Mondelēz's surprise on June 1, 2018, barely three months later, when Zurich announced it was denying its claim. How could they possibly deny it?

Fresh from the White House, press secretary Sarah Sanders communicated that NotPetya "was part of the Kremlin's ongoing effort to destabilize Ukraine and demonstrates ever more clearly Russia's involvement in the ongoing conflict. ... This was also a reckless and indiscriminate cyber-attack that will be met with international consequences."[51] When the US and the UK jointly attributed NotPetya to Russia, they effectively gave cyber insurance underwriters the legal grounds to deny claims by exercising the fairly standard "act of war" exclusion.

So, due to the nature of the GPCyber™ attack, Zurich was able to exercise a fairly standard "act of war" exclusion, which is featured in many insurance policies:

> B. This Policy excludes loss or damage directly or indirectly caused by or resulting from any of the following regardless of any other cause or event, whether or not insured under this Policy, contributing concurrently or in any other sequence to the loss:
>
> . . .
>
> 2) a) hostile or warlike action in time of peace or war, including action in hindering, combating or defending against an actual, impending or expected attack by any:
>
> (i) government or sovereign power (de jure or de facto);
>
> (ii) military, naval, or air force; or
>
> (iii) agent or authority of any party specified in i or ii above.

Corporate decision makers buy cyber insurance as a key line of defense to mitigate cyberthreats in order to sleep better at night. More often than not, this false sense of security ends up becoming a corporate nightmare. In essence, the refusal by an insurance company to pay out for a cyber breach further twists the damage. Instead of expecting any cash to support your recovery while you get back on your feet, you now must consider suing the insurance company, which requires further liquidity you may not have. You are literally pouring more fuel upon the flames ravaging your company.

At the core of this problem is the mechanism that the vast majority of corporations follow in procuring a cyber insurance policy. As always, it's a checklist by some department within their corporate governance committee or legal dept. The process is designed to be more of a compliance showcase, a dog and pony show.

It should be an acquisition of necessary information regarding the specific, relevant risks an organization is facing, in order to acquire the appropriate insurance policy and ensure its wording reflects and covers these threats. The most relevant risk information and necessary expertise to acquire the most suitable cyber insurance policy is often not available within its corporate structure.

CYBER INSURANCE STAKEHOLDERS

Governments are often involved in creating an insurance mitigation mechanism too large for any insurer to underwrite. This is intended to help the nation-state deal with natural disasters such as flooding. Overall, the insurance sector is typically regulated through the financial sector. In the UK, for example, the insurance industry is governed by the Financial Conduct Authority (FCA).

However, in the US, where no FCA equivalent exists, this responsibility is distributed across several federal agencies.

1. The Securities and Exchange Commission (SEC). This agency is mandated in regulating the conduct of publicly traded stocks, the companies that issue them, and the markets on which these stocks get traded. Its purpose is to ensure investors are on an even footing with each other. It also tries to prevent fraud against stock investors.

2. The Federal Deposit Insurance Corporation (FDIC). This agency issues low-cost insurance to guarantee the deposits in commercial banks. The FDIC helps regulate banks to minimize dangerous practices that can put banks in financial jeopardy.
3. The Federal Trade Commission (FTC). Last but not least, this agency is one of many organizations designed to protect consumers. It is supposed to monitor advertising to prevent illegal and unethical behavior (such as the exploitation of minors) and monopolies, which can unjustifiably increase prices on goods and services.

A major problem is that neither UK nor US governments are demanding that insurance players offer more details in their policy definitions. Therefore, stakeholders who buy these policies are left confused. The government leaves it to stakeholders such as the underwriters and brokers to self-regulate, which has remained the ethos for obvious reasons. I would hope by now you are thinking about the influence any given sector has on the government. Insurance as a sector has existed for a few centuries and therefore has a strong influence on government lobbying.

Established in the late 1600s, a company began offering marine insurance for the slave trade out of founder Edward Lloyd's coffee house. Most often you've heard of this company referred to as Lloyd's, or Lloyd's of London. Today, it is an insurance and reinsurance global marketplace operating and located in the city of London in the United Kingdom. Rather than simply being an insurance company, it is a corporate body governed by the Lloyd's Act of 1871 and subsequent Acts of Parliament.[52]

Investors are grouped into syndicates that are pooled together in the interest of spreading risk. All in all, members are known as underwriters and are a collection of both corporate and private individuals traditionally writing policies and claims backed by centuries of historical data.

In recent years, cyber insurance policies contracted by US businesses represent 80% of policies worldwide; 15% are in the EU, and 5% are in the rest of the world.

While the cyber insurance industry is growing very fast, it is young in comparison to other insurance, such as life, home, and auto; it can be considered an infant that is growing too fast for the clothes it is wearing. Companies that jumped into offering policies in this space had very little data on which to base their underwriting and risk exposure mitigation models effectively. This is why they incorporated conflicting and ambiguous clauses in these policies to give themselves legal grounds to deny paying out on specific claims.

When an insurance company offers health insurance coverage, it has already amassed data to assess risks of payout in case of a claim and underwrites accordingly in a manner that allows them to make a profit. When it comes to cyber insurance, because the data are young, and the historical data are very limited and short, underwriters are unable to do the risk versus payout calculation as extensively as they normally can. This means they must create wording within the policy that is often ambiguous and may conflict with other clauses.

Ambiguity is at the core of mitigating their risk of a payout. This is why you see standard exclusions clauses, such as the act of war policy used by Zurich, in order to decline Mondelēz/Cadbury's claim. The word "terrorist" is a significant one that is often used as an exclusion.

In the midst of all of this, the sector is predominantly a private/public partnership where governments encourage self-regulation; the wording within these policies and the standards which they must follow are often created by the insurance companies—not the regulators. The people have no real influence on the wording of these policies or the laws that govern what must be clarified and what can be left to insurance companies to self-regulate. Therefore, they have virtually zero influence on the process.

VULNERABILITIES WITHIN CYBER INSURANCE

Today, top decision makers around the world need to wake up and come to grips with this new reality. They are now targets of hackers motivated by politics, ideologies, terror, religions, extremism, and causing destruction. This is not a threat to short-term profitability or shareholder value. It's a threat to corporate and national Competitive Survivability.

Organizations relying on their existing cyber insurance policy to protect them, or those considering the acquisition of new cyber insurance coverage, are in for a shock. It is a fact that most cyber insurance policies available today contain specially injected ambiguities or conflicting clauses that render policies no longer fit for the purpose they were bought. This has added an even greater risk when a breach does occur.

Today, you need to be concerned not just with the security of your data and that of your customers but also with your Competitive Survivability. Ultimately, this means you will want a cyber insurance policy that will perform for you in the very likely eventuality of a cyber breach. The new necessity is a fit for purpose cyber insurance policy that will perform, as it can be the difference between a collapsed business and an effective, Competitive Survivability.

Organizations pay a premium for their cyber insurance, expecting it to pay out when they file a claim as a result of a cyber breach. This is no different than any household in the world that buys home/fire/earthquake/etc. insurance and expects it to pay out in the case of a claim, but hoping they'll never need to claim. Critical to the process of procuring the right policy for the right risks you need covered is the awareness of all the specific risks, individually first, and then looking at them comprehensively.

Most often, the insurance policy itself will tell you what it does cover, and the insurance company's agent will give you a list of other policies you should be considering. While their list will be close to what you and/or your organization needs, it will not be exact. At that, it's a generic list created by the insurance underwriter in a manner that helps them mitigate the risks of payout versus revenue from the premium. Then, the insurance broker will step in to explain how these policies are best suited for you so it becomes purchasable "as is."

Meaning ...

A. You (the organization) are buying the coverage generically created but not specific to your needs.
B. The broker, who is sales-motivated, is doing their best to identify the closest policy to the needs of the client (you) to secure sales/commission.

Take note: There is a large gap between what they offer and what you actually need.

In certain instances, when your organization is large enough, you may have the scale, purchasing power, and opportunity for your broker to offer specific riders of risks that are not incorporated in your policy. These riders generally come at high premiums and are seldom within the scope/ability of small and medium-sized enterprises (SMEs). And you need to know your risks in order to request those riders.

Another challenge is the internal mechanisms of the organizations in the way they procure cyber insurance policies. Many organizations in the West may be required to acquire cyber insurance as part of their corporate governance protocol, or government requirement. Therefore, having any insurance policy in place to administrators is more important than having the right policy.

If you've chosen the policy as is, then you are facing a particular problem. Your insurance company is already mitigating future payouts, and this is done through clauses, conflicting clauses, and exclusions added to the offered policy. For example, you've purchased a cyber insurance policy which "clearly" covers you against a cyberattack. You discover that you've gone through a cyber breach and there are damages because of it. You submit your claim. In principle, the insurance company should pay out. Every broker will tell you up to the point of sale that the policy covers the action of the breach, but not the motivation.

If the cyberattack was perpetrated by someone who publicly claims it in the name of "Allah," then their attack now falls under the category of terrorism. Or if a Western government decides to attribute a particular cyber breach to some other country, even without providing any evidence, underwriters can use this to exercise exclusions such as "act of war" to deny the claim. The same can apply if government leaders publicly acknowledge an attack between countries. As explained with Cadbury/Mondelēz's cyber breach, any such qualification means that the insurance company can now refuse to pay out.

In contrast to the Mondelēz/Zurich scenario, it's worth noting that the insurance company does not need a government to classify a cyberattack as terrorist activity to deny the claim. It can exercise that clause/exclusion if the cyberattack is reported in the press to have been claimed by a terrorist individual/group. Many perpetrators have taken the lead independently, and this will quickly escalate. The organization then takes claim of the attack. Does the insurance company investigate further into this? No, they can deny your claim purely due to the declaration.

There are then two possible outcomes after a GPCyber™ attack:

1. Either an individual claims it, who may or may not offer allegiance to a group (not always the case).

2. A terrorist group claims it.

Case in point, the hackers behind the NHS attack in 2017: they may have been individuals, but they attributed themselves to be the cyber caliphate. In either case, the moment a link to a terrorist individual or group, or even a terrorist motivation behind the attack is discovered, the underwriter now has sufficient legal ground to deny the claim.

Often, an insurance company may choose to pay out a claim it can legally decline for the purpose of maintaining good standing with an important customer because it manages an entire portfolio of insurance policies on its behalf. Invoking the terrorism clause within insurance policies is so common, and yet the majority of organizations that are buying cyber insurance policies do not have the necessary expertise to assess whether or not the policy it is being offered will cover it against GPCyber™ motivated attacks.

MLI GROUP'S SURVIVABILITY CYBER INSURANCE AUDIT

I want my readers to know about what MLi Group and I did and are doing about this significant problem and how we took leadership when most were just trying to make money no matter the means. This is not to generate business leads in any way, shape, or form, far from it. It is to illustrate what I did when I identified this huge problem and the unique solution we created to help those who asked us for help.

Before I illustrate the uniqueness of what we did and our services, I want you to consider the following questions.

- With corporate survivability at greater risk than ever, how do you find out if your current cyber insurance policy is fit for purpose?
- How do you, as a decision maker, know if your sales-motivated insurance broker has provided you the best options for today's latest threats, without any sales bias?
- How do you determine if you have or are buying the right coverage?
- How do you know if your current policy is truly protecting you?
- How do you know if it is up-to-date in covering the latest risk exposures?

- In case you file a claim, how confident are you in the policy actually paying out, especially if against GPCyber™ hacks?
- Above all, can you sleep well at night, confident that you will be covered when your company is breached?

As a corporate leader, if you are uncertain about any of the above questions, you are not alone. And I hope it comes with great relief when I tell you that there is another way to bring the necessary expertise into the equation.

MLi Group and I worked directly with and explored many underwriters, and we partnered with insurance companies to be able to suggest at least three policies that can cover against cyber terrorism by default. One of those policies features our trademarked terminology incorporated in the policy wording and included in the cover automatically: Poli-Cyber™ and Geo-Poli-Cyber™.

While we aren't an insurance company, disruption wherever and whenever possible is part of our DNA. So changing the modality of a sector that's more than a few hundred years old comes naturally. Being able to turn some of their policies around to properly protect their stakeholders was a mission of mine. At that, we've been invited to speak at many insurance events. Since 2016, the MLi Group has been offering the MLi Group's Survivability Cyber Insurance Audit™, which we rebranded recently to Survivability Cyber Insurance Audit.

This is a highly specialized, confidential, in-depth audit of your existing cyber insurance policy, if you have one, or of any new cyber policies you are considering buying. If you do not possess one, the audit becomes an assessment of your needs to recommend the ideal cyber coverage(s).

With organizations all over the world, especially in the West, becoming targets for GPCyber™ attacks, it is critical to undertake our Survivability Cyber Insurance Audit™ before you are cyber breached. Many learn this very costly lesson too late, when filing a claim after the fact and discovering that their insurer won't pay. This leaves only costly legal recourse and delays important actions in response.

MLi Group's precise audit looks at the new risk exposures of the stakeholder, their current corporate structure, model of operation, and internal processes in addition to many other areas. Then it audits their current cyber insurance policy or policies they are considering purchasing to identify ambiguities and/or conflicting clauses that may exist that would give their insurers valid legal grounds or sufficient cause to deny a claim.

The scope of the audit places special emphasis on GPCyber™ attacks, cyber terrorism, and terrorism. The audit results are provided in a confidential report that concludes with recommendations of actions to take, identification of more appropriate cyber insurance policies to consider, and other considerations where appropriate. As said, this special service is also designed to help organizations that do not possess a cyber policy but want help identifying "a fit for purpose cyber policy," without sales bias, to then tailor it around their specific needs and requirements.

Our audit is a highly specialized, professional, and confidential service for the client, not a sales instrument. Those interested in learning more can visit the MLi Group website or this book's website, where an expression of interest can be sent.

BUTTERFLY WINGS AND HURRICANES

In closing, I want you to think about the Cadbury/Mondelēz attack. Zurich was able to deny their claim because the virus and damage were the result of cyber warfare on the other side of the world. You could have an organization based in Australia, and a cyberattack in Iceland could very well spill over into your servers on the other side of the globe. Much like Mondelēz, your computers could be rendered useless, business shut down for days, and profit completely lost without warning.

WannaCry, NotPetya, RAT, Mimikatz, and Dyn are well known across the globe. And many viruses and exploited vulnerabilities such as these were designed by government entities with a single purpose against an enemy or adversary (and sometimes even allies). Others were designed by GPCyber™ organizations with the sole intent of leaving as much destruction as possible in their wake.

To mitigate your risks, you must become fully aware of every single risk you are exposed to. This is not possible for most top decision makers. Also, you often do not possess the internal expertise to understand your specific risk exposures to geopolitical, terrorist, extremist, and GPCyber™ motivations, and how they can impact you directly and indirectly, let alone be able to create and implement specific strategies, solutions, and protocols that go far beyond cyber security to mitigate them.

If you are hacked and receive a demand, consider yourself lucky. You are dealing with a financially motivated hacker who is driven by enriching themselves. Often, they give the ransom demand, you pay out, and the problem is sorted. How do you deal with GPCyber™ motivated perpetrators whose sole cause is to bring maximum damage, devastation, or destruction?

Clearly a new model of regulation must be considered to defend nation-states in mitigating today's and the 21st century's cyber and non-cyberthreats. We are headless, running through models and systems set in place by leaders and decision makers claiming we are protected—and that everything from "best" practices to actual requirements are created in our best interest.

Citizens are the most impacted by this damage in terms of national/international regulation. All impact falls on them. And if you disagree, keep reading. I think you'll be surprised at what I will be talking about next. In fact, the way things are currently going is an unprecedented threat to democracy and humanity.

For more information, please visit survivabilitythebook.com/ placeholder (or scan the code below) to see articles referenced as well as my recommended reading list. We have been very lucky to have journalists with integrity on the case. I encourage you to explore how the world received this story.

PART III

An Unprecedented Threat to Humanity and Democracy

17

Three Meals from Anarchy

(A Threat to Humanity)

MANY OF YOU might think I'm a pessimist by illustrating the potential disasters ahead rather than any utopian seeds that might happen to be planted today. I prefer to think of myself as a realist. And I believe the reality of life is that unless you're aware of the potential problems you're facing, you have no chance to prepare for them.

I do not believe that current Western models (economic, electoral, etc.), institutions, or players are capable of safeguarding democracy or honoring its core values in the 21st century. Overall, I have no confidence in the sustainability of these models/institutions, which will be to the detriment of citizens' lives and livelihoods. And within these variables, the corruption found represents the putrid stench of a cancer consuming any hope for sustainability—and it is getting worse every year.

So, the pessimist in me cannot ignore the obstacles between true survivability and the ongoing (albeit failed) status quo. These established Western institutions are part of their countries' mechanism to serve and maintain said status quo; it's not democracy or the people—regardless of any PR/narratives spinning the opposite. If Western institutions/systems were truly serving their people and democratic values, as professed, then true transparency would be in place; however, such a thing would reveal that foreign aid and international support is still provided to leaders stealing money from their people and in some cases abusing human rights that make Genghis Khan look like an amateur.

In the US, there are very well-known think tanks and nonprofits that have democracy as part of their label. But they are either funded by special interest or by governments to serve a particular cause. At that, their agenda is very polarized or polarizing, either serving a special-interest domestic political agenda or that of a foreign country.

After Part II, I hope it's become clear to you that Western governments and supported parties are not serving the public or true democratic values—counter to what seems to be in place. This is clear to me in that nothing of significance is being required or mandated via legislation. If their models were effective and their legislation required anything significant, we would not be observing the systematic failures throughout the unprecedented—and in some cases, much to their chagrin, even precedented—events leading up to or surrounding 2020.

One of the key objectives of my book is to draw your attention to Geo-Poli-Cyber™ (GPCyber™) attacks and their motivations, how we remain vulnerable to them despite the trillions spent worldwide on cyber security, and to provide you an understanding of how they will affect us now and in the future. I can predict with certainty that the current models and legislation will miss the mark by a mile as to what governments need to do to secure their nation-states as well as the lives and livelihoods of their citizens from GPCyber™ events.

In Chapter 3, I shared Alfred Henry Lewis's nine meals concept. Please recall his quote, "There are only nine meals between mankind and anarchy." Again, the pessimist in me strikes deep as I share with you the following statement:

We are no longer nine meals from anarchy, but three.

In Lewis's mind, if/when disaster strikes, people facing scarcity in terms of resources and supplies necessary to survive end up resorting to unprecedented actions. His words were written in 1906, and his meals were a measurement of days: three meals per day, and three days between stability and complete anarchy. As I was writing this in 2021, it only became more apparent to me that Lewis's scenario would play out much faster and harder than he could have anticipated more than 115 years ago.

As we begin Part III, I want you to keep in mind that we, the citizens of the world, are the double victims—once by the perpetrators, and again by the current regulatory models that are seriously failing to protect them. With every form of vulnerability in our systems and nation-states, one can find the flawed and misguided decisions behind it as made by our beloved leaders. Where we should be protected, organizations are given a slap on the wrist, and we are left with the bill following any cyber-attack of any motivation.

As further injustices come into focus, the people are falling further into civil unrest, protest, and desperation. We are in a pressure cooker today, and left to its own devices, it will not diffuse itself; it will explode. I'll share more on this later in the chapter, but picture the events after George Floyd's murder by a police officer: peaceful protests followed by fire and brimstone.

Counter to what we might hope for, and what we need, politicians brought some legislation to depressurize the situation, and they did so to maintain stability of (here we go again) the status quo; they did not solve the problem. Citizens remain lambs for the slaughter, and I believe that unless we as a society do something dramatically different, we will remain three meals from anarchy until there are no meals left.

CHECKS AND BALANCES (OF A FAILED POLITICAL, ECONOMIC, AND DEMOCRATIC WORLD ORDER AND MODEL)

Can we ever forget the "Mission Accomplished" speech by US President George W. Bush on the aircraft carrier USS *Abraham Lincoln* on May 1, 2003?

While he announced the end of the military operation in Iraq, little did the world know that the carnage was just about to begin. The US and the UK formed a narrative for launching the war, and their declared mission, many of you may still remember, was bringing democracy to the Iraqis and ridding the world of Saddam Hussein. On the ground, the reality, as we have learned over the next 17-plus years, is totally different.

For all intents and purposes, Iraq became segregated by religious sectarianism, which did not exist during the rule of Saddam. When the US was supported by the UK and others in its 2003 invasion of Iraq, the subsequent decisions allowed for unprecedented levels of corruption therein. New warlords were born and became richer than God.

A country that once had the world's third-largest oil reserves, and the best publicly funded free health care system in the world, faces power cuts 12 out of every 24 hours today—meanwhile, new Iraqi leaders and politicians are becoming billionaires. This was all under the watchful eye of the "allied" forces, namely the US and UK, which were busy ushering democracy to ungrateful Iraqis. Instead of delivering their declared promise of democracy and prosperity for Iraqis, the US and UK delivered mayhem and a failed state that enabled the birth of ISIS. Let me put it another way: without the mayhem of a corrupt Iraq, ISIS could not have been born or created.

For any supporters who might claim that the allies simply made mistakes in their strategies and implementation of policies after the initial invasion, allow me to disagree. The mayhem and destruction of Iraq was part of the plan from the beginning. It was no accident. It was not a series of unfortunate events.

Many readers may recall public statements by neoconservative American politicians about how the first invasion of Iraq in 1989 was intended to be followed by subsequent invasions of Libya, Lebanon, Syria, and eventually, Iran. This was no secret. As a result of this failed supremacist strategy, the world has been fully engulfed in the "War on Terror" since 2001.

In fact, I call on all Western citizens, especially fellow Americans, to watch and listen to General Wesley Clark's speech (it's included in my online resource page). Speaking at an event, Gen. Clark talks about how the Bush Jr. administration plan was to launch chaos in the Middle East as it was planning the Iraq invasion. He recounted that Bush administration officials knew there was no link between Saddam and Osama bin Laden but were determined to launch the war regardless.

Along the way, corrupt local politicians would become key figures in the implementation of this plan. Regardless of their record on human rights abuses, war crimes, etc., as long as they were supportive of the plan, the West turned a blind eye. The US and UK formed local alliances with Iraqi groups to serve these goals.

The Kurds, who became staunch allies of the US, were given exclusive rights to sell the oil in Kurdish territories, directly and outside of the control of Baghdad, the capital, and the central government of Iraq. This new wealth came at the disposal of the Kurdish leaders, with little or no transparency/accountability as to how such natural resources belonging to the Iraqi people would be used. Can you imagine any US president deciding overnight that their buddy (say, an NFL team owner), can now become the sole recipient of all the oil extracted in the state of Texas, just because they want his favor? Well, this is what successive American presidents were doing for decades while championing and promoting democracy around the world.

The favor that the US received was the Kurds becoming the US proxy army, implementing US special interest in Iraq that would segregate the country on ethnic, sectarian, and tribal grounds. This template was duplicated routinely in Syria, Lebanon, and other locations throughout the region. And many of these US proxy fighter groups end up abandoned to fend for themselves whenever a change of strategy or leadership takes place in the US. It's hardly the perfect recipe to create loyalties to the US.

In fact, the Kurds have been let down by the US on numerous occasions, some of which led to them being massacred. Meanwhile, incumbent officials remain in US pockets, and they renew terms every four years. While carrying out the "promise" of democracy, incumbency, special interest, and corruption have become the new unholy trinity. The resulting template of an imposed Western model can also be found in African, Middle Eastern, and Asian countries, as well as certain Western and Eastern European countries.

Are you scratching your head wondering how this relates to the threat to democracy and humanity?

Well, in April 2016, immediately south of the US, and on the other side of the world from Iraq, nearly 12 million documents were leaked from a Panamanian law firm and corporate service provider Mossack Fonseca. The global shockwave was called "the Panama Papers."

The Panama Papers revealed highly sensitive data detailing financial and confidential attorney–client information for over 200,000 offshore entities. This involved a list of who's who clients—specifically, government leaders around the globe including both current and former rulers, heads of state, ministers, top government officials, their family members, and many others. It behooves you to watch the short video.[53]

For a moment, you can try to consider these hackers who compromised Mossack Fonseca as the true implementers of checks and balances on global systems of our society in which the supposed checks and balances are failing us on unprecedented levels. Or you can consider them law breakers. Regardless, what they uncovered cannot be ignored if we value true democracy.

Western society likes to distinguish itself as better than other models by pointing with pride to our democratic values, institutions, and formidable true representation of the people and their wishes. But, from the names involved and the connections implied, such things practically became illusions spun by profiteers.

Wrong or right, the hack identified the following:

- Such leaders serve the establishment (or their deep state puppeteers) over their constituents.
- The West accepts human rights abusers as partners as long as they are willing to kiss the ring.
- Checks and balances in place are in fact a camouflage for a system that is captured by special-interest domestic and foreign political players and agendas.
- It is not just the frailty but the falsehoods of the transparency and mechanisms in Western society we must hold to account when it comes to promoting democracy in other countries.

Before I go into the specifics of this massive leak, let's recap and dive deeper into the ineptness in today's hailed world order and the gigantic corruption breeding more corruption.

CALLING A SPADE ... (THE FAILED STATUS QUO AND ITS UNPRECEDENTED VULNERABILITIES)

In defending the nation-state and securing its effective and competitive survivability and securing its sovereignty from threats, including coercion, we must recognize a very specific dynamic:

National security is dependent on economic security, and vice versa.

While economic security is dependent on national *stability*, it also requires the stability and security of organizations/corporations. Therefore, a stable nation-state requires stable and secure organizations/corporations. At the bottom of this food chain rests the lives and livelihoods of citizens.

Without the above balance, the nation-state cannot be secured in the 21st century, to the detriment of the citizen. In principle, organizations must comply with government regulation when it comes to their security posture, and many go beyond that. If the cyber security breaches scattered all over the news are any indication, government regulation currently in place in many countries around the world has proven to be toothless and inadequate.

Consider the GBPR legislation I have talked about numerous times so far. Breached companies that receive a ransom note ought to throw a party and celebrate; that's because they now have an idea of the perpetrator's most likely motivation: money. However, the more sinister non-financially motivated cyberattacks (which might not get reported as frequently) occur with massive cost/consequences, as you may recall from Part II:

Sector One: CNI (Critical National Infrastructure)

In December 2019, four US cities suffered massive cyberattacks within one month. For reference, that's Pensacola, New Orleans, Galt (California), and St. Lucie (Florida). Damages amounted to $7.5 billion. The impacted organizations included 113 state and municipal governments and agencies; 764 health care providers; and 89 universities, colleges, and school districts—with operations at up to 1,233 individual schools potentially affected.

Sector Two: IoT & Miscellaneous

The Dyn attack of 2016 meant hundreds of websites and services (public and private) shut down. The attackers requested no form of ransom. Damages of their attack included ATMs, traffic lights, and gas pumps, and it amounted to billions of dollars in losses.

Sector Three: "Smart" Environments (Cities, Buildings, and Homes)

In 2020, perpetrators took advantage of exposed NSC Linear eMerge E3 devices and compromised a "smart" building using a specific malware (CVE-2019-7256). After taking over devices, and downloading and installing further malware, the hackers launched distributed-denial-of-service (DDoS) attacks on other targets.

Sector Four: The Cloud

Attacks on Capital One and Deloitte resulted not only in high costs to the companies themselves but the compromised data of millions of users. In the case of Deloitte, hackers had been hiding in their systems for nearly a year.

Sector Five: Banking & Financial

Marriott and Verizon found themselves in horrendous purchases gone bad (Starwood and Yahoo!, respectively). Previous to the acquisition, perpetrators had already infiltrated Starwood, compromising 500 million guest records. In Yahoo!'s case, hackers remained undetected for more than three years, compromising 2 billion accounts.

Sector Six: Telecommunications

The Soft Cell major cyberattack of 2019, which was highly coordinated, impacted telecom operators located in Europe, Africa, the Middle East, and Asia. After compromising the IT infrastructure of many telecom network operators, Soft Cell acted as a shadow IT department, complete with administrative privileges. Using a modified version of Mimikatz in stealth mode, they collected information about the network and compromised usernames and passwords. They accomplished lateral movement around the targeted network, including access on demand. They were able to gain access to call records and geolocations of hundreds of millions of people. Worst of all, they had the capability to shut off the networks altogether.

Sector Seven: Transportation

In July 2015, Chrysler issued a safety recall. Of 1.4 million Jeeps in the US, hundreds of thousands of them were discovered to be hackable. Luckily, the hackers involved were financially motivated. However, had they been GPCyber™ motivated, the destruction could have been catastrophic. And in 2019, it was revealed that Honda's database was exposed. Thankfully, this was revealed in time, and they were able to address the issue. This was not limited to one location, however. The exposure included records on multiple offices around the world, including locations in Mexico, the UK, and the US—including sensitive information regarding Honda's CEO.

Sector Eight: Maritime & Shipping

A. Moller-Maersk (known simply as Maersk) fell victim to malware known as NotPetya in June 2017. Considered a success story, the company did a complete infrastructure overhaul in ten days. That's 4,000 new servers, 45,000 new PCs, and 2,500 applications. All the damage was the result of one bad email.

B. In 2018, a scheme from 2015 resulted in a complete shutdown of California's San Diego Port. While hailed as ransomware (the hackers demanded Bitcoin), I believe there was something far more sinister going on. The FBI later announced that the 2015 scheme originated from state-sponsored hackers operating inside the Islamic Republic of Iran, who targeted more than 200 public agencies and hospitals.

Sector Nine: Aviation

A Russian airliner seemingly disappeared in 2015 as a result of a terrorist act. It was discovered that the bomb may have been smuggled onboard in a branded soda can. This shows that the safety of Aviation stakeholders is as good as the sector's weakest link. Shortly after this tragedy, hackers nearly accomplished their goal of hacking more than half a dozen planes in order to crash them into the ocean. While international security agencies were able to thwart the attack at the 11th hour, we can never rely on luck when it comes to our safety.

Sector Ten: Cyber Insurance

Another NotPetya attack struck Cadbury (owned by Mondelēz International) in 2017. Nearly 2,000 servers and 25,000 laptops were rendered "permanently dysfunctional." However, as the company attempted to work with its insurance provider, it discovered that not only did the attack stem from destabilization efforts against the Ukraine, damages of the attack fell under a fairly standard "act of war" exclusion. Cadbury/Mondelēz's claim was denied.

The majority, if not all the companies breached in these attacks are highly likely to have been compliant with their national regulatory authorities' requirements (such as GDPR) under the jurisdiction of the governments where they operate. Still, none found this compliance of much help to be able to better defend themselves against these attacks. This means that legislation in the form of a checkbox list is an exercise in cyber futility, good enough only to offer a defense against being fined by their respective regulator, to showcase that they followed the process.

Why is this relevant?

The guidelines required by the legislation must be comprehensive enough to ensure not only the survivability of the corporation but also ensure economic stability of the nation-state (and therefore, the stability of the nation-state itself). As it currently stands, a mere handful of organizations are capable of surviving such breaches. This is due to their financial size, scale of business, and resources. The majority operate without such an asset base and will have no chance of defending themselves, let alone surviving. Therefore, their compromisability is of direct impact on their nation-state, and the impact on the nation directly impacts its national stability as it impacts its citizens' prosperity, lives, and livelihoods.

The stability of a national economy cannot be secured or defended if its businesses/organizations can be easily compromised or shut down, suddenly or repeatedly. And government assistance on keeping an economy afloat as a result is artificial and can only be expected for a short time, and will need to be repaid back sooner or later, as we witnessed of the furlough and assistance schemes by many Western nations during the COVID-19 pandemic. At that, in countries where governments are unable to assist, only more human disparity and hopelessness should be expected.

For governments that are determined to continue peddling self-regulation and best practices as gospel, good luck. They should bear in mind that very few corporations, if any, have the necessary in-house expertise to understand, analyze, and mitigate GPC attacks—let alone the motivation of cyber terrorists and extremist groups targeting them and the dire unfolding of events and consequences that will fall on them and the country they belong to.

CORRUPTION ON UNPRECEDENTED SCALES

With effective and Competitive Survivability as a goal, for the nation-state to defend itself, presiding governments must at the very least move to (a) improve and specify new mandatory requirements in their legislation/regulation that govern businesses and organizations, (b) significantly elevate their guidance, and (c) increase assistance in order to help and support these organizations in meeting the new compliance benchmark requirements. Such improvements are only the beginning. And while they will not happen overnight, time is of the essence.

The traditional approach to legislation and regulation, the institutions, modality, and timeframe of planning and preparation (etc.) inherited from the 19th and 20th centuries (and even further back to the Middle Ages in some cases), can no longer be relied upon to deliver what society needs urgently. Despite being updated with the latest high-tech-focused amendments, it's still a dinosaur with Christmas lights wrapped around it. Before it's too late, we need new and improved systems that can deliver credible results for citizens to believe in and feel pride in belonging to a society they are part of; only then will they actively engage in it, furthering real change.

I would say that we need to start now, but we should have started yesterday. The stability of nations is at stake. This applies to us in the West and countries all over the world.

For the West, also at stake are the real values of democracy. Not only are we vulnerable, unstable, and unsecured, but the corrupt actions and systemic failure of current leadership are increasing the scale of potential damage. The lives and livelihoods of all citizens will continue taking the brunt of any catastrophes ahead of us.

How is the aforementioned instability so prevalent today? During times of adversity, the action of law making only creates authority—it does not create legitimacy. To create legitimacy, the active approval and participation of citizens is imperative.

During the global outrage and reactions following George Floyd's murder at the hands of a policeman, many new laws around the world (including in the US) were passed, providing law enforcement with additional authority rather than legitimacy. The marchers continued marching, even though the threat of COVID-19 infection was rife. As I said at the beginning of the chapter, government motions were made in the interest of depressurizing the situation and maintaining the failed status quo. The passing of laws was unable to overcome the outrage of the people.

Current participation of citizens is pushed outside of the institutions, which only leaves room for protesting on city streets. Government's approach to regulation/legislation trades citizen involvement for that of the corporate world. The primary decision makers of politics are influenced by the outcomes desired by decision makers of prominent organizations.

This influence is garnered through ongoing efforts made by the many heads of special interest, such as lobbyists, think tanks, special advisories, etc. While some of them claim to be "champions of democracy," they actually push special-interest agendas cloaked beneath their guise. In the US, for example, the two- to four-year cycle of campaigning and elections keeps everyone in check, especially the incumbents and those who want to unseat them. Key to the process are the lobbyists/financial supporters, without whom no incumbent can reach power, let alone stay in power.

In essence, any given politician is in constant campaigning mode from the minute they walk into their new office. This renders them ultimately answerable to those who support their campaign, not the voters whose votes actually put them in power. In the US and other Western nations, this incumbency is the root of the problem.

With elections bought, sold, and marketed like laundry detergent (I am sure you have seen some of these cheesy political commercials), the tight grip of incumbents on power is easily manifested by the lopsided dollars spent against their challengers—despite decades of promises made to reform both elections and election contributions. At that, no matter what, special-interest groups often support multiple and opposing candidates, incumbents and challengers alike, to ensure they have a horse that can win the race. What about the other losing candidates/horses? you might ask. Well, just think what is in the food you feed your dogs. In essence, only horses that can cross the finish lines can be declared winners, with a role to serve their masters who funded them over the line. Whether in power or seeking it, to be allowed in the game with support, all must kiss the ring.

If you review OpenSecrets.org elections overview as to the incumbent advantage, you'll see a vast amount of spending on US elections.[54] At least in terms of Senate and House campaigns, for every $1 spent by a challenger, $5 to $6.50 is spent by incumbents. Incumbents are able to spend millions on their elections, which predominantly comes from special interest—not the individual citizen/voters who historically donate less than $10 each. Is it any wonder that lawmakers become more responsive to those buttering their bread?

Significant support from special interest leads to legislators advocating legislation that promotes the continuation of self-regulation, a consistent doctrine on corporate lobbyists' part. With their relationship in place, major upheaval can be anticlimactic, such as the response to the financial crisis of 2008. After the crash, the outrage at the abuses by the banking sector champions of "Greed is good" raised voices for the need for tighter regulation on the banking sector. This got championed by many politicians and was welcomed by almost all. However, the resulting regulation suffered significant pushback from the industry/lobbyists to the point that minimal changes were implemented.

It is within this system and these relationships that we find a proverbial blade of systemic elitism with two sides:

A. Special interest's influence on elections in order to secure leaders who will trade financial support for favored political decision-making.
B. Special interest's influence upon elected leaders in regulation, and therefore legislation, in order to maintain the status quo.

As long as this remains the case, legislation/regulation will remain unimproved and society will continue paying the price. Guidance on further improvement/specification sinks into the muck. The only assistance and support involved appears to be that of special interest keeping their incumbents afloat. And upon the very edge of the blade above rides the lives and livelihoods of citizens.

This is unsustainable ...

THREE MEALS

It was 1906 when Alfred Henry Lewis said there were only nine meals (three days) between us and complete anarchy. At that point in time, his assumption of everyone having three meals per day aside, the resources in his equation basically came down to food, water, and shelter. One might think with the addition of gasoline, energy, and various resources of modern infrastructure, we would be weeks and therefore many meals from disaster. However, the addition of the internet and our serious dependency on it in our daily lives changes everything.

In considering the breakneck speed at which technology is evolving, I believe the risk to citizens becoming three meals from anarchy (rather than Lewis's nine) is very real. Our lives continue to become more and more digitized, and we have a higher reliance on technology to live and consume products/services than ever before. The more dependent we are, the less we will be able to function when it's taken away.

Please recall the Dyn and other cyberattacks I've shared with you up to this point. The perpetrators are no longer driven exclusively by financial motivation. Some were successful in shutting down the internet for a significant period of time. GPCyber™ motivated hacks are becoming commonplace and as we continue deploying more technologies with such pace and vigor, such as 5G, we are creating new vulnerabilities at such scale we will not be able to patch them fast enough.

As more data become available through everyday interaction and services, the potential of artificial intelligence as a weapon grows further (not only between nation-states, but within each of them as well). To some of you, AI as a threat vector may appear to be mitigated if the internet is shut down, but that would not be the case; the parcel will have already been delivered and well planted within the operating systems to do its deed while the internet is out.

Current strategies/solutions are failing to defend nation-states and organizations, and therefore the citizen. If access to the internet is compromised or shut down, we are up shit creek. In fact, our ultra-dependence on the digital form, in the way we consume services available today and transfer money/credit in exchange for them, is underscoring Lewis's estimation.

The following is not meant to criticize any of my readers; however, it's very likely that you are subscribed to Apple Pay, Google Pay, Square, or any number of online services (through your bank or another company). At the very least, you may still use some combination of plastic, debit, and cash; after 2020, less of the latter and more of the former.

In 2009, global credit card transactions were measured at 10,000 per second, meaning over 800 million per day.[55] As the number of users online has nearly quintupled since 2009, from 1 billion to 4.8 billion as of June 2020, those transactions have increased further than imaginable over the last decade.[56]

Beyond finance, important information (personal, confidential, and classified) is transferred just as often, if not more. Cities and infrastructure continue to digitally upscale their systems, some of them doing so without updating security needs and posture. As explained earlier in this chapter, those very service providers simultaneously increase the unlikeliness of necessary improvements.

The very act of lobbyists pushing for continuous self-regulation causes companies to adhere to a lower standard of security, regulation, and compliance. It is catastrophic, myopic, and self-endangering to the companies and the special-interest lobbyists that actually promote unhindered self-regulation. This is because self-regulation increases the systemic GPCyber™ risk on business, which in turn increases it on the nation-state itself while neither has any defense in place.

The world turns amidst billions and trillions of clicks, and orbits the sun via lines of code. As I've explained over the course of Part II sectors, we remain vulnerable to attack through the very resource that currently sustains us.

The internet as an economic conduit is compromised, and we are dependent on the illusion of stability. A lone wolf could shut a city or even a country down in one single cyberattack. Please recall the hack mentioned at the end of Chapter 2, in which a telecom company paid a mercenary-hacker 25,000 UK pounds to shut down their competitor, which incidentally led to a complete shutdown of the internet in Liberia. This is an extreme example of corporate-on-corporate crime; nevertheless, it was the citizens, the people, who got caught in the middle.

In such cases as the above example, when organizations are punished for their actions, the "severe penalties" usually amount to a slap on the wrist in the form of fines. But the money received goes straight to the government—not the people who were directly affected. Citizens impacted by such an event rarely receive compensation for their troubles; but the companies in question continue making money off of them. Failure of governments to respond to the needs of citizens in times of adversity elevates the anger of protests and marches for real change.

What makes it worse is the conditions people continue to suffer as economic disparity expands, matched by the increase of injustices. Case in point, while the US was in the midst of the Iraq War, New Orleans was tragically struck by the infamous Hurricane Katrina. The disaster left people living in the richest country on the planet in a near third-world state—thirsty, hungry, and distraught, after being underwater. Government response was an absolute disaster in and of itself, in which the state government refused to evacuate despite early warnings—and the federal government was in a position where the pace of assistance was shamefully lagging and insufficient.

In 2008, when President Obama ran his campaign to become president, he did so on the platform, "Change we can believe in." Voters were inspired and mobilized, driven by their reactions to President George W. Bush's presidency overall, as well as the Iraq War, responses to Katrina, and the recession following the financial crash of earlier 2008. And when Obama won, he then declared, "Change has come to America." Americans and people worldwide celebrated, believing that maybe this time hope for change may be for real.

Eight years later, Hillary Clinton was dueling with Donald Trump for the next US presidency, which led to the most inconceivable turn of events. Many ordinary people who voted for Obama, hoping for change, decided to vote for Donald Trump because the hope they were sold never reached them. Fundamentally, despite the significance of the first African American president, the majority of US citizens were fed up with waiting for the future to happen; they wanted change in the present. Yet again, their vote was one of outrage at a broken and unjust system, and they were tired of endless broken promises.

In the land of the free and the home of the brave, where the American dream reigns free, their dreams were being extinguished like used match sticks. Ultimately, these voters wanted the American dream and economic prosperity to reach them and improve their lives; it never did—it turned out to be the gold at the end of a rainbow. Even worse, the economic crisis left them worse off. Little did they know, sadly, that those in power measure prosperity by how the stock market performs and how the quarterly earnings and profitability of big companies are reported.

We become slaves to the 21st-century pharaohs. But with supposed human rights, equal opportunity, minimum wage, and unions, while the rich and elite are becoming richer on scales never seen before, the poor are either stagnating or becoming poorer.

Unlike our incumbents (at least according to democratic legends), there seems to be no end in sight as to the term of dominant titan corporations. For any new businesses entering the game, they are startups and small companies. Within a short window of their successful existence, they are acquired by the powers that be and swallowed into the ongoing system, often to eliminate competition (see acquisitions by Facebook, Google, etc.).

While current legislation is designed to protect against monopolies (as implemented by the House Antitrust Subcommittee), it is hardly exercised and effectively useless; meaning the WhatsApps and Snapchats of the future are just as likely to be conquered by the pharaohs reigning supreme.

As an American, I ask you, where is the true competition promised by capitalism and supply-side economics? Where is the democracy enshrined by our Constitution as aspired for by our founding fathers? And where is the inspiration to individualism, which is meant to serve humanity?

In Chapter 3, I shared the story regarding my challenge to my professor at USC, Dr. Arthur Laffer, the creator of the Laffer curve. In the early 1980s, as a student during one of his lectures, I interjected a discussion focused on a flaw in supply-side economics. As we spoke, I illustrated my thoughts based on my background in Syria and Lebanon and experiencing a life in a civil war. I specifically presented a situation in which a man with two gallons of water can either aim for maximum profitability by selling two gallons of drinking water to the highest bidder or volunteer some of the precious resource to two children who have not had a drop for a week.

I said capitalism's supply-side economics was missing a critical variable: social responsibility. As I explained, within the next three decades, there were two moments (in 2002 and 2008, respectively) that proved me correct. As I'll share again in the next chapter, Alan Greenspan, chairman of the Federal Reserve Board, spoke before US leaders twice, in which he addressed flaws in the system. He spoke of infectious greed and Wall Street's civic duty to protect Main Street.

In fact, the lack of social responsibility I was referring to when I challenged Dr. Laffer permitted that very greed to take root in the economic system we follow like gospel. Furthermore, Wall Street's failure to self-regulate was a symptom, not the root cause. And what is the root?

A flawed economic model, both locally and globally.

People and society can ill afford the damage of continued self-regulation.

Are politicians worldwide listening? Or will they remain deaf until one day, overnight, they become extinct like the dinosaur?

Over the course of Part III, I will further explain how this affects democracy as well as humanity. But as long as the failed status quo continues at the forefront of special interest, lobbyists, and incumbent politicians, citizens remain on the blade facing more injustices.

On one hand, Western influence only further creates more possibilities of attack from other countries. On the other, special interest's influence on the nation-state increases the likeliness of foreign and domestic compromises.

Injustice often leads to blood boiling over and flooding the streets. Resources are quickly scarce, as we saw in the spring of 2020 as citizens scrambled during COVID-19's spread to secure what they felt was necessary to survive. Our instability drives us deeper, from nine meals as Lewis proposed in the early 1900s to my prediction of three meals—even less (God forbid) if things don't change fast.

A LONG LIST OF NAMES

The repercussions of the Panama Papers were raging across the world like a wildfire. The prime ministers of Iceland and Pakistan were forced to resign. And in the latter case, Nawaz Sharif was barred from holding high office, fined $10.6 million, and finally sentenced to imprisonment.

Canada's Royal Bank closed more than 40 accounts. In Germany, 170 police raided the headquarters of Deutsche Bank, Germany's biggest, as part of a money laundering investigation. The probe focused on whether Deutsche Bank helped clients set up offshore accounts to transfer money from criminal activities. And in Mongolia, the capital city council chairman, Sandui Tsendsuren, submitted his resignation.

You would be hard pressed to find American names directly mentioned in the Panama Papers. Perhaps one day, when Delaware and/or Las Vegas incorporating firms are breached/leaked, we may discover another level of unprecedented corruption within the US. The majority of names revealed may not be known to you but, in terms of Western leadership, at least one should stand out from the rest:

David Cameron, former prime minister of the UK.

The Panama Papers revealed he owned shares in a company worth half a million dollars. He explained that it was from his father, but records from the House of Commons revealed he never disclosed this. Before becoming prime minister, after the death of his father, Cameron inherited the company while he was a Member of Parliament.

UK politicians are expected to report foreign income and assets, in the interest of transparency and accountability. In fact, many Western countries have similar laws and regulations on transparency in place; yet, when it comes to foreign policy implementation, foreign aid, and serving other political or special interests overseas, these rules somehow stop applying. Cameron received a slap on the wrist, and he publicly apologized. Thankfully, his investment was not supporting any corrupt leaders directly.

Nevertheless, my point is more that he did not come clean independently at the proper time. Had the Panama Papers never seen the light of day, he would never have been required to explain or apologize. While the sum of Cameron's $500,000 might seem insignificant to the hundreds of billions revealed in the hack, leaders of Western nations are directly responsible for the corruption undertaken by foreign leaders through the political/economic policies they implement.

Please recall the template illustrated at the beginning of the chapter, in Iraq. Allied forces enter the country, remove current leadership, establish proxy armies, and select new leadership willing to align themselves with Western occupying forces' interest. In some cases, Western involvement is limited to selecting and supporting specific leaders in order to receive benefits by way of imported and exported goods, and to further Western geopolitical goals in that country as well as the surrounding regions.

In the Panama Papers, many of the Western-supported leaders' names revealed/disclosed for having stolen and hidden wealth of unimaginable levels were those in charge of countries that are not democratic—nor do they claim to be. Democracy aside, their regimes are fully propped up by the West. And in all honesty, if they're not propped up, they'll fall apart in a matter of minutes.

This gives us insight into Western politics and how it plays out throughout the world to serve political and financial interests, not necessarily the welfare of the people in those foreign lands. And they most certainly are not serving to advance democracy or democratic values overseas. Once you see the names and positions of government officials listed in the Panama Papers, you will come to terms with the breadth and width of not just the perpetual corruption of these countries but how Western democracies created the unbroken cycle of it.

While I've listed some of those names below, I encourage you to look further into this independently. My hope is that you will then realize the scale of the problem and recognize that it is unsustainable to continue as such, to the global detriment of all citizens.

Bear in mind, Mossack Fonseca is only under scrutiny because they were caught. They are but one company facilitating stolen/hidden wealth. Just imagine how many other Fonsecas are still out there, performing the same role for undisclosed, corrupt world leaders. The following were included in the Panama Papers[57]:

- King Salman and Crown Prince Mohammed Bin Salman of Saudi Arabia
- Khalifa bin Zayed Al Nahyan, president of the United Arab Emirates and emir of Abu Dhabi
- Hamad bin Khalifa Al Thani, former emir of Qatar
- Sheikh Hamad bin Jassim Al Thani, Qatar's former prime minister and foreign minister
- Mauricio Macri, former president of Argentina
- Rafael Correa, former president of Ecuador
- Ahmed al-Mirghani, former Sudanese president

- Former Prime Minister Bidzina Ivanishvili of Georgia
- Pavlo Lazarenko, former prime minister of Ukraine
- Petro Poroshenko, former president of Ukraine
- Prime Minister Ayad Allawi, a former vice president of Iraq
- Ion Sturza, former prime minister of Moldova
- Ali Abu al-Ragheb, former prime minister of Jordan

The leaked files also identified family members, children, and immediate associates of international leaders:

- Najib Razak, former Malaysian prime minister
- Tessa Tielemans Razak, daughter of former Malaysian prime minister
- Nawaz Sharif, former prime minister of Pakistan
- Azerbaijani president Ilham Aliyev
- Jacob Zuma, former South African president
- Former Kazakh president Nursultan Nazarbayev
- Moroccan King Mohammed VI
- Kofi Annan, former United Nations secretary-general
- Margaret Thatcher, former British prime minister
- Former Mexican president Enrique Peña Nieto
- Spanish Royal Family members (as well as the mistress of former King Juan Carlos I)

The Panama Papers named other less-senior government officials along with further relatives and associates from over 40 countries, spanning from Eastern/Western Europe, Africa, the Middle East, Latin America, to Asia. I believe that much of the corruption we are seeing is merely a symptom of a larger problem: special interest (which we'll be examining further in the next chapter).

Something I want you to consider is that in the last 30 years, no US president came to power without an American Israel Public Affairs Committee (AIPAC) endorsement or blessing. And as long as their agenda is served, and the leaders serving it are in place, the "War on Terror" will continue enabling further corruption around the world, feeding the unbroken cycle. Forces of "democracy" are enabling perpetual misery for citizens in foreign countries, and they do so for the benefit of their own nation-states' special-interest groups.

A continued corrupt third world is the fuel to elevated instability there and in the West. The greater the hardship of the people in those countries, the greater the likelihood their people's response to be outrage for their continued hardship and oppression by their leaders. In fact, the greater the oppression and disparity, the greater the likelihood for their anger to get aimed at the West for supporting and propping their oppressors in power.

Resistance to oppression is often manifested in domestic and international violence. Along the way, enemies, adversaries, and challengers of Western-declared values find new local partners that are desperate and willing to collaborate at whatever terms. All this makes for the perfect storm for us in the West to label them as terrorists and then point to their action as the validation why our 20-year-old global "War on Terror" remains never-ending.

After the US invasion of Iraq, and its disbandment of the Iraqi Armed Forces, hundreds of thousands of Iraqi soldiers found themselves left without a job and a salary to feed their families. Tens of thousands of them found economic refuge in joining the early days of ISIS, which positioned itself as the resistor of American occupation as the Islamic State in Iraq and Syria (ISIS). This is long before ISIS started spreading extremism and havoc across the Middle East and the world.

This might feel like it's out of your hands but remember this—it's in your name. These decisions are taken by our elected politicians who get voted in to represent us and act in our name. It is actually we who must break the cycle. Our tax dollars in the West feed this systemic failure, and our leaders' neglect is not exclusive to failed foreign policies and perpetuating the problems in third-world countries. We are left vulnerable by their allegiance and service to masters in the shadows, their special-interest hand, and the self-regulation and "best practices" put forward in an effort to please them.

Citizens' lives and livelihoods are on a knife's edge. It should be clear that our leadership is not delivering the values of their promises and propaganda. Special-interest needs are prioritized over the needs of the citizen, and in this instability, putting us in the West and citizens of other countries three meals from anarchy, or less.

Left unchanged, the relative stability grown accustomed to by Western citizens since WWII will turn upside down. And once flipped, citizens of the West will enter a new three-meal era as well. Our stubborn comfort and continued support of failing leadership will become our own demise.

For more information, please visit survivabilitythebook.com/ placeholder (or scan the code below) to see articles referenced as well as my recommended reading list. We have been very lucky to have journalists with integrity on the case. I encourage you to explore how the world received this story.

Don't forget to check out General Wesley Clark's speech!

18

A Threat to Democracy Part A

(The Symptoms of Special Interest)

NEVER IN THE history of mankind has man had so much information at his fingertips, and yet never before has he been so misled and misinformed. Where democracy is enshrined in the West, and aspired for in many parts of the world, it is now in peril. As I explained over the course of the previous chapter, the current standing of democracy is counter to the values projected and even spun into endless propaganda. It does not serve its people, their lives, livelihoods, or aspirations in any meaningful manner—let alone as a first priority.

Worse over, the fact is this Houdini trick has been figured out years ago by people all over the world despite it remaining a big secret only to Americans in America who keep asking innocently: "Why do they hate us so much?"

As far as I'm concerned, democracy is suffering stage four cancer, and its condition worsens by the hour. As I'll explain by the end of Part III, without an informed citizenry, democracy will not, and can never, survive. Before that, I want to explain a few symptoms of the cancer itself. The presence of special interest is in plain sight to shed light at possible cures.

GRAVE RISKS (AND COMPROMISES THAT FAIL TO DELIVER)

As a citizen, consider the fact that in the last 20 years, two US presidents (a Republican and a Democrat, respectively), identified the global threat of a pending pandemic and requested funding and global strategies from Congress to prepare and mitigate it: George W. Bush and Barack Obama. Both Bush and Obama served two terms, and therefore they each had eight years with which they could carry out their visions and plans. However, when it came to budget, neither received the full sum requested. President Bush received a little less than what he asked for while Obama faced much conflict and was seemingly castrated. Regardless, neither strategy was ready for America and the world when COVID-19 struck in 2020.

When I was writing this in the fall of 2020, the US had surpassed over 200,000 dead, and counting; the economy had already shrunk by 32.9% and was facing disaster.[58] Although I'm not the biggest fan of George W. Bush (for many reasons, including the invasion of Iraq), I will admit that he was 100% correct on the following. In 2005, President Bush read a copy of American historian John M. Barry's *The Great Influenza: The Story of the Deadliest Plague in History.* After requiring key officials in his administration to read Barry's book, Bush made it clear that he was determined to avoid the events of 1918.[59]

John M. Barry had predicted that humanity was looking at a 100-year cycle, which meant that Bush was attempting to mitigate an event around 13 years away. On November 1, 2005, Bush spoke before Congress to request $7.1 billion for pandemic preparedness:[60]

> Our country has been given fair warning of this danger to our homeland—and time to prepare. It's my responsibility as President to take measures now to protect the American people from the possibility that human-to-human transmission may occur. So, several months ago, I directed all relevant departments and agencies in the federal government to take steps to address the threat of avian and pandemic flu. Since that time, my administration has developed a comprehensive national strategy, with concrete measures we can take to prepare for an influenza pandemic.

> Today, I am announcing key elements of that strategy. Our strategy is designed to meet three critical goals: *First, we must detect outbreaks that occur anywhere in the world; second, we must protect the American people by stockpiling vaccines and antiviral drugs, and improve our ability to rapidly produce new vaccines against a pandemic strain; and, third, we must be ready to respond at the federal, state, and local levels in the event that a pandemic reaches our shores.*
>
> To meet these three goals, our strategy will require the combined efforts of government officials in public health, medical, veterinary and law enforcement communities and the private sector. It will require the active participation of the American people. And it will require the immediate attention of the United States Congress so we can have the resources in place to begin implementing this strategy right away.
>
> *The first part of our strategy is to detect outbreaks before they spread across the world.* In the fight against avian and pandemic flu, early detection is our first line of defense. A pandemic is a lot like a forest fire: if caught early, it might be extinguished with limited damage; if allowed to smolder undetected, it can grow to an inferno that spreads quickly beyond our ability to control it. *So, we're taking immediate steps to ensure early warning of an avian or pandemic flu outbreak among animals or humans anywhere in the world.* (emphasis mine)

It's critical to acknowledge President Bush's desire to produce a game-changing approach: focus globally to save lives domestically. By preemptively identifying outbreaks anywhere in the world, American lives could be saved. Bush received most of his requested budget (minus a few million or so). And by the end of the following year, 2006, the Pandemic and All-Hazards Preparedness Act (PAHPA) was passed, which I'll address in the next chapter.

His administration was also able to launch www.pandemicflu.gov, which remained active for years to come. This is a man who had a House majority, he gave direction, and it was followed. Where was PAHPA when COVID-19 struck at the end of 2019?

Before we answer that together, let's take a look at the second president to identify critical preparedness for looming pandemics. Eight years after PAHPA was put into effect, it must have been clear to the Obama administration that neither the US nor the world would be ready for the next flu or influenza pandemic. During the Ebola pandemic of 2014, Obama spoke in front of the National Institutes of Health (NIH), in Bethesda, Maryland. Scientists there had recently made progress on an Ebola vaccine, and the president had been pushing Congress for an increase in funding for pandemic preparedness.

From Obama's speech on December 2, 2014, in Bethesda, Maryland:[61]

> There may and likely will come a time in which we have both an airborne disease that is deadly. And in order for us to deal with that effectively, we have to put in place an infrastructure—not just here at home, but globally—that allows us to see it quickly, isolate it quickly, respond to it quickly. And it also requires us to continue the same path of basic research that is being done here at NIH that [Dr. Nancy Sullivan] is a great example of. So that if and when a new strain of flu, like the Spanish flu, crops up five years from now or a decade from now, we've made the investment and we're further along to be able to catch it. It is a smart investment for us to make. It's not just insurance; it is knowing that down the road we're going to continue to have problems like this—particularly in a globalized world where you move from one side of the world to the other in a day.
>
> So, this is important now, but it's also important for our future and our children's future and our grandchildren's future. And the last few elections, the American people have sent Washington a pretty clear message: Find areas where you agree, don't let the areas where you disagree shut things down, work together and get the job done.
>
> I cannot think of a better example of an area where we should all agree than passing this emergency funding to fight Ebola and to set up some of the public health infrastructure that we need to deal with potential outbreaks in the future. How do you

> argue with that? That is not a partisan issue. That is a basic, common-sense issue that all Americans can agree on.
>
> Now, I have to say I've been very encouraged so far by the bipartisan support in our various visits with members of Congress. For the most part, people have recognized this is not a Democratic issue or a Republican issue—it's about the safety and security of the American people. So, let's get it done. This can get caught up in normal politics—we need to protect the American people and we need to show the world how [America] leads.
>
> I have to tell you, I traveled to Asia, we had the G20 Summit—if America had not led, if I had not been able to go to CDC, make a major announcement about the commitments we were going to make, be able to go to the United Nations and basically call on other countries to step up, and know that we were following through with our own commitments, had we not done that, the world would not have responded in the same way. American leadership matters every time. We set the tone and we set the agenda.

I feel that Obama was unambiguous. The mere fact that he was calling for pandemic preparedness on a global scale to save American lives is a clear indicator that the US was not ready. Therefore, it is conclusive that any form of PAHPA inspired by President Bush had not materialized by 2014. And the US response to the pandemic, under the Trump administration, is further evidence that the aspirations and preparedness plans of the Obama administration also never materialized.

All American citizens should be asking questions. Two US presidents identified the grave risks of a pending pandemic, made the case for creating preparedness plans, and yet, the United States failed miserably when struck by COVID-19. Why?

Why didn't politicians approve the necessary legislation so that the US would be more prepared? What was holding them back? To whom was their allegiance when they were passing or failing to pass legislation?

Clearly, not the American people.

In requesting an increase in the budget for combating Ebola, Obama also wanted to appropriate funds to set up public health infrastructure.

How much was approved for the latter? A little more than a tenth of what he requested. Within the month, Congress approved a $5.4 billion budget for Ebola efforts.[62 63]

While fighting the current fear and viral conflict was successfully a bipartisan decision, Congress did not show any interest in providing the $2.43 billion requested for Obama's preparedness plan for potential outbreaks in the future. Of that $2.43 billion, the CDC would have received $1.83 billion for planning and stockpiling. According to ProPublica,[64] only $165 million was provided to the CDC.

To my knowledge, nothing further along these lines was passed until 2019, which was a new version PAHPA from 2006 (which was reauthorized in 2013): The Pandemic and All-Hazards Preparedness and Advancing Innovation Act. Clearly, in 2014, the politicians did what they normally do. They created compromises that would not deliver on what is needed but which satisfied their political positions and posturing. And that compromise added up to the tune of 200,000+ American citizens dead by the end of September 2020, and 750,000+ by the end of December 2021. And as usual, the political blame game continues as no one takes responsibility for their roles in these failures.

Of course, despite being three years into their term—and being briefed by the CIA in November 2020, and twice by trade advisor Peter Navarro—the Trump administration blamed the pandemic response on Obama and China. Whenever we face a national threat, very little real change happens and the citizen ends up paying the biggest price. Our actions are superficial, and we seldom go to the root cause of the problem. This was seen throughout each term of the last three presidents.

Clearly, something is seriously wrong with our system. We are misdirected, misinformed, and misled. We are constantly bombarded with talking points that drain our energy and stifle any form of real progress.

Even the leaders who claim they are taking action to serve humanity, upon closer inspection, are contributing to the very cancer consuming democracy as it stands today. As I'll share at the end of the chapter, Obama himself, a champion for climate change, elevated the narrative of President Bush's "War on Terror" to further fund the military-industrial complex. Before I share more on that, as you read about the ongoing threat to democracy, I want you to think about the fact that Obama had no issue working with Congress to increase military spending by billions of dollars.

Why is that?

THE SYMPTOMS OF SPECIAL INTEREST

COVID-19 caught us with our pants down. This can be a warning. Man-made or natural disaster, preparation is needed, and we have been shown to be incapable. Our significant lack of capabilities, our symptoms of failure in this regard comes down to the fact that our leaders do not seek to serve the public first and foremost.

Everything in place keeps the powers that be in power. And the result of their effort can be seen in the symptoms of democracy's cancer. The following are examples in the US where special-interest agendas were prioritized at the expense of the people:

1. Financial crisis of 2008
2. Climate change
3. Mass shootings

SYMPTOM 1: FINANCIAL CRISIS

We all know that the crisis was caused by banks/bankers who had no care whatsoever to trade/deal with toxic loans as long as they could sell them off and make their profit. They ignored fundamental mechanisms in ensuring they operated in a transparent, well-regulated fashion. They knew fully well that the loans they were buying, selling, and trading were tainted. The only reason they didn't mind buying them at overinflated prices was because they knew they could sell them off to other financial institutions and make their arbitrage profit margin.

Many of these tainted loans were against real estate properties. At the time, those loans were taken out by citizens/businesses that had a positive loan-to-value. Before a bank would allow you to receive a loan, they would require 10–20% as a down payment, and the same applied for commercial property. When the real estate market started going down, the equity that was put into those down payments evaporated; however, on the books of the financial institution, it appeared that the banks still had those deposits.

When a financial institution trades billions of dollars in commercial paper, it's based on the values of the past, in the books, not on the values in the present. The bankers knew that the value at the time of purchase was not reflective of the book value. The system worked as long as all parties were willing to buy, sell, and trade with shutters over their eyes.

Then came the day that someone decided to lift the lid, ever so slightly, releasing a rotten stench. This triggered a financial crisis. When the lid was lifted wide open, that stench manifested an unprecedented financial abyss, which was clearly draining the global market.

In both Chapter 3 and 17, I've already shared with you the 2002 and 2008 quotes from Chairman Alan Greenspan of the Federal Reserve Board. Once again, in 2002, he specifically said, "An infectious greed seemed to grip much of our business community. ... It is not that humans have become any more greedy than in generations past. It is that the avenues to express greed had grown so enormously."[65]

And then, in 2008, in response to what he called a once-in-a-century credit tsunami: "We share the outrage of most Americans at the greed that blinded Wall Street to its civic duty to protect Main Street."[66]

Their civic duty, indeed. Citizens across the world ended up paying the price for the failures and seismic practice of US bankers and regulators. Western governments stepped in to bail out banks/bankers who perpetrated this global disaster at the expense of Main Street. As a result of this, what game-changing reforms did we see in the western hemisphere after the financial crisis?

None.

Even Greenspan could see flaws leading to our destruction a full half decade before the housing bubble. And still, there were no reforms put in place to counteract the very greed he spoke of. Any changes enacted after the financial crash of 2008 were not substantial; Western leaders were tweaking legislation and calling it progress.

The system is broken; we are beyond the point where a few tweaks can lead to any promising results. COVID-19 showcased this failure of governments in which other broken systems led to the detriment of citizens' lives and livelihoods. Although Greenspan identified the infectious greed by 2002, he was personally unable to place mechanisms to regulate it in the financial sector, specifically in Wall Street.

From his 2008 testimony: "We did try to regulate in some on our side and were stopped from the other side of the aisle from bringing regulation in earlier."

This is exactly what I want this chapter to help you see, and my reference to "tweaking" is specifically pointing to Greenspan's attempts to regulate. It's addressing the possibility that where he said he was stopped is most likely the pushback from legislators and lobbyists who wanted no heavy regulation in place.

Up to this moment, neither he nor those legislators would be inclined to add substantial regulation. They were and remain spiritually, philosophically, and practically married to laissez-faire, supply-side economics, where minimal government regulation is gospel. In fact, many US leaders are on the same page as him, in which any manner of touching or altering this gospel would be sacrilegious—somehow more so than taking advantage of it.

Even though Wall Street's greed was palpable, it seemed more important to him that the gospel remained according to custom, than it was to ensure the cancer stopped spreading. As said in Chapter 3, he was "shocked" that the model resulted in these toxic outcomes, as he was under the impression everything was working well (God bless him ... was it?). What's painful to me is twofold:

1. The failure of the man who is tasked with leadership, regulation, and oversight not only of the US financial system, but on its global influence.
2. The fact that he foresaw the cancerous flaw in that system, and despite his claim of attempting to fix it and seeing he could not (because of the pushback), he did not remove himself from the equation.

He was intelligent enough to know that the prospect of such greed would have serious, perhaps disastrous consequences—not only on Wall Street but on the economy, both nationally and globally. Why did he not resign in protest of what he was blocked from doing? People are still paying for this today and directly. As with all flaws in current models of Western democracies, self-regulation, minimum government intervention, and "best practices" led to preventable problems—and in this case, a preventable catastrophe.

Yet, these models remain gospel today. And in the post–COVID-19 world, upon any attempts to fix it, or change it, our leaders will tell us we are committing sacrilege; that we are the ones spreading misinformation and the very toxicity endangering our own lives and livelihoods. We remain in, return to, and are forced into the failed status quo.

SYMPTOM 2: CLIMATE CHANGE

You must be living on Mars if you're unaware that the Earth is suffering a major threat due to climate change. Governments, people, and organizations all over the world have recognized the need to respond positively and proactively to the challenge (such as methods of plastic waste, emission standards and goals, etc.). Yet, all experts tell us that we need to do things much faster.

In 2015, toward that endeavor, the Paris Agreement gathered and committed nations together (including China, Russia, and the US) to begin taking serious action and acting responsibly. From the United Nations' Climate Change website:[67]

> The Paris Agreement builds upon the Convention and for the first time brings all nations into a common cause to undertake ambitious efforts to combat climate change and adapt to its effects, with enhanced support to assist developing countries to do so. As such, it charts a new course in the global climate effort.
>
> The Paris Agreement central aim is to strengthen the global response to the threat of climate change by keeping a global temperature rise this century well below 2 degrees Celsius above pre-industrial levels and to pursue efforts to limit the temperature increase even further to 1.5 degrees Celsius. Additionally, the agreement aims to strengthen the ability of countries to deal with the impacts of climate change. To reach these ambitious goals, appropriate financial flows, a new technology framework and an enhanced capacity building framework will be put in place, thus supporting action by developing countries and the most vulnerable countries, in line with their own national objectives. The Agreement also provides for enhanced transparency of action and support through a more robust transparency framework.

In late 2015, an agreement was drafted, and by April 2016, 195 signatories were confirmed. The intention was for the accord to take effect later in November of that same year. To summarize, the Paris Agreement can be labeled as "the biggest collaboration by nations around the world to address climate change."

And here are a couple million-dollar questions:

Is any of it working?

What enforceability does it place on signatory nation-states that don't comply?

Greta Thunberg is probably the most famous activist on climate change. In her impassioned speeches at the UN and from her interviews throughout worldwide media, she has unapologetically voiced how the older generations have failed younger generations along with the planet itself. She'll be the first to tell you that no, none of this is working. Clearly, what we are doing is not enough.

In the case of the US, we are doing worse, as President Donald Trump discounted climate change as fake science to the American people. After his decision to withdraw the US as a signatory of the Paris Agreement, policies were soon put in place that directly contradicted any and all collaboration toward improving the climate. He also revived the usage of coal, one of the biggest polluters. His claims were at least twofold: (1) he was creating jobs, and (2) methods of mining coal were somehow cleaner than ever before.

By 2019, the efforts of the Trump administration resulted in Environmental Protection Agency (EPA) analysis to no longer include impacts on public health. At that, by dissolving advisory boards from providing apolitical guidance, he opened even more doors to business interest and influence. Further dismantling included plans for reducing emissions/pollutants in oil and gasoline refineries, the automobile industry, and power plants, along with air-conditioning and refrigerators.

How great a collaboration can the Paris Agreement possibly be if a signatory nation can withdraw faster and easier than going through a McDonald's drive-through? What about pulling out and immediately implementing policies that actually do more polluting—without punitive consequences?

It is incumbent on us to correctly label the Paris Agreement for what it really is: a self-regulation, laissez-faire model of governance (or lack of). It permitted signatories to enter their core and allow them the ability to self-regulate their compliance and their reduction in emission contribution. It also permitted them to leave the agreement without consequences—or even reparations to other signatory nations—for not fulfilling their obligation.

The primary Western governments leading the agreement were already advocates and implementers of a laissez-faire model of self-regulation of one form or another, and therefore collaboration was doomed to fail from day one. The agreement itself is serving the self-regulation modality of its stakeholders (the governments), and their sub-stakeholders (corporations and special-interest groups). Regardless of any effective efforts, the goal was to limit the warming of the Earth's temperature to less than 2 degrees Celsius in this century.

All adults living today, and especially all politicians involved, will be long gone by 2100 ... we don't need to wait until then to determine if this failed or not. I don't know your position, but I can tell you that I believe it is failing.

How is any of this a serious attempt to mitigate the urgency of climate change? It's yet another symptom of the problem, yet another example of social responsibility lacking as a core value in the models our leaders choose to maintain.

SYMPTOM 3: MASS SHOOTINGS

When the children of Dunblane Primary School in Scotland were massacred in 1996, the outrage by Scottish and British people was seismic. The call for radical change was deafening. As a result, the Scottish and British governments implemented a major overhaul of guns, ownership, etc. Within a year, the first Firearms (Amendment) Act was passed, banning citizen ownership of all handguns, with the exception of those using .22 rimfire cartridges. And by the end of 1997, a second version was passed to ban ownership of .22 caliber single-shot weapons. Since the shooting and the following legislation, no similar tragedies have occurred, thank God.

And in March 2019, New Zealand suffered its own unprecedented massacre. An extremist white supremacist, Brenton Harrison Tarrant, walked casually into two mosques during Friday prayer and started shooting innocent men, women, and children, killing 51 worshippers and injuring 49. Not only did Tarrant livestream the attack on Facebook but prior to the shooting, he shared an online manifesto detailing his extremist motivations.

A global outrage took place, and the New Zealand government responded emphatically by instituting a new law on gun control. Within a month, the House of Representatives were introduced to The Arms (Prohibited Firearms, Magazines, and Parts) Amendment Act 2019, and upon the first reading, it was passed for the next stage. Before officially becoming law by mid-April, the bill was supported by the majority of Parliament.

Interestingly, the only objectors were the Association of Consumers and Taxpayers (ACT), who stand for freedom and personal responsibility—their primary concern being the velocity of the bill being written and set in stone. In fact, New Zealand independent news source *The Conversation* published an article[68] titled, "New Zealand Gun Owners Invoke NRA-Style Tropes in Response to Fast-Tracked Law Change." In this, they shared online discourse paralleling American discussions on the topic, specific to NRA as the title suggests. One of their main points regards the difference between New Zealand and the US, in that the former perceives gun ownership as a privilege, not a right.

Some citizen responses to the tragedy did indeed mirror US NRA-esque responses to their own massacres. Do the following statements sound familiar?

- "Guns don't kill people. People do."
- "*STOP* terrorizing firearms owners! You extremist ... you're a disgusting human being."
- "I would rather see people with the right to carry for self-defence. ... If a handful of those worshippers had been packing [carrying guns] that could have stopped this tragedy in the early minutes."

Through December 2019, New Zealand implemented a buyback program, in which guns were turned in to the authorities and removed from the equation or were altered for owners who wanted to keep them.

While this topic is not necessarily recurring in all parts of the world, Americans witness mass shootings on a monthly if not weekly basis. I'm not here to explain the true constitutionality of guns nor am I here to debate the validity of the right to bear arms (or not). What is blindingly obvious is that innocent Americans are dying routinely by mass shootings and nothing we have done as a society has actually stopped this or even significantly reduced it.

Yes, we've seen tweaking of laws, and the media battleground of narrative against narrative, but the fundamental result remains unchanged. Any call for gun reform is matched and overpowered by other calls for the constitutional right to bear arms. Much of this gets centered on the symbolic word "freedom," and (as seen in the online forums of New Zealand) the usual cliché that repeats throughout immediate history: Guns don't kill people, people do.

So, whenever we go through a mass shooting, there are three constants:

1. From the people, an amplified outcry for change.
2. Seemingly from traditional and new media, systemic and consistent redirection.
3. Across the nation, debates focused on tangential talking points.

Both sides of the argument are happy to point a finger at the media for twisting their focus. Do you believe that this is true? Are they the only culprit? Is there another stakeholder who might be responsible?

Someone is coordinating them all to stay on message. Who is this master puppeteer? Who is the true source of these counter narratives? And who ends up disseminating these sound bites so that ordinary people can start repeating them like parrots?

You might recall how serious conversations and debates on virtually all talk shows and television programs drown the focus on addressing the root cause by focusing on symptoms. Typically, the distraction twists the spotlight onto mental illness, the dangers of policy making (and its unintended consequences), or it places all bets on the idea of guns being a source of our salvation.

With regard to mental illness, Wayne LaPierre (NRA executive vice president) replied to the 2013 Navy Yard shooting:[69] "We have a mental health system in this country that has completely and totally collapsed. We have no national database of these lunatics ..."

For policy, Chris Cox (chief lobbyist and principal political strategist) had a deleted reply on TexasCHLForum.com to the Charleston shooting, commenting on the pastor of the Methodist church (2015):[70] "[Clementa C. Pinckney] voted against concealed-carry. ... Eight of his church members who might be alive if he had expressly allowed members to carry handguns in church are dead. Innocent people died because of his position on a political issue."

Similarly, the following was his reply to the shooting at the Orlando nightclub Pulse (2013):[71]

> Americans were shocked and disgusted to learn of another act of terrorism on our soil, this time in Orlando. In the aftermath of this terrorist attack, President Obama and Hillary Clinton renewed calls for more gun control, including a ban on whole categories of semi-automatic firearms. They are desperate to create the illusion that they're doing something to protect us because their policies can't and won't keep us safe. This transparent head-fake should scare every American, because it will do nothing to prevent the next attack ... Repeating the same thing but expecting a different result is the definition of insanity. Law-abiding gun owners are tired of being blamed for the acts of madmen and terrorists. Semi-automatics are the most popular firearms sold in America for sport-shooting, hunting and self-defense. ... It's time for us to admit that radical Islam is a hate crime waiting to happen. The only way to defeat them is to destroy them—not destroy the right of law-abiding Americans to defend ourselves.

And I have two examples of the "guns will save us" mentality. After Sandy Hook (2012), LaPierre said at a press event:[72] "The only thing that stops a bad guy with a gun is a good guy with a gun. ... With all the money in the federal budget, can't we afford to put a police officer in every single school?"

Second, I will now refer to Trump's response after Parkland (2018):[73] "Armed Educators (and trusted people who work within a school) love our students and will protect them. Very smart people. Must be firearms adept & have annual training. Should get yearly bonus. Shootings will not happen again—a big & very inexpensive deterrent. Up to States."

The Parkland youth movement was an unprecedented move in the US. Virtually every city/state had people mobilizing. But what real change was it able to accomplish?

None.

This is not on the people in the marches. Special interest is so well entrenched in the current system, little will change within it. This is because the political representatives do not represent the will of the people for new laws to be adopted for the real change desired and needed. The previously provided quotes go to the heart, showcasing how tremendous outcries are bombarded with counternarratives that drown, diffuse, or change the topic.

Specific to NRA representatives, one must admit the creative genius of the following stance/slogan: Guns = Freedom.

In terms of PR, this keeps everything simple, and simplicity is the key power behind their efforts and successes. Essentially, the idea itself keeps everything at bay, ensuring all supporters and stakeholders stay on message. How can you, and who can possibly argue against freedom? Such a thing would be un-American, God forbid!

Such grand designs and planning and great detailed implementation does not happen out of thin air. It requires strategic thinking, exceptional operational execution, and the necessary funding/support to push it forward. It is self-serving, not the will of the people. It's entirely about power.

THE TOTAL INFLUENCE

At this point of the chapter, if you are waiting for me to pull the white hood from the master puppeteer to reveal the NRA, you're gravely mistaken. While they are a powerful and significant implementer, they are purely advocates for gun rights, and they most definitely have higher authorities to serve. Historically, weapons and ammunition manufacturing were drivers of the military sector. Today, high-tech and cyber warfare defense solutions are the significant drivers of the US military-industrial complex (MIC).

Many of you might know the details surrounding the concept of an MIC, as well as its capabilities. If you don't know, the MIC is essentially an unofficial coalition of a military and its supplier, the defense industry. For the purposes of this chapter, they are a key example of special interest bringing democracy's cancer to stage four.

In the US, their collective ability to influence public policy is detrimental and should not be underestimated. In fact, in 1961, former WWII five-star general and US president Dwight D. Eisenhower specifically included the MIC in his Farewell Address to the Nation:[74]

> A vital element in keeping the peace is our military establishment. Our arms must be mighty, ready for instant action, so that no potential aggressor may be tempted to risk his own destruction ...
>
> This conjunction of an immense military establishment and a large arms industry is new in the American experience. The total influence—economic, political, even spiritual—is felt in every city, every statehouse, every office of the federal government. We recognize the imperative need for this development. Yet we must not fail to comprehend its grave implications. Our toil, resources and livelihood are all involved; so is the very structure of our society. In the councils of government, we must guard against the acquisition of unwarranted influence, whether sought or unsought, by the military–industrial complex. The potential for the disastrous rise of misplaced power exists, and will persist.
>
> We must never let the weight of this combination endanger our liberties or democratic processes. We should take nothing for granted. Only an alert and knowledgeable citizenry can compel the proper meshing of the huge industrial and military machinery of defense with our peaceful methods and goals so that security and liberty may prosper together.

What Eisenhower predicted and warned against is exactly where we are today. Clearly, we did not heed his visionary warning. So, how did we get here?

As a result of the September 11, 2001, terrorist attacks, the US launched its global "War on Terror," with the invasion of Iraq in 2003 (I referred to this as the "unbroken cycle" at the end of the previous chapter). Before that, in the late 1980s, President George H. W. Bush formed an international coalition for the first invasion of Iraq, to end Saddam Hussein's occupation of Kuwait.

Many may not recall that right after Desert Storm, subsequent US narratives flourished regarding a domino effect of further invasions and regime change in the Middle East. This was cheered by many neoconservatives, as to how they would start with Iraq, and the regime change would soon be followed by Syria, Lebanon, Libya, Iran, and so forth. These narratives were pushed by the majority of the US MIC, if not the entirety. It was marketed as bringing democracy to the citizens of those countries, as if it were the long-awaited arrival of Coca-Cola, KFC, and other American goods. I urge readers who question what I am saying, and all democracy-loving Americans, to watch the *National Geographic* video of General Wesley Clark talking about his shock of what he learned before the 2003 US invasion of Iraq (see online resource page for Chapter 17).

Of course, the regime-change plan never materialized—not yet anyway. This was because the first war on Iraq did not unfold in the manner its many proponents hoped, nor how it was justified and manipulated. However, the seed, foundation, and momentum for the global "War on Terror" had been successfully established.

Before 2003, while the US was carrying out its counterattacks on terrorists in Afghanistan, UN inspectors searched Iraq and found no weapons of mass destruction. US intelligence advised the White House and Pentagon that Saddam Hussein had zero link with Al Qaeda and the 9/11 attacks. Despite this, in 2003, to ensure that the invasion of Iraq went ahead—as prompted by the elder President Bush—British Prime Minister Tony Blair made the public statement that Saddam possessed biological warfare that put Europe within a 45-minute threat.

The US government and its security agencies were very prompt to corroborate this. In fact, US Defense Secretary Colin Powell spoke at the UN about this threat, showing a test tube to the audience and telling them if it were filled with the chemicals that Saddam possessed, it would kill the population of a major city. It turned out that all of the intelligence to make this claim was entirely fabricated.

Tony Blair later said he was "misled" by UK and US intelligence agencies. And years later, Colin Powell had the decency to apologize. By that time, the next invasion of Iraq had already taken place, and the wheels of the global "War on Terror" had already reached full motion, as planned.

As said in Chapter 17, this invasion along with the overthrowing of Hussein led to the creation of ISIS and the birth of an extremist version of Islam that would justify the continuation of the "War on Terror" as well as its funding. Many might claim that this was accidental or an "unintended consequence" of the invasion. I do not subscribe to that belief.

The funding and the direction that led to the birth of ISIS came from Arab Gulf State money and Western planning, including MI6 and the CIA. For those who may not see an immediate link between the NRA and the perpetual "War on Terror," I can understand. However, if you follow the series of linkages, you might see how it all connects.

The NRA advocates "freedom" (right to bear arms and constitutionality) in the US, and civilians hold gun ownership as a fundamental right. Within a month of 9/11, President George W. Bush addressed the nation, saying:[75]

> Our war on terror begins with Al Qaeda, but it does not end there. It will not end until every terrorist group of global reach has been found, stopped and defeated. Americans are asking 'Why do they hate us?' They hate what they see right here in this chamber: a democratically elected government. Their leaders are self-appointed. *They hate our freedoms: our freedom of religion, our freedom of speech, our freedom to vote and assemble and disagree with each other.* (Emphasis mine.)

Since Bush's declaration of war on such freedom haters, the MIC has actually been the primary financial benefactor beyond their staunch support of the Bush administration's doctrine of preemptive strike. Worth noting, Vice President Dick Cheney was previously the chairman and CEO of Halliburton (1995–2000), a major MIC stakeholder, which became the sole defense contractor in Iraq after an exclusive $7 billion bid. His direct connection to the MIC illustrates the corruption within our leadership and goes to the heart of our political system.

The resulting "War on Terror" was not unique to the Bush administration; in fact, the Obama administration maintained it and even furthered it by increasing funding. The MIC accomplished this unbroken cycle through the very same technique of twisting the narrative into a debate surrounding "freedom," just as the NRA continues to do so following all mass shootings. In the case of MIC, this strategy created impetus for never-ending wars, and they continue profiting from it, which means the US continues to provide funding.

While championing an era of great change, President Obama actually increased military spending by $150 billion. Under Bush, it was $600–700 billion. Immediately after the 2008 financial crisis, which was paid for by the people, Obama raised it to $850 billion. While bailing out the very bankers that caused the crash, which led to many American citizens going broke, the US awarded contracts for defense.

Were the people outraged?

No. Of course not.

For any who were aware of such decisions, it was easy to support. As Bush established, the terrorists don't believe in our values, they hate us, and they hate our freedom! Meanwhile, when discussing domestic policy and "freedoms" at home, the mindset falls further into, "Get the government out of my face!" To this end, patriotism is spun into upholding democracy, "We keep the government in check!" And citizen roles are romanticized into good guys with guns protecting the vulnerable Constitution, and passionate speakers voting necessary changes into it.

Any dissension to the narratives on democracy renders people as unpatriotic. We saw this immediately after 9/11. Anyone asking what drove the hijackers to do this were easily labeled unpatriotic and un-American. Only if you were 100% in support of launching a war and invading Iraq in retaliation for 9/11 would you be classified as patriotic.

And while the people squabble over true patriotism, freedom, and rights, special interest continues driving the stock market. In the MIC's case, this means they are pushing for citizens to drown in a fruitless number of arguments. Meanwhile, corporate and military stakeholders profit from war and death.

SEISMIC INSPIRATION

The financial crisis of 2008–2009 may have resulted in seismic consequences. And yet, events such as shootings and climate change have not yet caused the necessary catalyst to inspire a movement big enough to call for change in the US and around the world. The pushback of special interest is so formidable that it would not allow these causes to reach substantial fruition like they have in other countries.

The people then find themselves in a dissonant choir, the cacophony of which is caused by everyone singing their own tune. Some sing for change and are driven by feeling and passion. Some sing for the past and are driven by nostalgia or fear. To make matters worse, there are the people who manage to do much of the singing for their own leaders.

In all cases, no matter the proof or validity of any given statement, the people will exercise the freedom of their expression and cancel each other out. And when the majority of a nation, or the entire world itself, is not facing the dilemma attached to the cause, it's easy to get caught in the noise and sour notes. Bear in mind, remaining in this conflict of expression means only one assured outcome: status quo. Therefore, Western democracies continue forward as "normal," purely driven by a well-oiled methodology that throws out counternarratives to cancel out initiatives, securing an outcome of no change.

If the mother of all democracies in the world (US) is captured by special interest, then neither the people nor democracy get served, and therefore the will of the people is never delivered. If the US is not truly democratic, we're no better off than anyone else. However, we are uniquely positioned to aspire and reach this ideal because of our Constitution.

The universal values of living in peace with dignity, opportunity, and security are within reach; our inability to deliver that dream to the citizen is a failure to humanity. While all aspects of US legislature appear to serve the citizen, you are unlikely to see a bill/act that's contradictory to special interest. While you might see some diluted legislation delivering something to the citizen, upon a closer look, if it does not actually benefit special interest, it seldom goes far enough to inconvenience them or hold them to account.

It is this apparent priority that puts democracy in stage four cancer. And if we allowed it to die, you can probably imagine the result to us in America and in countries all over the world aspiring for our ideal and hoping that similar rights are enshrined in their laws and constitutions. If true democracy fails, humanity is in peril.

For more information, please visit survivabilitythebook.com/ placeholder (or scan the code below) to see articles referenced as well as my recommended reading list. We have been very lucky to have journalists with integrity on the case. I encourage you to explore how the world received this story.

19

A Threat to Democracy Part B

(Strategies of Special Interest Groups and Corrupt Leadership)

AS WE MAKE our way into this second installment of exploring the threat to democracy, I want you to ask yourself this question: Who is the primary stakeholder? At that, my intention is for this chapter to be a call for representing the will and welfare of the people.

As the citizen remains motivated by passion and feelings—and many take part in a variety of well-intended but sporadic initiatives—without real unity, they have no chance of withstanding the ongoing barrage. To accomplish real change, you need unity, critical mass, perseverance, and continuity. Most important of all, you need political leverage and staying power.

Political leverage is the people's ability to get their elected politicians to adopt their aspirations instead of delivering on the demands of special interest. In the meantime, special interest contributed to the elections of those leaders in return for scratching backs by blocking or diluting regulation or legislation aimed to serve the people. Without staying power or initiatives, there will be no critical mass. And without real numbers, leverage is out of the question.

Our system of representation is intended to carry forth the needs of the critical masses across the nation. We find ourselves needing to empower citizens with leverage to curb the decision-making of our leaders, who should be securing our lives and livelihoods. Who are they representing instead? Who are they serving first and foremost?

- The banks (Symptom 1: Financial Crisis)
- Industrial manufacturers, mining companies, and energy (Symptom 2: Climate Change)
- Gun manufacturers, the NRA, and the military-industrial complex (Symptom 3: Mass Shootings)
- And a variety of others as well

As established in Chapter 18, our leaders' top priority seems to fall on special interest, such as the groups above. We have yet to have an election without the significant presence of their influence. Traditionally, this can be found in the systemic influence consistently present in election contributions as well as lobbying.

More recently, their influence has evolved into driving the people apart through the use of populism (and even anti-populism, as I'll touch on briefly at the end of the chapter). While citizen voices are distracted over passionately debated national topics, special interest continues impacting the outcome of democratic processes. Ultimately, they are maintaining the failed status quo.

TRADITIONAL INFLUENCE: ELECTION CONTRIBUTIONS AND LOBBYING

Does anyone today subscribe to the illusion that when an organization contributes funds to a political candidate's campaign/career, there is no back-scratching expected in return? Does anyone believe that corporate social responsibility by most Western organizations is anything other than a marketing tool to associate their companies with good causes in order to increase sales?

Recently, how many political candidates have stated that they will not accept funding in the form of corporate, lobbyist, or special-interest contributions? How many prospective politicians could afford such a high level of morals and ethics in adopting a unilateral approach to their campaigns (and win)? How many of our current US elected officials (House/Congress/state) have won their elections without the money and influence of special interest?

Help me, because a Google search could not ...

Google had no answers as to any political candidates winning without such contributions, nor did they offer any suggested edits to my question (as they normally would during any internet search whatsoever). For a moment, I felt like I was living in a third-world, autocratic country where certain questions must not be asked, for fear of losing my life. *Is it possible that Google has now reported me for asking such a sacrilegious question?*

Ultimately, I want you to begin your journey toward active engagement with your own fact-checking (start with FEC.gov or OpenSecrets.org). As of 2019, my research was that none of the candidates aspiring toward occupying the White House in 2021 had clear policies/proposals on election contributions. While I'm not endorsing any politician in this book, Bernie Sanders was the main, if not sole candidate making statements against election contributions from anyone but the citizen.

Some things will surely remain a mystery, but I assure you that contributions to campaigns can be found and are available to the public:

www.opensecrets.org/elections-overview/
business-labor-ideology-split

At the time of this writing, Democratic candidates appear to be receiving more contributions from business than their Republican counterparts. Just imagine what US elections and outcomes would look like if funding was only allowed from citizens. Imagine what the political landscape and the incumbents would look like.

A good percentage of currently elected politicians would not secure the funding necessary for a repeat term. Imagine the new blood and new faces of politicians. Imagine the possibility of new policies legislated by them that would serve the people as their first priority. In fact, can you see any real change happening without election contribution itself being curtailed?

Sure, campaign media could lose some of its razmataz. But would it really be the end of the world if there was less show business and more substance? I'm happy to pay that price if it means the people are less misinformed, better informed, and aptly represented.

LOBBYING

According to Wikipedia, "Lobbying in the United States describes paid activity in which special-interest groups hire well-connected professional advocates, often lawyers, to argue for specific legislation in decision-making bodies such as the United States Congress."[76] Before the American term "lobbying" came into being, the concept was born in British Parliament. Leaders of the country met in a main hall, and people with various agendas would wait for and attempt to meet with these leaders in an intermediary room found outside the hall.

Supposedly, President Ulysses S. Grant coined the term as we use it today. The story goes that he grew tired of people attempting to influence him in the lobby of the Willard Hotel, near the White House. Nevertheless, from the 1800s (at least) through today, special-interest groups await politicians in the corner, offering luxuries, donations, and opportunity in the hopes of currying favor. There have been times when lobbyists have represented the people in a private room, but more often these lobbyists are serving the agenda of powerful individuals and organizations. Overall, throughout history, citizens remained wary of the lobby and its influencers. What happened?

Even as recently as the 1980s, if you operated a brothel, managing women as prostitutes, what would you have been labeled as?

You would be called a pimp.

Today, if you manage prostitutes, call girls (also euphemistically called escorts), or operate porn websites, you are called an entrepreneur. The adult industry currently hosts award ceremonies for their superstars, production houses, and crews that rival the glitz of Hollywood. The pimps, entrepreneurs, and lobbyists alike are in the business of making money. So, what's the common change for these professions?

Our standards and values as to social taboos.

Over the years, new socially accepted job roles and descriptions became the new normal. New ways of approaching business, and new acceptable professions have formed. How does that pertain to special interest? you might ask.

Special-interest groups are not operating in the spirit or the letter of how our founding fathers intended. In fact, their accepted practice along with their lobbying today is undermining our democracy and its processes. Our founding fathers wrote the Constitution in such a way that factions would compete against each other in the interest of maintaining democracy to serve the people.

"Factions" was defined by James Madison, in "Federalist No. 10," as "a number of citizens, whether amounting to a minority or majority of the whole, who are united and actuated by some common impulse of passion, or of interest, adverse to the rights of other citizens, or to the permanent and aggregate interests of the community."

In theory, the inherent competition would ensure that there could be no faction in control of the nation. Lobbying, in this sense, meant contributing to certain groups in order to improve positioning toward being able to capture decision-making in the government. There was a time when this may have allowed like-minded individuals to form community and representation for a louder voice in debates surrounding policy and candidates. But today, the allowance of these factions has enabled like-minded corporations to directly funnel money into the system in order to gain advantages or maintain the failed status quo.

Obviously, the decision-making of our government is swayed toward the benefits of certain groups and organizations—not the citizen. The pimp still offers cigars, good liquor, and "entertainment," but the banner behind him now says it's for a great cause. I can hardly imagine our founding fathers supporting the $3.47 billion funneling into campaigns and movements in 2019. Contributions had not reached that amount since 2009 and 2010, at $3.50 billion and $3.51 billion, respectively.

Those two years remain the highest between now and 1998. This information can be found at Statista.com, along with the following:[77]

> Since the turn of the millennium, the amount spent on lobbying in the United States has more than doubled. The intention of firms employing lobbyists, who in turn lobby government officials, is to gain a degree of influence on the legislative process in the hope of legislation more favorable to their business or cause being passed. Lobbying occurs at all levels from local government to presidential elections. The industries utilizing lobbying as a means to gain influence come from a range of industries with the biggest spenders including pharmaceuticals, insurance, business associations as well as oil and gas. The U.S. Chamber of Commerce, a pro-business association, was the largest lobbying spender in 2018 by a considerable margin.

Meanwhile, on Investopedia, their literature veers from descriptions of influence and gain, focusing instead on the importance of the function. In their article, "Why Lobbying Is Legal and Important in the US," the excerpts below can be found.[78]

> Lobbying is an important lever for a productive government. Without it, governments would struggle to sort out the many, many competing interests of its citizens. Fortunately, lobbying provides access to government legislators, acts as an educational tool, and allows individual interests to gain power in numbers ...
>
> ... Lobbying provides access to government legislatures that no single individual could possibly hope to achieve. By grouping individual goals together into a lobbying aim, lobbyists represent the interests of many and are more likely to be heard by legislatures than if they came bearing the concerns of one voter. With the number of tasks and matters required of a legislature ever-growing, populaces need lobbying to bring issues front and center, otherwise, the government can fall into an "out of sight, out of mind" trap.

Their spin would have you believe that lobbying is as important to democracy as oxygen is to living. "As alluded to above, lobbyists serve an important purpose in aggregating the interests of many individual constituents." Really? I thought we elected representatives to do this on our behalf?

At this point, the presence of lobbyists hangs by a very specific thread: free speech. Apparently, this is due to specific phrasing in the First Amendment, "to petition the Government for a redress of grievances." Recently, in 1995, The Lobbying Disclosure Act was passed, defining lobbyists, required registration, legal actions, and compliance.

Since then, the number of lobbyists has risen and fallen with each year, reaching an all-time high of 14,825 in 2007, and an all-time low of 11,188 in 2016.[79]

Presently, that total remains under 12,000. As far as I'm concerned, this drop in activity parallels the echo of 2008's financial crisis. Is it any surprise that spending decreased? What money was there to spend?

Nevertheless, I don't imagine the founding fathers intended their ideas to allow such influence. And the attention of the lobby is not exclusive to our leaders. They specifically sway public opinion as well. Which returns us to the end of the previous chapter: manipulation, smoke, and mirrors.

MODERN INFLUENCE: POPULISM

By populism, I mean the anti-Semitism, Islamophobia, extremism, and racism (etc.) that has become so prevalent in modern politics. Previous to traces of it in the US in 2016, Nigel Farage could be considered the father of 21st-century populism in the UK. Blaming immigrants (such as Polish workers), he threatened to split David Cameron's Conservative government majority in Parliament over conflicts regarding UK membership in the European Union (EU). This forced Cameron to promise a Brexit vote in advance of a general election.

Cameron's promise was made in the hopes of keeping the party together—and it did, but it split the country and severed ties with the EU. The wave continued spreading from the UK through the US. Farage was a major force to Trump's 2016 populist election campaign, following the very same template of blaming immigrants (such as Muslims, Mexicans, and others).

Upon entering the presidential race, Trump's presence split the votes and communities, which paved the road to his first term. Beyond receiving support of the people, Trump elevated Farage's creation to a new level, quickly focusing on reversing legislation regarding fracking and coal. The ramifications of this started not just a new trend but a well-entrenched new political movement that swept the world.

Populism then captured many other countries (including Brazil, Hungary, and India), in which new political leaders very successfully leveraged populism as part of their strategy toward rising to power. Since the financial crisis of 2008, virtually all governments around the world, with exception to oil-rich Arab nations, went through serious financial austerity. This meant that many government programs serving the people needed to be cut due to lack of funding.

Austerity led to citizens being fed up; they wanted to know why their livelihoods were damaged and how there were no improvements. This made for fertile ground for populist leaders (such as Trump, Jair

Bolsonaro, Viktor Orbán, and Narendra Modi). These leaders championed nationalism (country first), which gave the pretext to start blaming immigrants and foreigners for the problems faced by their country—rather than the actual perpetrators of the financial crisis and therefore the very austerity driving civil strife to an all-time high.

History unfolds as we live and breathe through the continual toxicity of the ultra-populist movement. As the common point of blaming others (immigrants, impoverished, etc.) spread throughout global politics, each populist leader shared the goal of implementing special-interest mandates.

HUNGARY AND ORBÁN

Europe was flooded with Muslim immigrants through 2018 and 2019. Hungarian prime minister Viktor Orbán already made his stance known, in that he was vastly against their presence. From BBC News,[80] in January 2015, Orbán joined 40 leaders in solidarity after the infamous *Charlie Hebdo* terrorist attack:

> He told Hungarian TV: "We will never allow Hungary to become a target country for immigrants. We do not want to see significantly sized minorities with different cultural characteristics and backgrounds among us. We want to keep Hungary as Hungary."

Later that year, in May, he stood his ground on the topic when the European Commission was attempting to redistribute asylum seekers: "No one will tell us who we let into our own house." His decision that following June was a 110-mile barrier along the Serbian border. After his party, Fidesz, lost two by-elections earlier that spring, critics claimed that Orbán saw value in playing the migration card. "In the following months his party won back anything up to a million supporters, pollsters estimated."

This should sound familiar to US readers except, in this case, the barrier was actually built as opposed to Trump's "wall."

> ... Crossing or damaging the fence became a crime punishable by up to three years in prison. Most who do so are caught and summarily expelled from the country ... Two "transit zones" built into

> the fence at Tompa and Roszke, initially allowed 20 asylum seekers a day to apply. That figure is now down to two a day, according to the UNHCR.
>
> In April 2017 the zones were enlarged into "container camps" where asylum seekers, including unaccompanied minors as young as 14, could be detained for many months …

In 2020, during the spread of COVID-19, Orbán was being interviewed on the radio. His interviewer inquired as to decisions made regarding schools remaining open unlike the universities. His reply, according to France 24,[81] was, "There are lots of foreigners there. … Our experience is that primarily foreigners brought in the disease, and that it is spreading among foreigners."

Immigration continues to be the football kicked around by the majority of populist leaders. Orbán, in this case, was not unique. However, in addition to the classic populist playbook, Orbán was surrounded by cronies who became super rich from a land grab facilitated by him. In November 2019, *The New York Times* published a report,[82] "The Money Farmers: How Oligarchs and Populists Milk the E.U. for Millions." As a member of the European Union (EU), Hungary is one of 28 countries receiving annual funds in farm subsidies from the EU. Totaling $65 billion, the intention of this money is to support rural communities.

> But across Hungary and much of Central and Eastern Europe, the bulk goes to a connected and powerful few. The prime minister of the Czech Republic collected tens of millions of dollars in subsidies just last year. Subsidies have underwritten Mafia-style land grabs in Slovakia and Bulgaria …
>
> Specific to Hungary:
>
> Mr. Orban's government has auctioned off thousands of acres of state land to his family members and close associates, including one childhood friend who has become one of the richest men in the country, the Times investigation found. Those who control the land, in turn, qualify for millions in subsidies from the European Union.

And neither Orbán's use of EU funds nor his network of friends is exclusive to the farmlands of Hungary. In 2018, Reuters investigated the use of taxpayer money by them in special tourism projects, such as the shores of Lake Balaton, in the city of Keszthely.[83] Reuters has coined Orbán's group "the Keszthely 10," after their involvement in the formation of waterfront properties. In terms of further accepting EU funds, and aside from any investigation or claims from EU's antifraud office (Office Européen de Lutte Antifraude, or OLAF), Orbán seems to think he and the Keszthely 10 are entitled to not only take the funds but use them for their own gain:

> [Orbán] has long defied oversight by what he calls the "global political overlords" and "liberal elites" and portrays himself as a pioneer among eastern European leaders whose countries are part of the European Union, but who rebel—in his case by saying Hungary deserves the bloc's cash in exchange for opening up its markets, and that he should be free to form his own class of loyal industrialists.
>
> "What some call corruption is essentially the main policy of Fidesz," Andras Lanczi, an Orban supporter at the think tank Szazadveg, said in a 2015 newspaper interview that Szazadveg put up on its website. "By that I mean the government has set goals like forming a layer of domestic businessmen, building pillars of a strong Hungary in rural areas or in industry."
>
> Orban and his associates have a clear system, said Peter Kreko, chief analyst at the Political Capital think tank in Budapest: They build positions in sectors and prepare for the arrival of public funds. "Close associates of the prime minister get fat on state money," he said.

While populism strengthens its grip on Hungary, Orbán sees his economic doctrine/model (see below) as "a revolt against international capital and liberal values." Similar to surrounding regions in Eastern Europe, his revolt appears to affirm nationalist-oriented supremacy.

> "We were among the first, or maybe the first, to revolt in 2010," Orban said in his state of the nation address last year. "In seven years of hard work we built our own political and economic system, a Hungarian model tailor made for us ... the *System of National Cooperation*." He told a gathering of friendly intellectuals in 2013 that this involves nurturing a supportive moneyed class: "The system cannot work without international capital. But ... Hungarian national capital must be empowered as well." (emphasis mine)

From the hard work of *The New York Times* and Reuters, I would say that it's more likely that Orbán is empowering the capital lining his own pockets, and the pockets of the Keszthely 10. The EU always flaunts its leadership on democracy, values, freedom (etc.), as well as its democratic institutions for the world to emulate. Yet they allow Orbán and many others to act like banana republic leaders while benefiting themselves. The EU seems happy to keep them at the table unchecked. Perhaps this is because they are allies against Vladimir Putin.

Through the use of populism and essentially obvious service to special interest, Orbán has shown that his government does not reflect the true values flaunted by the EU. Again, he is not the only one doing so, nor is any of this exclusive to Hungary. Nevertheless, with their presence in mind, there should be no wonder as to the fact that Western democracy is in stage four cancer.

BRAZIL AND BOLSONARO

Brazilians were notoriously easygoing people until the recent past. During the rise of now-President Jair Bolsonaro, his campaign and leadership focused on blaming the previous corrupt politicians as well as the presence of Middle Eastern immigrants from across the Atlantic. Brazilians are now facing segregation while Bolsonaro focuses on pleasing his special-interest backers.

From UK news outlet, Reuters:[84]

> Conservative caucuses ranging from evangelicals to farmers and pro-gun lawmakers have visited the front-runner at his home this

> week to make sure their agendas are on the front-burner if as expected he becomes president-elect on Sunday.
>
> Industry leaders told Bolsonaro they opposed the combining of the ministries of finance and planning with the industry and trade portfolio into a super ministry that would be headed by his economic policy guru Paulo Guedes. "If this is their interest, for the good of the country, we will maintain the trade and industry ministry, no problem," Bolsonaro said in a *Facebook live appearance* ...
>
> ... But his most controversial plan to merge the ministries of agriculture and the environment set off a storm of criticism from environmentalists who say it would undermine Brazil's *commitment to protect the Amazon rainforest.* (emphasis mine)

Bolsonaro's bedfellows illustrate the use of populism to its worst extent. While the people were swept into the toxic storm of blame, he chose very specific players in his efforts that directly countered the above-mentioned commitment. From *The Guardian*, during the fires in the Amazon that followed his successful campaign:[85]

> Bolsonaro's choice for his environment minister, Ricardo Salles from the so-called New Party (Partido Novo), exemplifies the radical and even violent anti-environmentalism fueling these fires. Last year, Salles, while serving as a state environmental official in São Paulo, was found guilty of administrative improprieties for having altered a map to benefit mining companies ...
>
> ... In 2018, Salles—now the custodian of the Brazilian Amazon—ran for federal Congress with a political ad that displayed bullets from a rifle as his solution for environmental activists, indigenous tribes impeding the destruction of their land, and "leftists." Salles lost his bid for congress, but was rewarded with a much more powerful position: Bolsonaro's environment minister.
>
> Bolsonaro and Salles view deforestation as such a pressing priority that they openly despise anyone who seeks to impede it.

> Earlier this month, Bolsonaro fired a top scientist after he warned the country that deforestation was taking place at an unprecedented and dangerous rate ...

As you can see, the smoke and mirrors, along with the blame, never ceased. Meanwhile, the fire spreading parallels that of democracy's stage four cancer. And they have no problem finding further "enemies" of the people to skew the conversation away from their actions.

As I'll explain after the next example, Brazil is a signatory of the Paris Climate Change Accord, and Bolsonaro's actions counter that agreement. Retrospectively, what does it say about the accord if signatories remain compliant by terms and conditions but deforest at such scales? As you'll soon read, he's not alone in this course of action. While claiming to be a force against the very austerity that inspired problems in Brazil, Bolsonaro seems fit to continue working with corrupt figures (convicted felons, in the case of Salles) to fulfill special-interest agendas.

INDIA AND MODI

It should be clear after Trump, Bolsonaro, and Orbán that voters in most democratic elections end up voting for new politicians out of protest for the corrupt leaders they want removed from power. The US, Brazil, and Hungary (along with many others) are not unique. In India, Narendra Modi, a member of the Bharatiya Janata Party, won his first campaign based on India's equivalent of "draining the swamp."

His success was a testimony that Indians were fed up with the corruption revealed up to that point and were willing to give him a chance. In addition, Modi's formula for success also included nationalism and populism. In May 2019, after Modi secured a second five-year term, BBC released their article, "How Narendra Modi Has Reinvented Indian Politics," in which they shared vital context to his effect on the nation:[86]

> In a bitter and divisive campaign, Mr. Modi effortlessly fused nationalism and development. He created binaries: the nationalists (his supporters) versus the anti-nationals (his political rivals and critics); the watchman (Modi himself, protecting the country on "land, air, and outer space") versus the entitled and the corrupt (an obvious dig at the main opposition Congress party) ...

> Aligned to this, deftly, was the promise of development. Mr. Modi's targeted welfare schemes for the poor—homes, toilets, credit, cooking gas—have used technology for speedy delivery. However, the quality of these services and how much they have helped ameliorate deprivation is debatable …

And of course, no story of populism would be complete without some form of blame being thrown upon an unwelcome people.

> After a suicide attack—claimed by Pakistan-based militants—which killed more than 40 Indian paramilitaries in disputed Kashmir and the retaliatory air strike against Pakistan in the run-up to the election, Mr. Modi successfully convinced the masses that the country would be secure if he remained in power.

Further context: Pakistan was created by the British Empire to be a Muslim state for Muslims fleeing from India during the empire's long colonial tenure of India. Where India once included both Hindus and Muslims, the vast majority were pushed into an exclusive territory in a British game of divide and conquer, in which regions were manipulated into conflict with one another. Many Muslims still decided to remain. In fact, today, there are more Muslims in India than in Pakistan.

After securing his second five-year term, in December 2019, Indian parliament passed the Citizenship Amendment Act. On the surface, this act appears to implement a fast track for refugees from Bangladesh, Afghanistan, and Pakistan. In February 2020, *The Guardian* released further information as to the truth:[87]

> Refugees of every south Asian faith are eligible—every faith, that is, except Islam. It is a policy that fits neatly with the RSS [Rashtriya Swayamsevak Sangh] and the BJP's [Bharatiya Janata Party's] demonisation of Muslims, India's largest religious minority. To votaries of Hindutva, the country is best served if it is expunged of Islam.

The Bharatiya Janata Party is essentially the right-wing of India. Over time, their actions have reflected Hindu nationalism. As of late, they are clearly linked to Rashtriya Swayamsevak Sangh (RSS). The RSS is a paramilitary volunteer organization, and the arrival of Modi as prime minister has amplified their Hindu nationalist presence since his first term.

> When Modi won his first term as prime minister in 2014, it was difficult to know how to read the result. Were those who voted for the BJP frustrated with the alternatives, or did they believe Modi to be the economic miracle-worker he claimed to be? Had they simply chosen to disregard the fact that he had allowed mobs of Hindu fanatics to murder hundreds of Muslims in riots during his chief ministership of Gujarat in 2002, or did they actively approve of this overt anti-Muslim agenda?
>
> Only after Modi settled into power did many BJP voters begin to clearly voice their sympathies for Hindutva. These revelations felt sudden and shocking, to the point that you wondered if these voters had silently longed for a pure Hindu nation well before Modi. Relationships ruptured the way they did after Trump's election or the Brexit referendum. Families bickered on WhatsApp groups, and friends fell out. "Before 2014, you'd have found a pro-ABVP student and a pro-left student who were friends with each other," Cheri Che, a PhD student in history, told [Samanth Subramanian]. "After 2014, that was increasingly difficult."

Modi's actions have turned citizen against citizen, and his anti-Muslim stance may have encouraged violence. As per the prompt, while unrest settles across the country, their prime minister serves special-interest groups, as we can see with the deforestation he allows on behalf of the coal industry. Once again, *The Guardian*, in August 2020, shared insight from their investigation:[88]

> The war being waged in Hasdeo Arand, a rich and biodiverse Indian forest, has pitted indigenous people, ancient trees, elephants and sloth bears against the might of bulldozers, trucks and hydraulic jacks, fighting with a single purpose: the extraction of coal.
>
> Yet under a new "self-reliant India" plan by the prime minister, Narendra Modi, to boost the economy post-COVID-19 and reduce

> costly imports, 40 new coalfields in some of India's most ecologically sensitive forests are to be opened up for commercial mining.

Modi's decision has resulted in a privatized, commercial coal sector. As these 40 coal blocks are being auctioned, massive organizations, owned by the rich and powerful, are bidding for ownership. *The Guardian* draws specific attention to the Adani Group (worth $14 billion), which is led by billionaire Gautam Adani, "who operates India's largest coal power plants and has close ties to Modi."

Arguments supporting Modi's decision include rising demand from Indian citizens. As India has the fourth-largest coal reserves in the world, this is claimed to be a cost-effective action. And while there are objections, Modi's party seems to think the "benefit" of development, employment, and money are well worth the loss of nature. Meanwhile, opponents to this plan see it as a loss, and they see it as a direct result of Gautam Adani's influence on their government.

> Among the prominent opponents to the project is the former environment minister, Jairan Ramesh, who also wrote a letter to Modi condemning coal auctions. It was during his time in office that a survey was carried out in 2010 on India's biggest coalfields and determined that 30% were "no-go areas" due to their biodiversity or resident tiger or elephant populations. Yet since Modi came to power in 2014, that 30% has been reduced to about 5%.
>
> Ramesh alleged this was a direct result of pressure from the powerful corporate coal lobby, Adani in particular. The Adani group is contracted to operate two of the mines currently open in Hasdeo Arand, and has been pushing to expand mining operations in the forest for years, even reportedly offering microloans to local tribal people in order to win their support. "Adani is behind this," claims Ramesh. "He is one of the most influential forces on the government."
>
> "Modi poses as a great environmental champion globally but his track record is one of complete loosening of environmental laws and regulations," Ramesh added. "The corporate lobbies are just

too powerful and in the name of ease for businesses, environment has become the biggest casualty."

Much like Brazil, the above deforestation is perpetrated by yet another signatory of the Paris Accord. Policies and decisions made by Modi and Jair Bolsonaro are resulting in profits for special interest, personal friends, and influential organizations alike. The new formula of rising to power has proven to be a great "success."

FARAGE'S WAKE

Nationalism, populism, and blaming others for failure in serving citizens are the anchors that divide society all over the world and create opportunities for inner-circle profiteers to benefit at the expense of ordinary people. Viktor Orbán, Jair Bolsonaro, and Narendra Modi are opportunistic politicians who wanted to win at any price, and they chose this new poisonous and divisive playbook as their strategy. And they succeeded.

Nigel Farage's pivotal influence on Brexit and Trump's divisive campaign and presidency may pale in comparison. Nevertheless, they are certainly the beginning of the movement still taking hold of the world today. If Farage is the messiah of modern populism, Trump, Bolsonaro, Orbán, Modi, and others like them are surely his disciples. These are the new founding fathers of systemic divisiveness and resulting critical failures in exchange for rising to power, at any cost.

Specific to the Paris Accord, the loose restrictions of self-regulation rear their ugly faces in the actions of leaders like Modi and Bolsonaro. The challenge facing humanity is that adopted models such as the accord, touted as saviors to the planet, are designed and structured to permit signatory countries not only to self-regulate but self-monitor. There are no penalties or punitive recourse on governments that do not meet requirements or standards. At that, there is no incentive to remain on the "good" side of such agreements or legislation. The cases of India and Brazil are examples of how signatory nations remain inside the treaty while increasing damage to the planet.

This celebrated model is not fit for purpose. It remains adopted because of the corrupt global economic and political system we live under—the failed status quo. Unless we fix them, we will not be able to save the planet, nor will we be able to secure mankind's survivability.

Therefore, allowing existing leadership and legislation to remain unchallenged is allowing this status quo to continue—this is a threat to humanity.

ANTI-POPULISM

As if the situation couldn't be more complicated, further distraction can be found in the use of anti-populism (anti-anti-Semitism, anti-Islamophobia, anti-racism, etc.), in which the opposite narrative is used to call attention upon unwanted change or progress. Minnesota US Representative Ilhan Omar was brought into focus by Trump's infamous controversy back in the summer of 2019.[89]

At the age of 12, Omar fled civil war in Somalia and came to the US as a refugee. In 2016, she became one of the first Muslim women to win a seat in the House of Representatives (in District 60B). In 2018, she then transitioned into Minnesota's 5th District. And in early 2019, political rivals and conservative media began drawing attention to statements she had made and was making on Israel. In January, a tweet from 2012 was brought into focus, in which she said:

"Israel has hypnotized the world, may Allah awaken the people and help them see the evil doings of Israel."

She wrote the post in response to an Israeli offensive on Gaza, where conflicts are yearly recurring activities, with heavy and disproportionate Palestinian civilian casualties. Judging by the deluge of statements against her, it would seem that no actions taken by the Israeli government can be criticized in America. In February, after reports were published saying that Republicans wanted her punished for her words and responses, she added a new tweet to the mix:

"It's all about the Benjamins, baby."

Though she was commenting on the financial relationship between American politicians and Israeli lobbyists—implying that the US was turning a blind eye to further casualties in Gaza and profiting from it—the standard template of anti-Semitic claims against her doubled down, accusing her of resorting to Jewish stereotypes. She apologized and then seemingly dug herself an even deeper hole. In an attempt to clarify, she shared material on the American Israel Public Affairs Committee (AIPAC), also recognized as the primary Israeli lobby in the US.

During a panel in Washington, Omar later shared her two cents on questionable influence from pro-Israel activists:

"I want to talk about the political influence in this country that says it is O.K. for people to push for allegiance to a foreign country."

Criticism of her statement ranged from her being anti-American to an echo chamber of claims that she was further anti-Semitic. Quickly, a doctored quote was fabricated and shared online making it seem like Omar was saying she didn't need to pledge allegiance to any country, let alone the US. More to the point, accusations of anti-Semitic language remained at the forefront as others claimed she was addressing "dual loyalty," which touches on old propaganda against Jewish immigrants. In defending herself against a fellow Democratic congresswoman, Omar tweeted:

> Our democracy is built on debate, Congresswoman! I should not be expected to have allegiance/pledge support to a foreign country in order to serve my country in Congress or serve on committee. The people of the 5th elected me to serve their interest. I am sure we agree on that!

Omar was attempting to expose the American public to the darker nature of AIPAC and how it puts the interests of Israel above that of America. Her own party, led by Nancy Pelosi, asked her to apologize, and she did. And yet, her statement was accurate.

While self-governing, Gaza is an occupied territory by the state of Israel, along with the West Bank. Its inhabitants/citizens are under occupation. They are entitled to resist occupation by any means possible according to UN charters. Worth mentioning, they live lives worse than that of dogs. If Israel does not allow them water, supplies, or other material, there is nothing they can do about it.

Israel continues breaking UN resolutions by building settlements on this Palestinian land, yet the US is the only country supporting and blessing this course of action. The Palestinians are expected to be good dogs while Israel makes the next Beverly Hills at their expense. From BBC News, "Gaza crisis: Toll of operations in Gaza," the number of casualties from such attacks is and should be shocking.[90]

In 2014, Israel launched an attack in response to rockets being launched from Gaza. Over 50 days, 2,104 Palestinians were killed, as well as 72 Israelis and 1 Thai national. Of the 2,104 Palestinians, 1,462 were civilians, and of those, 253 were women and 495 were children. There is no country in the world where its government could carry out a military offensive on one of the most densely populated areas in the world and get away with calling it self-defense. Casualties aside, in March, the House of Representatives passed a new resolution.

Racism, bigotry, and specifically anti-Semitism were condemned.

As this was in response to Omar's statements and responses, some Democrat voices were concerned that the resolution did not include her by name, as they wanted to separate their party from her opinions. On Monday, July 15, 2019, President Trump personified Republican strategies against Omar when he said she "says horrible things about Israel, hates Israel, hates Jews, it's very simple." Much to the DNC's chagrin, he then proceeded to claim the Democrats themselves were anti-Semitic.

The idea that any criticism of Israeli government actions should be considered anti-Semitic has in turn become criticized as anti-Semitic as American Jews themselves have increased their criticism of Israel over the years. The idea did not decrease in speed, nor did it lose any support over the course of 2019. By December, Trump passed a bill declaring Judaism (both culture and people) as a nationality (Title VI), decreeing any criticism of the state of Israel as hate speech. Moving forward, if you disagree with or criticize *any Israeli government policy on any topic*, be it economic, political, educational, or policy, you would be breaking US federal and state laws and would be labeled as anti-Semitic.

Powerful American Evangelical Christians are more Zionist than many Jews around the world—who seriously object to the many policies of the state of Israel on multiple levels. For any Jews who deplore Prime Minister Benjamin Netanyahu's policies, and continue vocalizing their criticisms of his decisions, would you consider them anti-Semitic? Well, US federal law now classifies them so, regardless of the fact that the people of such voices are Semitic themselves.

In a land long championing freedom of speech, you are now considered a racist criminal bigot—and potentially face jail time—for criticizing Israeli policies on human rights, economics, or the apartheid conditions imposed on millions of Palestinians living under Israeli occupation (as defined by the UN). In fact, many US states still require a promise not to engage in any criticism of Israel or boycotts of its products as a condition of any state or federally funded job or event. The constitutional right, freedom of expression, is not just out the window on this topic—it's been desecrated by law.

Measures of this sort are designed to drown any initiatives for transparency, accountability, fair play, conversations, or positive developments, etc. Such debates within debates within debates are meant to lead us nowhere by design, drowning us in order to maintain the status quo. If this is possible in a country supposedly abiding by the model of Western democracy, one can only imagine the extent it can be taken to in a country ruled by despots.

WE ARE THE PRIMARY STAKEHOLDERS!

The American dream of job security, home ownership, freedom of expression, and the pursuit of happiness are not exclusive American ambitions. These are universal hopes within every possible culture around the world. In fact, they are the common denominator aspirations that bind us all as human beings.

And yet, no global mechanism exists that can actually link local citizens of one country with those of another under the same aspiration. There is no model that connects ordinary people at any magnitude. We only see static and scattered dreams.

As it stands, without real unity on a local level, citizens have no leverage or staying power. In my mind, this is a short-term goal, as we truly need unity on an international level in order to accomplish real change. What we continue seeing is corrupt leadership implementing their own visions toward control and the longest possible terms of "service." And if we listen, I think we'll soon find that we are all tired of the ever-repeating story playing out year after year: decision makers ignoring their primary stakeholders. However, we are continually drowned by special-interest-sourced narratives, and we continue to remain in a state of being "purposely disinformed."

Overall, the remaining thought I want you to keep in mind from Part II of my book is that we need to not just reform how we legislate, regulate, and are governed; we need to seriously overhaul it. Self-regulation is the form of governance that has led to the same leaders serving themselves and special third parties over the people. This leaves the true primary stakeholder at risk and abandons them with the bill when GPCyber™ attacks storm through the system. The same result applies to most if not all other forms of vulnerability, be it market crashes, climate change, or mass shootings.

At this point of Part III, I want you thinking about true reformation in the transparency and accountability of our leaders, as well as our systems and models. No more tweaks. No more bills with counterintuitive addendums in the small print. No more passing bills with 5,000+ pages left unread by the majority of legislators (see COVID-19 relief deal). No more solutions watering down over the course of bipartisan processes, losing the original intention to compromise and pride.

We need our elected leadership to remain honest as they explain how they're putting tax dollars to the best use while serving their citizens. In the world of our aspiration, their election contributions would be exclusively from the people. Rather than counting on third-party groups and organizations, our elected officials would manifest real leverage by actually representing our voices.

At the risk of angering the corporate gods, lobbying as we know it must be caged. Left to their own devices, many leaders and organizations seem fit to keep us distracted while they corrupt celebrated models, furthering agendas and fortifying their continued grip on power. As long as safeguarding the failed status quo remains the ongoing goal, our nine meals will only further deplete. As it stands, I continue believing we are three meals from anarchy. They aren't exactly adding food to the table. In fact, they seem perfectly content to take even more for themselves.

If all of this were the result of GPCyber™ hacks at the hand of bad actors, the gauntlet would be thrown—the hunt would begin for justice, vengeance, and retribution. And yet, in the Era of the Unprecedented, the hunt would lead right back to our own doorsteps. These problems are at the hand of our own politicians. Beyond being a threat to democracy, the failed status quo is truly a threat to humanity.

For more information, please visit survivabilitythebook.com/ placeholder (or scan the code below) to see articles referenced as well as my recommended reading list. We have been very lucky to have journalists with integrity on the case. I encourage you to explore how the world received this story.

20

A Broken System, Part A

(Corrupt Regulation and One Last "Gift" from 2020)

IF YOU STILL have doubts that our system is broken, reconsider the Panama Papers from Chapter 17. Hackers were responsible for revealing 12 million documents detailing financial and confidential attorney–client information for over 200,000 offshore entities. While it would indeed be a challenge to find Americans directly named, clients of Mossack Fonseca included a cross-continental list of government leaders, current and former rulers, heads of state, ministers, as well as family members.

Again, one can almost consider the hackers responsible for compromising Fonseca as implementers of checks and balances in a global system and society where current checks and balances are no longer effective. As far as I'm concerned, this leak revealed at least three things:

1. Such leaders serve the establishment (or their deep state puppeteers) over their constituents
2. The Western checks and balances in place are in fact camouflage for political agendas
3. Not just the frailty but the falsehoods of the transparency and mechanisms in Western society when it comes to promoting democracy in other countries

As I was writing about this very topic at the beginning of Part III, September 2020 had one last "gift" for humanity. Our leaders claim we are fighting a war on terror, and it can now easily be seen that they've been turning a blind eye to the enemies declared to the people. Before regifting this to you, let's take a look at a few infamous leaks before and after the events surrounding Mossack Fonseca in 2016.

The Panama Papers was not an anomaly; it was one of many systemic disclosures of how broken the system was and continues to be. And, calling it for what it is, the following events led to slaps on the wrist, at most:

- LuxLeaks (2014)
- Swiss Leaks (2015)
- The Paradise Papers (2017)
- FinCEN (the last "gift" of 2020)

LUXLEAKS

In 2014, a top-four accountancy firm, PricewaterhouseCoopers, found themselves embroiled in a leak from whistleblowers within their firm. The LuxLeaks were the focus of a collaborative effort by the International Consortium of Investigative Journalists (ICIJ), which reviewed nearly 30,000 pages. PricewaterhouseCoopers is based in Luxembourg, which is one of the smallest countries in western Europe. The LuxLeaks revealed they had more than 500 tax rulings with a little over 300 companies around the world.

Essentially, PricewaterhouseCoopers was assisting their clients in reducing tax payments. For companies incorporating themselves in Luxembourg, moving their headquarters therein meant benefiting from the lowest taxes available. And technically speaking, this was legal, but it was a loophole. PricewaterhouseCoopers's clients included Amazon, Fiat Finance and Trade (now Fiat Chrysler Finance Europe), Ikea, McDonald's, and Starbucks.

Use of this loophole was traceable in the form of Luxembourg tax rulings from 2002 to 2010. During the formation of these rulings, Jean-Claude Juncker was serving as prime minister of Luxembourg. Coincidentally or not, a few days into being appointed President of the European Commission, the LuxLeaks had the world's attention. Two years later, the European Commission concluded that such dealings were illegal, which meant collecting over half a billion euros from nearly a tenth of PricewaterhouseCoopers's clients.

Juncker went on to complete his term in 2019 ...

SWISS LEAKS

A year after LuxLeaks, in 2015, the ICIJ assisted in revealing yet another international/financial crime, but this story begins in 2006. Hervé Falciani worked for the Swiss branch of Hong Kong and Shanghai Banking Corporation Ltd. (HSBC). According to his own story, in 2006 he personally revealed to his bosses that their data management was fostering tax evasion and proposed a new method. After HSBC rejected his idea, Falciani spent the next two years collecting potential tax fraud evidence against over 100,000 individuals.[91]

Falciani attempted to put this information in the hands of Swiss authorities but was unsuccessful. According to his version of the story, this inspired him to capture the attention of Swiss prosecutors by arranging an overt/shady business deal. He traveled to Beirut, Lebanon, and took steps toward selling private client information to Bank Audi. His supposed intention was taking actions that would specifically trigger alarms for the appropriate authorities to not only pursue and capture him, but to legally gain access to the records in question.

If this was indeed his plan all along, it was successful, in that he was arrested and the Falciani lists ended up in the "right" hands—not to say that justice was served. These lists covered five months (from November 2006 to March 2007), and the information showed activity for more than 100,000 HSBC accounts (and 20,000 offshore companies). Allegedly, Falciani revealed 180.6 billion euros passing through those accounts in Geneva.

The "right" hands were those of the French authorities, which focused their investigations on a meager portion of the list: roughly 3,000 French citizens colluding with HSBC. They sat on this information from 2009 to 2015, and during this time, account managers illegally alerted at least some of those 3,000 clients. French newspaper *Le Monde* did not receive anything for research until 2014.

As the scale of the crimes in question was so large, journalists and publishers from around the world were invited to assist in researching the Falciani lists. ICIJ once again returned to the scene and released their findings in early 2015, "Swiss Leaks: Murky Cash Sheltered by Bank Secrecy." In this they named the top countries involved by total finances involved. Of the 203, here are the top 10:[92]

1.	Switzerland	$31.2 billion
2.	United Kingdom	$21.7 billion
3.	Venezuela	$14.8 billion
4.	United States	$13.4 billion
5.	France	$12.5 billion
6.	Israel	$10 billion
7.	Italy	$7.5 billion
8.	Bahamas	$7 billion
9.	Brazil	$7 billion
10.	Belgium	$6.3 billion

And they also ranked countries by the number of clients. Again, here are the top 10:[93]

1.	Switzerland	11,235
2.	France	9,187
3.	United Kingdom	8,844
4.	Brazil	8,667
5.	Italy	7,499
6.	Israel	6,544
7.	United States	4,183
8.	Argentina	3,625
9.	Turkey	3,105
10.	Belgium	3,002

Ultimately, the Swiss Leaks project was able to reveal that HSBC's clients included people accused of arms dealing, corruption, drug running, and money laundering. Not only that, it showed that HSBC assisted in helping such clients conceal billions of dollars through their Swiss branch. While French authorities were able to successfully begin a criminal trial in 2015, HSBC negotiated paying over $350 million to avoid going to trial in 2017. The case was dropped, wrists were slapped, and success was declared by all parties involved. Sound familiar?

And by the way, no individuals served time for their decisions.

HSBC continued handling money.

And thankfully, the ICIJ continued their great work. Soon after publishing their article about the Swiss Leaks, they revealed the Panama Papers to the world in early 2016 (the details of this were shared in Chapter 17: "Three Meals"). After three significant leak-journalism efforts (the Panama Papers being the largest ever), ICIJ struck uranium yet again the following year.

THE PARADISE PAPERS

Hints as to the existence of the Paradise Papers emerged in late October 2017. An anonymous user on Reddit insinuated as to the existence of information leaked from Appleby, along with corporate service providers Estera (which had been part of Appleby until 2016) and Asiaciti Trust, and business registries in nearly 20 tax jurisdictions. The ICIJ actually dove straight into the action on this one, as they directly approached Appleby with allegations.

The company diverted attention to a cyberattack the year before, essentially claiming (1) crimes were done against them and (2) they had no tolerance of illegal behavior. Similar to the Panama Papers the year before, the hacked information was sent to German newspaper *Süddeutsche Zeitung*. The events continued unfolding much faster than previous leaks, as the ICIJ most certainly formed a routine for necessary research and international cooperation. It took them more than a year to sift through the Panama Papers, which involved 2.6 terabytes of information.

This time they were focused on 1.4 terabytes, 13.4 million confidential electronic documents related to offshore investments (the locations of which inspired the name "Paradise Papers"). A mere portion of the Paradise Papers was shared with the public in early November, a little over two weeks after hints were made on Reddit. Stories continued to be published beyond this date as the world turned its attention upon people and organizations implicated (more than 120,000).

Former leaders around the world included:

- José María Figueres (President of Costa Rica)
- Juan Manuel Santos (President of Colombia)
- Ellen Johnson Sirleaf (President of Liberia)
- Petro Poroshenko (President of Ukraine)
- Shaukat Aziz (Prime Minister of Pakistan)
- Jean Chrétien (Prime Minister of Canada)
- Alfred Gusenbauer (Chancellor of Austria)
- Yukio Hatoyama (Prime Minister of Japan)
- Paul Martin (Prime Minister of Canada)
- Brian Mulroney (Prime Minister of Canada)
- Gerhard Schröder (Chancellor of Germany)
- Hamad bin Jassim bin Jaber Al Thani (Prime Minister of Qatar)

People implicated in the UK:

- Queen Elizabeth II
- Charles, Prince of Wales
- Michael Ashcroft (formerly of the House of Lords)
- George Magan (House of Lords)
- Jacob Rees-Mogg (Lord President of the Council, and leader of the House of Commons)
- James Sassoon (House of Lords and former Commercial Secretary to the Treasury)

Former US leaders:

- Randal Quarles (Former Chair of the Financial Stability Board)
- Steven Mnuchin (Secretary of the Treasury)
- Wilbur Ross (Secretary of Commerce)
- Rex Tillerson (Secretary of State)
- Penny Pritzker (Secretary of Commerce)
- Wesley Clark (presidential candidate and Supreme Allied Commander Europe)
- Gary Cohn (director of the National Economic Council)
- Jon Huntsman Jr. (ambassador to Russia and Governor of Utah)

US companies:

- Amazon
- Apple Inc.
- Baker McKenzie
- Bank of Utah
- Disney
- Facebook
- Goldman Sachs
- McDonald's
- Nike, Inc.
- The Blackstone Group
- Twitter
- Uber
- Walmart
- Whirlpool Corporation
- Wynn Resorts
- Yahoo!

Beyond the world giving in to speculation during the initial release of the Paradise Papers, the situation fizzled out. Amidst international calls for reform against the tax offshore industry, Appleby issued legal proceedings against both the *Guardian* as well as BBC for publishing confidential information that had been seized illegally. This was announced at the end of 2017, and the publishers argued that because the names of clients involved were international public figures, it was in the public's interest to disclose and report on this event. Within six months, both publishers settled Appleby's disputes.

In October 2018, companies were still navigating the resulting conflict of the leak, and one in particular attempted a daring feat. Multinational mining company Glencore tried to block the Australian Tax Authority from being able to use information from the Paradise Papers. Similar to the suit against BBC and *The Guardian*, Glencore's claim was entirely based on the idea that the cyberattack against Appleby leaked privileged/confidential client information.

Glencore's efforts did not end in success. The courts ruled that Australia could indeed use the documents in any legal action following the release of the Paradise Papers. Glencore's proceedings were not the end of this story, and unfortunately, the next court case went poorly for the cause of journalism.

At the beginning of 2019, in Turkey, Pelin Ünker found herself on the other side of legal action due to publishing information from the Paradise Papers regarding former Prime Minister Binali Yildirim—and more importantly, his two sons. Due to loopholes in the maritime industry, Yildirim's sons were avoiding their own country's high tax rates by setting up their companies (Hawke Bay Marine Co. Ltd. and Black Eagle Marine Co. Ltd.) in Malta.

While the brothers admitted the facts surrounding them in controversy, Ünker was fined and sentenced to 13 months in prison. Meanwhile, she was also taken to court by Turkey's finance and treasury minister, Berat Albayrak, son-in-law to President Recep Tayyip Erdoğan. Thankfully, the latter case was dismissed and her industry rose to her defense.

Her prison sentence was overturned but the fine was left in place. The world returned to pre-COVID normalcy for another year. And then, in the midst of the pandemic, another leak briefly graced headlines around the world.

FinCEN LEAK

After President John F. Kennedy's assassination, people have said that they will always remember where they were and what they were doing when they received news of Kennedy's death. Do you remember where you were and what you were doing when you heard about the Panama Papers? How about the Paradise Papers? Or the FinCEN leaks?

What does the phrase "FinCEN" mean to you?

If you don't recall, don't feel bad. This is why I've asked the question. In principle, these specific leaks were as detrimental to the world (you included) as the killing of an American president. And the most recent of them was doomed to slip through the cracks of newsfeeds and speculation.

A presidential assassination is understandably more capable of holding the world's attention. An untimely death can result in world war, and the international whodunit carries with it a morbid sense of curiosity. But in the case of leaks, we don't have an intended high-profile victim (outside of any firms being hacked), and we don't have a single perpetrator.

Where newspapers and news stations displayed photographs of JFK, they also had mugshots of Lee Harvey Oswald. The loss of JFK affected an entire nation, and Oswald's face was front and center for blame and resolution. Ironically, each of the leaks in this chapter have bigger and more direct ramifications on people worldwide. But they never have a face to associate with victims nor do they have one for the killer(s). In the world left exposed by hackers and the ICIJ, there are many organizations and head figures involved in activities that affect many people in many countries.

Today, we the people are the target, and the culprit's face is the broken system. You may not recognize the name Natalie Mayflower Sours Edwards, and likely, you have no reason to care who she is. But in 2016, when she caught a glimpse of the "face," she took action.

After September 11, 2001, Natalie Edwards claims she was inspired to pursue a government career. In an effort to do her part in mitigating similar attacks against the United States, she worked at the CIA, as well as the Bureau of Alcohol, Tobacco, Firearms, and Explosives. More recently, in 2014, she began working for FinCEN (Financial Crimes Enforcement Network) in the US Department of the Treasury.

After a little more than a year, she grew concerned as she observed the US Treasury transitioning FinCEN employees to the Office of Intelligence and Analysis (I&A) within the Department of Homeland Security (DHS). This was troubling because there was a lack of congressional authorization throughout this equation. At first, this was specific to the movement of employees, but then something else caught Edwards's attention. I&A did not seem to have the right authorization in place to collect information, nor did she believe they were adhering to basic safeguards in doing so.

Why would they need authorization? Because they were specifically collecting information on people in the US—including American citizens. Similar to the story of Edward Snowden vs. PRISM (Planning Tool for Resource Integration, Synchronization, and Management), this environment and speculation inevitably boiled over.

Natalie Edwards blew the whistle, nationally, in 2017. On the record, she filed an internal whistleblower complaint, which is acknowledged. She also reached out to people in Congress; however, these attempts were not completely related to her final blow. After her efforts failed to inspire any corrections by her superiors, BuzzFeed journalist Jason Leopold entered the scene.

Over the course of their communications from October 2017 to October 2018, Edwards allegedly shared confidential information, including 18 years' worth of Suspicious Activity Reports (SARs). Originally, this material was used in the *BuzzFeed News* series, "The Money Trail," detailing financial movement and information within the suspected relationship between Donald Trump's political circle and Russia.

I find their use of "The Money Trail" strange, as they seemed to assume the "trail" was exclusive to the White House. While they managed to receive international data from 1999 to 2017, they initially kept their journalistic execution to a small pond—completely missing the big picture. One could surmise that BuzzFeed was attempting to reveal a "face" in their work implicating Trump, his family, and colleagues.

Eventually, they must have realized their angle was not leading to anything conclusive, as they followed suit on previous leaks by reaching out to the leak journalism experts: the ICIJ. Before going further into that, let's take a side-step. I should spend a little time on the details of FinCEN and Suspicious Activity Reports (SARs). You will see the great importance of this shortly.

When a financial institution begins to suspect any of their clients are planning, executing, or profiting from financial crimes, they submit SARs to the appropriate government branch (in this case, the US Department of the Treasury). Typically, SARs are prepared and sent by compliance officers who are often far from the action, working with minimal materials and research. These reports are then handled by respective financial crimes departments, and for the US Treasury, that's FinCEN.

FinCEN specifically gathers (and ideally investigates) information regarding money laundering, tax evasion, and even terrorist organizations/activity support. SARs are basically red flags for FinCEN, as opposed to evidence. And leaking this information is a criminal offense, as doing so can affect ongoing investigations or even reveal the identity of both FinCEN investigators and compliance officers.

Whether or not SARs instigate any kind of response (either reading or further investigating), financial institutions are required to fulfill appropriate actions on their side. From Natalie Edwards, BuzzFeed allegedly received 2,657 documents, and of those, 2,121 were SARs. Whether or not compliance officers or FinCEN investigators are limited, BuzzFeed took their analysis to the next level, combing through bank data and public records, unsealing information through federal courts and many uses of the Freedom of Information Act.

Eighty journalists from BuzzFeed and ICIJ were able to piece together 200,000+ transactions, as guided by information in each SAR. This involved diving into spreadsheets of bank information, examining the exact details of withdrawals and transfers, and overall, reviewing 2,942,000 words of SARs data and notes (more can be read about their method online).[94] In total, Natalie Edwards's 2,121 reports revealed more than $2 trillion in suspicious activity.

Yes, that's 2 trillion, as in 2 thousand billions, and 2 million millions.

A LITTLE TASTE OF THEIR FINDINGS ...

The journalists in action discovered the total number of organizations reported and arranged them by country. In this case, the UK and the US were the top two, and the UK took number one with 622 organizations tagged in SAR subject lines.

Organization Subject Locations

Country/Territory	# SARs
United Kingdom	622
United States	435
British Virgin Islands	423
Cyprus	328
Hong Kong	318
United Arab Emirates	278
Russia	267

In terms of individuals named in SAR subject lines, BuzzFeed/ICIJ found that 25 people or more were previously featured in *Forbes* billionaire list from 2018 to 2020. In this case, while the US and UK once again reached the top, the US was number one at 259 individuals mentioned, followed by Russia (121) and then the UK (45).

Person Subject Locations

Country/Territory	# SARs
United States	259
Russia	121

United Kingdom	45
China	33
Germany	24
United Arab Emirates	24
Canada	21
Ukraine	20

And the results are in for the highest amount of money reported by a financial institution in a single SAR. While JPMorgan Chase takes the number one slot, at $335 billion, Deutsche Bank appears most frequently on the following chart, comprising 60%. JPMorgan's three record-breakers account for a total of $492 billion. And Deutsche Bank's top six transactions account for $426 billion.

Largest SARS in FinCEN Files

Month Filed	Filer	Amount Flagged	Industry
Aug 2014	JPMorgan Chase	$335 billion	Precious metals
Aug 2014	Deutsche Bank	$111 billion	Finance
Oct 2013	Deutsche Bank	$94 billion	Precious metals
Apr 2016	JPMorgan Chase	$81 billion	Electronics
Aug 2014	JPMorgan Chase	$76 billion	Petroleum
Apr 2014	Deutsche Bank	$74 billion	Commodities
May 2013	Standard Chartered	$68 billion	Commodities
Jul 2013	Deutsche Bank	$61 billion	Petroleum
Oct 2014	Deutsche Bank	$45 billion	Finance
Nov 2014	Deutsche Bank	$41 billion	Petroleum

Seeing as Deutsche Bank was included in the above chart six times, it makes sense that they're number one for total number of SARs filed as well. At 982 SARs filed, they flagged $1.3 trillion. While JPMorgan Chase arrives in fourth place, the amount of money flagged technically puts them in second. At 107 SARs filed, $514 billion was flagged. And in truth, their top three SARs numbers account for the majority of that amount.

By these numbers, for Deutsche Bank, the average SAR flagged $1.3 billion. With their top six SARs in mind, the average is closer to $895.4 million. And for JPMorgan, the total SARs makes for a whopping average of $4.8 billion; however, with their top three SARs accounted for, the remaining average is closer to $211.5 million.

Number of SARs filed + Total $$$ Reported

Institution	**# SARs**	**Amount Flagged**
Deutsche Bank	982	$1.3 trillion
Bank of New York Mellon	325	$64 billion
Standard Chartered	232	$166 billion
JPMorgan Chase	107	$514 billion
Barclays	104	$21 billion
HSBC	73	$4.4 billion
Bank of China	35	$1.3 billion
Bank of America	35	$384 million
Wells Fargo	21	$57 million
Citibank	18	$251 million

What can we learn from all this?

There are still questions worth asking in this story. My research could not ascertain how many of these SARs were subsequently investigated by FinCEN. Of those, I could not identify how many investigations led to any indictment of any kind—or a conviction, for that matter. Were any financial executives held responsible?

Natalie Edwards pled guilty for leaking FinCEN information in 2020, and her maximum sentence could be up to five years. There was some gossip circulating the internet that she'd go through a retrial in 2021. As of June 2021, according to the Department of Justice, she was sentenced to six months in prison, followed by three years of supervised release.[95]

For the banks, some of the information revealed by Edwards was previously addressed. According to their representatives, they were already in the motions of improving their systems and their behavior. Whether or not that improvement is real or gaining momentum, I guess we'll see.

As I've argued throughout Part II of this book, I believe our focus should be on improving legislative and regulatory models and processes. At the end of BuzzFeed's "FinCEN Files Explainer," they point out the limitations surrounding our current reporting system. To date, FinCEN requires no spreadsheets to be provided by the banks filing a SAR. And the details that would be on hand if this provision were a requirement would likely make the next step much easier to accomplish. They quoted Peter Djinis, who was one of the FinCEN analysts who set up the original SAR system:

> There's nothing of greater value than being able to take a look at a series of wire transfers or a series of deposits or a series of withdrawals ... All of that information is so useful.

As BuzzFeed, ICIJ, and even Wikipedia are not hesitant to share, there were more than 2 million SARs filed over 2019, following the leak in 2018. Unfortunately, over the last decade, FinCEN's staff remains in decline, dropping under 90% capacity in 2019. Not only is the system flawed, it doesn't have enough investigators available to do what needs to be done. It's been said that the effort involved with security clearance approval is part of the problem. In the meantime, supposedly, FinCEN employs contractors to assist in SAR analysis.

At this point, it seems like the powers that be have designed an elderly penguin to do the job of a hawk, while calling it a bald eagle. FinCEN looks like it can fly, but the support required for it to simply slide down the hill appears to be draining with time. Was the system intentionally designed to *not* be an effective legislative/regulatory framework? Or is this an example of political incompetence?

In either case, without the risk taken by Natalie Edwards in leaking the information, and without the extra effort provided by journalists across the globe, no institution or executive would have been exposed—let alone, potentially held accountable. While institutions can report suspicious activity, lack of requirements on spreadsheets and further data resulted in an impotent and ineffective process. FinCEN investigators are drowning and will continue to drown in a deluge of SARs—and for any they might process, they remain incapable of effectively investigating such reports any further.

NURTURING THE PENGUIN

Is it possible that legislators with the final say in formulating this lame duck of a regulatory model wanted something that would showcase a success story? A system that can catch some fish but not one that can catch the big fish?

In the West, we pride ourselves on a process called public–private partnership (PPP). This is when government players and sector stakeholders work collaboratively to ensure new legislation/regulation is conducive to the sector, while allowing the government to govern it. For most industries/sectors, governments don't have respective experts on staff, and being laissez-faire advocates, they would never dream of hindering innovation—so they lean on the professionals. While such partnership can be good, it is important to recognize when it becomes a detriment.

PPP essentially leads to business owners, CEOs, lobbyists, and other private leaders offering criticism throughout the drafting and formation of regulation. As these are the same stakeholders contributing to political campaigns—some of them contributing enough to make or break careers and outcomes—this makes for high-risk development. The end result of these interactions are policies and models that don't piss the wrong people off.

While the majority of sectors can agree that monitoring the financial sector for terrorist activity is important, there are clearly plenty who would still like to keep a few doors open for their own—or for their friends' and relatives'—money laundering, tax evasion, and offshore banking. Depending on the wording of policy and the limits of regulation, these actions remain legal until an actual hawk/eagle replaces the penguin sliding down the mountain. We should be asking all kinds of questions, but for now, I will limit myself to a few:

> **Question #1:** How involved were business sector leaders, players, and lobbyists in the process of developing and proposing all things FinCEN and SAR?
>
> **Question #2:** How much of the resulting model was contributed specifically by banking sector players lobbying industry-led "best practices" and "stronger" self-regulation?

Obviously, the concocted framework allowed more than $2 trillion of SAR activity to move unchecked for 18 years. And it took an alleged whistleblower jeopardizing her life (and that of her family) and an international journalism co-op digging through neglected details to expose a huge wrong. This brings me to my third question ...

Question #3: Isn't this the job of our regulators?

For more information, please visit survivabilitythebook.com/ placeholder (or scan the code below) to see articles referenced as well as my recommended reading list. We have been very lucky to have journalists with integrity on the case. I encourage you to explore how the world received this story.

Specific to this chapter, you will also find more regarding MLi Group's National Cyber-Survivability™ Strategies (including a Legislative Road Map).

21

A Broken System, Part B

(Corrupt Leadership . . . and the Bush Doctrine Lives On)

BY THE END of 2006, after President George W. Bush pushed for global focus on pandemics in order to save lives domestically, the Pandemic and All-Hazards Preparedness Act (PAHPA) was passed. As I shared in Chapter 18, while efforts against Ebola were a bipartisan decision, anything regarding the future did not capture the full attention of the Senate and Congress. Nor did the topic appear to appease lobbyists and special interest, even through Barack Obama's term.

PAHPA itself remained a somewhat sore subject until 2019. When it was introduced for renewal to the Senate in 2013, it did not receive a full vote; however, the same legislation was passed in the House, and later signed by President Obama. It was a similar story in 2018, when updates were also required beyond reauthorization, which led to the creation of the Pandemic and All-Hazards Preparedness and Advancing Innovation Act (PAHPAI). Once again, the bill failed to receive a full vote in the Senate.

While it was later approved by the House, both PAHPA and PAHPAI were considered dead after Congress completed its 115th term. However, after the first quarter of the 116th Congress, PAHPAI received President Trump's signature on June 13, 2019. At first look, PAHPAI appears to continue President Bush's original goal; however, it also appears to be incomplete.

On first impression, one might think the act is off to a great start. Title I involves the National Health Security Strategy (NHSS).[96] It provides a vision to strengthen our nation's ability to *prevent, detect, assess, prepare for, mitigate, respond to, and recover from disasters and emergencies.* It describes strategies to improve readiness and adapt operational capabilities to address new and evolving threats. By coordinating a whole-of-government approach that engages external partners and supports public health authorities and health care stakeholders, we can better safeguard the health and well-being of people across the country.

Beyond Title I, littered throughout the remaining titles, you'll find the phrase "requires a report," or even the completion of a "guidance," which means there were/are next steps to be finished by the government. In an actual pandemic, so much is happening at breakneck speed that we don't have the luxury of the usual five to ten years it takes to develop plans. PAHPAI is the result of our leaders chewing the cud of PAHPA, mulling it over for over 15 years. That's a zero deliverable, considering the unfinished quality of the outcome.

Look for yourself (try Wikipedia[97]). But just knowing that legislation was put in place by our government, how was the overall coordination of the preparedness throughout COVID-19? How was the coordination between the federal administration and state governors? Between state and their local administrations?

Even through the diagnosis of President Trump himself, COVID response is still lacking. How many times have you heard the performance of governments around the world described as an "unprecedented failure"? In my experience, throughout pandemic coverage, this phrase was repeated on every news network at least a dozen times a day.

At that, it was not as if there was any lack of red flags or early warning. Outside of anything direct, in my mind, two events concluded that governments were not prepared for the events of 2020—both of which were simulations of flu outbreaks.

1. Exercise Cygnus (UK, 2016)[98][99]
2. Event 201 (US, 2019)[100]

EXERCISE CYGNUS

Nearly four years before COVID-19 and its effects, the British government ran a three-day flu outbreak simulation. Over the course of those 72 hours, they fought a "worst-case scenario" in which 50% of the population were affected (400,000 deaths, for reference). In the interest of specificity, nearly 1,000 government officials participated, as did prisons, emergency response planners, and NHS organizations. After the fictitious death toll reached up to 400,000, nearly half the entire world was affected.

The Cygnus Report stated, "The UK's preparedness and response, in terms of its plans, policies and capability, is currently not sufficient to cope with the extreme demands of a severe pandemic that will have a nationwide impact across all sectors." This validated the concerns of US presidents Bush and Obama, as Cygnus findings showed that UK resource distribution was indeed a problem: "The lack of joint tactical level plans was evidenced when the scenario demand for services outstripped the capacity of local responders, in the areas of excess deaths, social care and the NHS."

Beyond issues regarding oversight, and lack thereof, organizations were attempting to communicate and coordinate with discontinued services and others that were no longer available—plans were clearly out of date. The government kept the report under lock and key without offering any reasoning for doing so. A redacted version of the report was released in May 2020 by *The Guardian*, and officials claimed that it was kept secret due to its influence on new policy and strategies.

Through the majority of 2020, UK officials were still facing legal action to release the Cygnus Report in full. As of October 12, 2020, the Information Commissioner's Office announced an order for the Department of Health and Social Care to release the unpublished report. If they chose not to, the department was required to explain the decision behind withholding it by October 22.

The "official" suggestion is that the health secretary, Matt Hancock, is the decision maker responsible for delaying any release of the report.[101]

In response to the Information Commissioner's Office (Freedom of Information Act 2000 [FOIA] Decision Notice) the following communication was included from the DHSC:

> DHSC has been awaiting Ministerial opinion on a submission provided. As you will probably be aware, this relates to leaked material and is extremely sensitive. We are unable to respond until the Secretary of State for Health and Social Care is satisfied and, understandably, are not able to determine when this will be. We would certainly consider this to be an exceptional circumstance under which the Department would continue to PIT extend until a Ministerial verdict on our submission is granted ...
>
> ... We have used the lessons learned from Exercise Cygnus to rapidly respond to this unprecedented global crisis. This included being ready with legislative proposals that were the initial basis of the Coronavirus Act 2020, planning for recruitment and deployment of retired staff and volunteers, and improving plans to flex systems and expand beyond normal NHS capacity levels.

Four years late, and the actions referenced by Hancock were after the pandemic began, not in preparation. The final grade, in my book, would be an F for both effort and responsibility. I leave it to your imagination why a government would hide such results for four years, and why they would continue doing so. The same goes for any curiosity surrounding FinCEN and the SARs leaked by Natalie Edwards (see Chapter 20).

Nevertheless, this event provided UK leaders ample warning. Their government claimed that necessary steps were taken to mitigate a potential catastrophe. And yet, with more than 43,000 dead and almost 600,000 infected, at the time of their statement, indications showed that their COVID-19 response was disastrous and the total opposite of their claim.

EVENT 201

More recently, in October 2019, the Johns Hopkins Center for Health Security organized and hosted a simulation of their own. Participants worked toward determining the efficiency of public/private health bodies working with national governments through a "pandemic," demonstrating gaps in preparedness along with elements of solutions between the public and private sectors necessary to fill any demonstrated gaps. Two months before the very real COVID-19 outbreak, starting in Wuhan,

China, Event 201 saw a shocking 65 million people killed within 18 months.

Within six simulated months, there were cases in every country on the planet. Travel and tourism were ruined, and humanity entered a global financial crisis. Does that sound familiar to you? It's eerie how this mirrored reality within such a short period of time.

Event 201 resulted in the following recommendations:[102]

1. Governments, international organizations, and businesses should plan now for how essential corporate capabilities will be utilized during a large-scale pandemic.
2. Industry, national governments, and international organizations should work together to enhance internationally held stockpiles of medical countermeasures (MCMs) to enable rapid and equitable distribution during a severe pandemic.
3. Countries, international organizations, and global transportation companies should work together to maintain travel and trade during severe pandemics.
4. Governments should provide more resources and support for the development and surge manufacturing of vaccines, therapeutics, and diagnostics that will be needed during a severe pandemic.
5. Global business should recognize the economic burden of pandemics and fight for stronger preparedness.
6. International organizations should prioritize reducing economic impacts of epidemics and pandemics.
7. Governments and the private sector should assign a greater priority to developing methods to combat mis- and disinformation prior to the next pandemic response.

In contrast to Cygnus—in which the UK government dragged its feet for four years, requiring its Information Commissioner's Office (ICO) to intervene in 2020 to force it to publish its test findings—at least Event 201's results were published soon after completing the table-top exercise. The resulting recommendations are just dandy. Who could possibly argue against them? And for those who might argue that they would have needed time for implementation, rightly so. However, history teaches us that while recommendations do get submitted, substantial action seldom follows.

PANDEMIC PUDDING?

President George W. Bush and President Barack Obama both set out strategies and dedicated millions to billions of dollars to deal with the threat of a global pandemic. Their strategies became academic processes that failed disastrously when COVID-19 hit the world. The proof of the pudding was found in the immediate impact of its arrival.

Do you really think the US government would have done anything differently if Event 201's recommendations were instead received in 2016?

As established, our systems and models are designed for very little real change to happen. The Trump administration was happy to divert the blame for COVID response to Obama's presidency, and the democratic party was happy to continue keeping it on Donald's lap. The reality is that both parties failed US citizens.

Obama had three years to replenish stockpiles of necessary resources after reauthorizing PAHPA in 2013. And Trump had three years after stepping into power. As established in Chapter 18, Obama pushed for an increase in budgeting for pandemic preparedness and received a fraction of what he said was needed.

Left to bipartisan politics, the empty cupboard Trump repeatedly mentions remained unreplenished, and the usual "party" paid the ultimate price—the American people. Both US political parties are failing, and this is the consequence of a broken system. All the while, the stage four cancer of democracy continues to metastasize and worsen, and citizens continue singing in their dissonant choir.

REAL HAWKS IN THE FLOCK

In January 2020, presidential candidate Tulsi Gabbard sued Hillary Clinton for $50 million over her "Russian asset" remark, for defamatory statements, claiming Clinton was making a deliberate attempt to derail Gabbard's presidential campaign. As a war veteran, Gabbard was running her campaign on ending the perpetual US wars and bringing our troops back home. This was in contrast to the years of Clinton's position during her time as Secretary of State under the Obama administration as well as her US presidential candidacy in 2016.

It seems that Gabbard dealt a serious blow to Kamala Harris's presidential campaign long before Harris was selected as vice president. What many people may not know is that Harris is Hillary Clinton's protégé. After Clinton lost to President Donald Trump in 2016, she passed most of her resources, Rolodex contacts, and top donors to Harris. They already had a close connection through Maya Harris (Kamala's sister), who was one of the main advisors for Hillary Clinton's campaign, structuring and choreographing Clinton's 2016 platform.

Kamala Harris also inherited Clinton's foreign policy advisory team, most important of which is a woman by the name of Michèle Flournoy. During Obama's presidency, Flournoy was the Undersecretary of Defense. She also worked for the Bill Clinton administration. More crucially, in 2007, Flournoy became the founder and CEO of a think tank called Center for New American Security (CNAS). This is where the picture starts getting very troubling. Flournoy founded CNAS right at the end of President George W. Bush's last term, and their mission was to influence future presidents and administrations.

While Harris did inherit quite a few other foreign policy advisors from Clinton, Flournoy and CNAS should hold your attention. By 2020, CNAS already mastered a model for infiltrating successive US presidents and administrations and influencing their American foreign policy visions, strategies, agendas, and plans. They successfully gathered top Republican and Democrat figures like General David H. Petraeus, James Clapper, and many others of the George Bush Jr. and Reagan administrations.

To be frank, their "nonpartisan" approach was genius. With the added guise of being unbiased and politically neutral, their recommendations were rendered more receptive to both parties and whoever ends up in the Oval Office. Most notably, CNAS advocated and promoted the Bush Doctrine, which asserts that it is acceptable to strike another country if the administration believes they are a threat to the US—even if it contradicts UN charters.

As established at the end of Chapter 17, this doctrine led to launching the global war on terror, spreading from Afghanistan to Iraq. If you recall, in the latter, it did not take long for it to be revealed that the US and UK governments fabricated proof regarding Saddam Hussein's weapons of mass destruction. And yet, CNAS's influence was so significant that Obama hired several employees for key jobs. So much for "real change" coming to America. Michèle Flournoy became Undersecretary of

Defense for Policy, and her cofounder, Kurt Campbell, served as Assistant Secretary of State for East Asian and Pacific Affairs.

In essence, CNAS and its former employees were exceptionally successful in maintaining the Bush administration's hawkish, invasionist, and warmongering policy under Obama. Later, they may have been one of the parties responsible for undermining Trump's promise to withdraw US soldiers from Syria, Iraq, and Afghanistan. You may recall the way he was second-guessed by the Pentagon and various security agencies upon stepping into office.

Another organization of concern was introduced at the end of Chapter 19. The American Israel Public Affairs Committee (AIPAC) is a lobbying group advocating pro-Israel policies to Congress and the Executive Branch of the United States. Claiming over 100,000 members, AIPAC has more than enough donors to continue their agenda. Interestingly, the group itself does not raise funds for political candidates; however, its members raise money for them through political action committees unaffiliated with AIPAC.

Some have characterized AIPAC as an agent of the Israeli government. US Representative Ilhan Omar fell through a rabbit hole of clarification attempts after addressing Israel's hypnotism of the world. While facing conflict against other representatives, she drew attention to how AIPAC's influence made it seem like she needed to pledge allegiance to two countries, not just the US. As of 2019, it became criminal to criticize Israeli action or policy, which means the US continued its support of the ethos of the ultra-hard-line position of then Prime Minister Benjamin Netanyahu even after he left office. Netanyahu has always been an unapologetic implementer of the Bush Doctrine. He was replaced as PM by Naftali Bennett in 2021.

As we approach the end of my book, I want you to think about how our democratic system continues allowing special-interest players like CNAS and AIPAC to spread their influence. Think about CNAS's rise to power. It went from obscurity under President Bush to having multiple members placed throughout the Obama administration (and they've been waiting for the door to open once again). Think about US politicians' efforts to appease AIPAC. We have gone so far as to make it illegal for anyone to vocalize so much as simple disagreement with Israeli actions (see NBC's apology after anti-Semitic claims against *Saturday Night Live*'s Michael Che on February 20, 2021, yet another example of anti-populism).

Special interest's ability to influence is contributing to (if not causing) the demise of our cherished democracy. I believe CNAS, AIPAC, and other organizations like them are responsible for the world remaining three meals from anarchy. Why? you might ask.Their goals and influence maintain the failed status quo, which means we are stuck and further depleting.

CNAS is mostly funded by the military-industrial complex (MIC). CNAS's major donors are Northrop Grumman, Boeing, Raytheon, Lockheed Martin, along with big tech and security firms. All of these players have great vested interest in maintaining and further gaining large defense and security contracts from the US administration—especially the Pentagon. CNAS and its funders are surgically influencing successive US presidents and administrations to keep wars going that do not serve the interest of American citizens.

Whose interest do these wars serve? In part, these wars contribute to MIC profits and company share values—which only further enable CNAS to increase their influence and power through other lobbying activities. As long as their donors have cause for contracts, manufacturing, and respective services, CNAS continues to receive funding.

Meanwhile, as Israel receives multiple billions in US aid and other forms of assistance, that funding recycles directly through the MIC's inventory. AIPAC doesn't just represent a foreign ally; it represents one of our top buyers of weapons and defense manufacturing. For guaranteed fresh revenues, every presidential candidate will kiss the ring long before stepping into office. And that includes Trump. In fact, Benjamin Netanyahu himself was the mastermind behind four of Trump's presidential actions:

1. The overpromised wall between the US and Mexico was inspired by the one Netanyahu constructed between Israelis and Palestinians—on Palestinian land no less.[103]
2. US exiting the UN Iran deal—which the EU, Britain, China, and Russia also signed and remained committed to.
3. Recent peace agreements between Israel, UAE, Bahrain, Morocco, Sudan, and other Arab/oil nations.[104]
4. Trump's "deal of the century," which was meant to provide security to Israel's borders while providing nothing to Palestinians,

especially, in the form of permanent annexation of their occupied territories.

Essentially, Trump's deal empowered Netanyahu in claiming land obtained through warfare (against the UN Charter). For nearly two decades, Israel was already building settlements at the cost of further displacing Palestinians. Such actions took place while AIPAC continued securing weapons and defense and while Israel continued launching MIC provisions on a besieged Gaza (once again, against UN resolutions).

The Palestinian National Authority and all other Palestinian factions rejected Trump's deal and peace agreements outright. EU nations and other US allies voiced their criticisms, but it was AIPAC's influence that kept US politicians in driver mode. And US support allows Israel to get away with disproportionate responses and with murder under the label of "self-defense"—especially when said defense involves US weapons manufacturing.

As explained over the course of Part III, the US has personally been involved in the perpetual war on terror since at least the 1980s. All costs associated with this seemingly infinite conflict come at the expense of the wants and cares of its citizens. And it appears that crimes against humanity are not enough for them to relinquish their support. Despite Trump's promises and Obama's timely marketing on "change," we did not see true reduction in the warring activities of Syria and Iraq. Both escalated and the US maintained its number of troops.

For any readers embracing the idea that the actions and results of populism are exclusive to the leaders exampled in Chapter 19, I implore you to reexamine the impact of Western leadership. US leadership especially requires our consideration, as it appears to be the most captured by special-interest groups. We expect US leaders to represent the US people, showing moral leadership to the world. Therefore, I believe the impact of a captured US leader is higher than capturing any leader of a banana republic. We expect corruption from tyrants and despots. The world looks to America for hope and justice; perpetual US corruption undermines that cause.

And for any readers operating under the assumption that corruption of this sort ends with the arrival of President Biden, think again. Please recall the hawkish presence lingering in our government through Vice President Kamala Harris. CNAS will have more of a foothold than the last four years, and the MIC will likely benefit from that. AIPAC will yet again arrange for another ceremonial kissing of the ring, and the MIC will maintain their business.

The 46th presidency will be cloaked by the same hope of Obama's campaign, intertwined with "decency" and "humanity." It will be haunted by the same repercussions, as well as the same foreign interventionism of Trump's policies. The perpetual war continues, and it will likely be labeled as "progress." We must not allow ourselves to take hold of the false sense of security offered by our leaders in transition. It's the same old world, and the same geopolitical motivations—just a rebranding of the "hope" offered 12 long years ago.

RED FLAGS OF FAILURE

Returning to FinCEN, from Chapter 20, unlike JFK's assassination, this most recent leak seemed incapable of capturing the attention of citizens as to the corruption spanning from 1999 to 2017 under the watchful eye of Western officials. Ironically, everything exposed from the leaks have an even more direct impact and consequence on our lives. There are leaders and bad actors who need to be brought to justice; this will never happen while they remain involved with the constitutionality, legality, inner workings, and functionality of processes.

With so many fingers pointing around the room and deflecting blame, resolution is caught in an eternal whirlwind. Without a singular mugshot, without an identified perpetrator, it's no wonder that this story and other stories like it fizzle from the eyes of the world. And yet, a Kardashian rear end spans international and infinite.

Implementing change through a common enemy is as ancient as the second oldest profession (politics). In early 2021, a new mugshot appeared to be shared around the world. While some readers/viewers might feel they finally have an Oswald for the corruption exposed by multiple leaks, and frankly, for 2020 itself, the following train of thought clarifies nothing as to the "assassination" of ourselves. For the *Times* article "Growing Risk of Attacks as World Order Crumbles," at Porton Down, they interviewed UK Secretary of Defense Ben Wallace at the Defence Science and Technology Laboratory.

On the topic of current global threats, he said the following:[105]

> Globally, I think there is a growing threat of chemical or biological (attack). ... It depends on what is at hand for people using the internet. ... It is unfortunately what happens in a sort of *breakdown of world order* where you see countries like Syria use it on its own people ... There has been a worry that some states think it is acceptable to use that type of method to carry out or further their aims. (emphasis mine)

His interview referenced both the 2018 poisoning of Sergei and Yulia Skripal by the Russian military in Salisbury, Wiltshire (United Kingdom), as well as the chemical attack in Syria. I believe a better question to ask Mr. Wallace is, "When the Skripals were poisoned, did that contribute to the breakdown of world order?"

The answer is No.

And how about the alleged chemical attack in Syria he referenced? Did that contribute to said breakdown of world order?

Again, the answer is No. Attributing the breakdown to these events and other cyberattacks is a falsehood. Perhaps Wallace should read further into FinCEN, the Paradise Papers, the Panama Papers, and other ICIJ adventures.

Currently, I think we can all agree that Wallace's breakdown of world order is due to COVID-19. And the worldwide incompetent responses to COVID-19 are due to the now exposed frailty and injustice of Western financial/democratic models and systems—along with elected leaders of Western governments and their failure to safeguard the needs of citizens and the economy. Headlines following Wallace's interview already started spinning new narratives that quite nearly admit the current condition of humanity, while feeding the echo chamber.

- From *The Independent* (UK): "Threat of chemical and biological attacks on the rise as *world order crumbles*, defence secretary warns" (emphasis mine)
- *Daily Mail* (UK): "Chemical attacks more likely as *world order collapses*, minister warns" (emphasis mine)
- *Metro* (UK): "UK faces growing risk of chemical and biological attack after '*world order breakdown*'" (emphasis mine)

Some publishers, such as *Express* (UK), did not keep Wallace's coin of phrase: "UK at risk: 'Growing threat of chemical or biological attack' amid *soaring global tension*." (emphasis mine) And as the story spread further across the globe, the key phrase faded from focus, and all that remained is a particular threat. Publishers such as Yahoo! MSN, and many others kept it simple:

"Threat of international chemical attacks is on the rise, warns Wallace"

For those referencing the breakdown, on one hand, admitting the problem is a good thing. We are currently experiencing a breakdown of world order. On the other hand, they are allowing this to be attributed to the usual scapegoats/enemies, such as the internet itself, as well as China, Russia, Syria, etc. Purely within the headlines and associations, this is a classic case of misleading readers/citizens.

While some of these countries and other bad actors may have plenty to answer for, they most certainly are not responsible for the breakdown of world order. This is squarely on the shoulders of Western leaders and the democratic systems they represent. As if our own leaders played no part in the failures revealed by 2020.

Don't get caught in the hype.

Just as we have now received red flags and crisis warnings from the travesty of this new decade, our leaders were informed of the same flaws and detriments. Our disadvantage is that we aren't looking at the results of an intimate table-top game. We are looking at reality, corruption, casualties, and loss.

The UK specifically received their warning nearly four years in advance of COVID's arrival. Exercise Cygnus showed them where they needed to improve their systems and organization. What did they do with this information?

They "buried the lede" until they were legally forced to share the truth.

Again, the US received their warning less than a month before any trace of the pandemic emerged. Event 201 was hosted at the very end of 2019. Up to that point, pandemic preparations were neglected to a series of bipartisan volleys for 14 years. Left to their own devices, US leaders allowed the protection, safety, and well-being of citizens to remain incomplete from 2006 to 2020.

In 2006, Bush wanted a strategy to protect US citizens and people around the world. Two presidents later, after the evolution of PAHPA to PAHPAI, any hope of being prepared was tarnished by "requires a report," and "requires the government to finish writing a 'guidance.'" While there was a framework in place, this wasn't even the bare minimum of what the strategy required. This result is either due to incompetence or profit-focused ignorance.

We are living the horrors of table-top epics. From the leaks uncovered by ICIJ to the failings of our own leaders amidst COVID-19's tyranny, we are receiving a variety of red flags. A common denominator across these narratives is a lack of oversight. Is that lack accidental? Or is it by design? In either case, we are looking at an ongoing, not so early warning.

When President Joe Biden began his transition into power, people seemed to be of the belief that this would mark the end of our crumbling world order. But before you start rejoicing that a better tomorrow is here, best you realize the following. President Biden, Vice President Harris, their cabinet members, and their allies are simply the next wave of badge-laden lapels. And while those badges are intended to represent the holy trinity of legitimacy, legality, and authority, these have been repurposed into shelter and fog machines.

The powers that be will continue relabeling the post–COVID-19 world in a way that will maintain them in control. This cannot be accomplished without the admission that our current system is breaking down or already broken, which people all over the world already believe to be the case. Leaders are simply appeasing their constituents by acknowledging some kind of breakdown, while they spin new narratives and fears to avoid taking ownership of their failures. Nor will they voluntarily usher in real change to fix the root cause of the problem.

Current systems do not allow the people to effectively hold their leaders accountable for failed policies and actions. Systems need to be improved and leaderships need to be overhauled. In either case, we will not have a better post–COVID-19 world unless we find a way to break the cycle. Currently, the relay race exchange of badges provides ongoing shelter for corrupt politicians while they serve special interest and their own lifestyles/aspirations over the citizen.

Since early 2020, I've said many times that the world before 2019 will never return as we knew it. As important as finding who the responsible party is, we should also be asking what kind of world order we will end up with. What kind of a society do we want our children and their children to grow up in? One that serves a failed status quo, or one that serves the citizen first, and above all?

Are we to remain continuous observers of our own tragedy?

Or do we want to help bring about a better reality?

How do we do that peacefully?[106]

2020 HINDSIGHT IN THE UK

October 12, 2021. A damning report by UK House of Commons inquiry finds the UK government's early handling and belief in "herd immunity" led to further deaths during the COVID-19 pandemic. The report, "Coronavirus: Lessons Learned to Date," involved more than 50 witnesses. The list of those involved included the former health secretary, chief scientific/medical advisers for the UK government, along with key individuals involved with vaccines, testing, and tracing.

Readers should recall the 2016 Cygnus simulation from the beginning of the chapter and how the results illustrated that the NHS would fail on multiple levels; it was identified that current systems would fail in the face of a hypothetical pandemic. Lessons were intended to have been learned and improvements implemented, and yet, when the pandemic struck in early 2020, the results were seen by all of humanity.

> We must conclude that no formal evaluation took place, which amounts to an extraordinary and negligent omission given [South] Korea's success in containing the pandemic, which was well publicised at the time ...

The damning House of Commons report includes recommendations and lessons learned as well as a scathing reprimand of Boris Johnson's government and its handling of the pandemic. Included in the summary were the following points:

- The forward-planning, agility and decisive organization of the vaccine development and deployment effort will save millions of lives globally and should be a guide to future government practice;
- The delays in establishing an adequate test, trace, and isolate system hampered efforts to understand and contain the outbreak and it failed in its stated purpose to avoid lockdowns;

- The initial decision to delay a comprehensive lockdown—despite practice elsewhere in the world—reflected a fatalism about the spread of COVID that should have been robustly challenged at the time;
- Social care was not given sufficient priority in the early stages of the pandemic;
- The experience of the COVID pandemic underlines the need for an urgent and long-term strategy to tackle health inequalities; and
- The UK's preparedness for a pandemic had been widely acclaimed in advance but performed less well than many other countries in practice.

What can we conclude from this official report? With real clarity, it tells me that the current UK establishment is ready to throw the kitchen sink at Boris Johnson and his presiding government—basting a sacrificial lamb to be given as a peace offering to the people in order to preserve the status quo. In essence, this report is an attempt for the broken system to safeguard itself by trading heads rolling for public grace.

If we lacked any further proof of a broken system that is incapable of delivering real change, the report above is it. A committee chaired by the ruling Conservative Party in the UK has officially condemned its own government for its monumental failure in handling the pandemic from the beginning. There is a question readers must now ask themselves. PR-inspired tweaks and pandering statements aside, are we to expect real change to come out of this? I don't know about you, but I'm not holding my breath.

You can find more information at committees.parliament.uk!

UNCOMPROMISING CHANGE

I believe there is real hope in the actions of active, engaged, and mobilized people. We are the manipulated domino piece awaiting the right time to fall. Before any change to world order takes place, it's imperative that citizens participate in current corrupt systems; once they're inside it, they can aim to change it—not tweak it. The alternative is changing it from the outside, which usually involves destructive means.

Current Western leadership needs to recognize that they cannot maintain the status quo while keeping power indefinitely, as this will lead to the destruction of their own system. When Biden says we need to come together, he is not talking about ushering global unity; he's talking about aligning Americans in support of his plans/approach/strategies, serving him and his masters. This is where we need to be careful.

Get in. Participate. But push for real and uncompromising change.

Gone are the days in which we can simply settle for symbolic measures. Left to its own devices, the system will keep producing the same leaders and same results. Left to their own agendas, our leaders will continue turning people into slaves of the 21st-century pharaohs.

For more information, please visit survivabilitythebook.com/ placeholder (or scan the code below) to see articles referenced as well as my recommended reading list. We have been very lucky to have journalists with integrity on the case. I encourage you to explore how the world received this story.

Specific to this chapter, you will also find more regarding MLi Group's Chief Survivability Officer™, as well as recruitment and training.

REAL HOPE

(Survivability Must Become the New Priority Focus, or Else ...)

There's a shared responsibility, not just across government agencies but across the private sector and even the average American.

—FBI Director Christopher Wray

AS I BRING *Survivability* to a close, I want to call two key stories to your attention: (1) the timely words of FBI Director Christopher Wray in spring 2021, and (2) the events surrounding OPEC in 2020. You might wonder why and how these stories are related. Well, as you will soon see, I believe they will help encapsulate the case as to why unprecedented Geo-Poli-Cyber™ (GPCyber™) attacks will continue getting eclipsed and outdone by even more unprecedented attacks and events—to the detriment of the citizen.

Wray's words and OPEC's actions illustrate a new reality most are not seeing with clarity. Added to unfortunate ignorance, when we the citizens are told something, we must improve our ability to determine if it is fact, spin, or fiction. This will lead to all of us asking better questions as to why the state of our respective regulatory affairs are in such a state of shambles.

In June 2021, *The Wall Street Journal* (WSJ) published an interview with FBI Director Wray, "FBI Director Compares Ransomware Challenge to 9/11." Wray's words spread across the media like wildfire. In particular, the following quote struck a chord with the world, regarding the recent challenges of ransomware and those posed by the 9/11 attacks:[107]

> There are a lot of parallels, there's a lot of importance, and a lot of focus by us on disruption and prevention. ... There's a shared responsibility, not just across government agencies but across the private sector and even the average American.

Publishers followed WSJ's suit and the following headlines caught the eyes of many citizens:

- The *New York Times*: "F.B.I. Director Compares Danger of Ransomware to 9/11 Terror Threat"
- *Fox News Business*: "FBI Director Chris Wray Compares Ransomware Attacks to 9/11"
- *The Guardian*: "FBI Director Sees 'Parallels' between Ransomware Threat and 9/11"
- The *Washington Post*: "The Biden Administration Seeks to Rally Allies and the Private Sector against the Ransomware Threat"

With regard to *The Washington Post*'s headline, I'll circle back to that. Meanwhile, Wray's remarks are timely with discussions regarding how we need to treat ransomware like terrorism is an incomplete fact. His comparison to 9/11 is raising an alarm to a portion of the truth. We need the whole truth, and nothing but the truth, so help us all, God.

I would compare the current state of this discussion to ignorant claims of saying violence in the home is the reason why marriages break up. Violence at home may be one of the reasons for marriage breakup; however, giving the impression that violence in the home is the only or the main reason for marriage breakups would be gravely misleading. I think the same can be said about Director Wray's words. This is because significantly more than ransomware must be equated to terrorism.

More importantly, Wray's warning is also ten years late. And I believe although his reality-check revelation may be very sincere, it is misleading and incomplete. Equally worrisome is that it proves two things:

1. An utter failure of our current national cyber security regulatory framework touted as gospel and followed by governments worldwide
2. A systemic failure in leadership by successive US administrations, and democratic and legislative models

I will always try to remain respectful, but let's not confuse bluntness and straight talk with disrespect. The following questions are what I want you to ask yourself as the discussion surrounding Wray's words and ransomware continues and expands:

- By specifically focusing on ransomware needing to be treated like terrorism, what is Wray's position on cyberattacks that never demanded a ransom?
- What is his position on the hacks of Equifax, Yahoo!, and Marriott's Starwood?
- How about the breach of The White House's *ultrasecure* communications in 2020, the brain of the greatest empire on the planet?
- If ransom is not the endgame, what is Wray's direction on how to mitigate these ever-growing and unprecedented attacks that threaten national stability, the economy, and security?
- Is the plan bigger cyber security budgets and "better" implementations of the recommended cyber security "best practices"?

None of the cyberattacks above had any ransom demands. As explained in Parts I and II of this book, in some cases the compromised/stolen data was never offered for sale on the Dark Web. So, clearly the motivation was not simply financial but something else more sinister. And in the case of Yahoo!, Equifax, and Marriott, the hackers were in the system monitoring data flow unnoticed and unhindered for years.

Neither the FBI nor other US government agencies have provided any significantly different or improved guidance on how to mitigate nonransom-demanding cyberattacks. Yet, the continued policy pattern seems to remain focused on voluntarily following "best practices." This cannot stand. Truth and facts need to be told. Stakeholders need to come to terms with how to mitigate all types of ever-growing threats. Above all, we need a significantly better regulatory framework than what we have now to protect the nation-state and all its stakeholders—including businesses and people (as citizens first and as consumers second).

Consider that ten years ago, the MLi Group and I identified and predicted the very threat Wray is warning about. It was part of a new, larger wave of cyberattacks that will debilitate and destroy businesses and economies, and devastate national security. This led me to create the MLi Group terms Poli-Cyber™ and Geo-Poli-Cyber™ (GPCyber™) in 2012 and 2013, respectively, in order to distinguish them from traditional cyberattacks that have been predominantly financially motivated. Not only that, but we went one step further by creating survivability strategies, solutions, and processes to upscale existing cyber security strategies and solutions. I predicted long ago that the existing "best practices" will fail. And they have been—on unprecedented scales.

This is not to say, "I told you so." This is more to say that I could identify, predict, and begin creating mitigation strategies, solutions, and services a decade ago. I have been able to improve on them with the help of very few but very smart people and team members I brought in and trained. And since we are not the only smart people around, nor are we endowed with the biggest budgets or privileged access, how is it that those who are much smarter than me (and my people) and who hold high ranks in high offices, and who have budgets in the billions of dollars, hardly scratched the surface?

I do not doubt there are much smarter people around than me. This is what makes me wonder why global leaders and decision makers are still peddling out-of-date strategies, policies, solutions, and narratives to existential threats. How are they not offering better ways that can truly and effectively mitigate these threats?

Remember Chapter 2, in which I said, "If you cannot name the threat, you cannot mitigate the threat." Well, by now you know what constitutes GPCyber™ motivated threats. Do you not think the ransomware attacks Wray wants us to treat like terrorism, if mitigated, is the comprehensive solution to GPCyber™ threats and the gold at the end of the rainbow?

Now ask yourself, on a scale of 1 to 10 (10 being astoundingly effective), how effective do you think Wray's advice and guidance on how to mitigate ransomware was? Below or above 5?

The unintended or perhaps intended consequences of Wray equating terrorism with ransomware keeps the conversation exclusively within the realm of cyber security—regardless of how much terrorism salt, pepper, and other spices you sprinkle on it. The conversation is kept to a focus on tech, not on strategic and board risk focus, unlike survivability.

Additionally, his lack of offering specifics on what and how organizations need to act moving forward also fails in elevating the strategic risk focus needed. However, the misfocus did not stop there. Here I return to the previous headline of *The Washington Post*. By summer 2021, the Biden administration announced a $10 million bounty for information on ransomware—and only ransomware. Somehow, it's as if ransomware is the holy grail that will secure everything if fixed.

Huge resources have been allocated to pay for these bounties, while, of course, "best practices" continue being highly recommended. If you also are finding it hard to fathom how this is, in any way, an effective and practical mitigation for unprecedented cyberattacks and disasters, you are not alone. We and society can no longer afford the ongoing "missionary style" mindsets—especially the failed regulatory frameworks and their "best practice" gospel.

Just remember what I wrote in earlier chapters. Whatever the US implements is often followed by most of the rest of the world strategically and operationally. So, this is also a failure to lead. Wray's words were also more unhelpful than helpful. Many ransomware cyber security service providers have jumped on the bandwagon, quoting the director in order to promote their ransomware protection services as a must-have.

I cannot judge if this was done intentionally or inadvertently. However, Wray may have given a grave false sense of security to top decision makers who authorized additional funds for ransomware services to be purchased, thinking they are now protected from enemy nation-states, terrorists and other bad actors.

The simple and unfortunate truth is that they are not protected in any way, shape, or form. All of this said, I'm not sure if Director Wray knew in advance that he would become the flagship salesman for many of these service providers.

And there is something else he said that weighed heavy on my mind: the thing about "shared responsibility." Sorry, Mr. Wray, there is no shared responsibility here. Government has the ultimate responsibility to lead, pass laws, regulate, and protect its citizens and all stakeholders. Are you waiting for Microsoft or Google to come up with the needed regulatory framework for all American stakeholder compliance before elevating US national security preparedness? This is not the leadership needed to prevent disasters hitting a nation, especially one that presents itself as a world leader.

By now, when I categorize an attack as GPCyber™ motivated, you know what I am referring to. I want you to ask yourself why governments and their leaders and officials are often very late in recognizing how serious a problem is. It cannot be because they are not smart enough. To the contrary, they are smarter than most people.

Bottom line . . . if you think following or becoming compliant to the regulation you are expected by law to follow will safeguard you from GPCyber™ motivated attacks, you are delusional, and I have a certain bridge in Brooklyn to sell you.

FREE MARKET? REALLY? (THE DECISIONS OF THE FEW AND POWERFUL)

Another worthy case, to anchor some of my conclusions, manifested itself on March 8, 2020. I say manifested because it had been percolating for a while before that date. In essence, two of the largest oil-producing countries ended up in an oil price war that had seismic shockwaves on markets and people globally.

Russia was in the process of direct engagement with OPEC (the Organization of the Petroleum Exporting Countries) to join the global club. OPEC and its members set and control global oil production, which directly impacts oil prices worldwide. Prior to the discussions starting, all indicators looked positive and amicable. Then news broke of a major rift between Saudi Arabia and Russia. This was followed by the Saudis announcing a big increase in their own daily oil production. The announcement sent oil prices in markets all over the world into a drop, like a hot potato.

In the first few weeks of March 2020, US oil prices fell by 34%, crude oil fell by 26%, and Brent oil fell by 24% according to many reports. Added to this, in the same month, the world was fully engulfed by the COVID-19 global pandemic. Many countries around the world, especially Western ones, were already implementing major lockdowns on their citizens. This meant people's demand for gas/petrol/oil for their cars and their business machinery also dropped overnight. As a result, oil storage facilities became full and unable to take deliveries of scheduled supplies.

The net effect of the Saudis increasing production overnight has led to the fall of the oil prices by 30% since the start of 2020. In fact, at one point, oil prices became a negative price. Yes, they dropped below zero. Seriously below. Just imagine going to your local coffee shop and instead of paying for your vanilla latte, the shop pays you to get it off its hands.

In fact, on April 20, 2020, US crude closed at -$37 a barrel, surpassing by a mile the zero mark that few ever imagined could ever be seen or crossed. This price war was one of the major causes of the global stock-market crash that started in early February and lasted till late April 2020. Are you still wondering what is the significance of this story? Have you figured out why I am telling it yet?

Think about it for a moment. And for those who are puritan and devout religious believers in the market economy, the market place, and its economics, prepare to have your beliefs shattered or massacred. The facts remain. The oil price war between Saudi Arabia and Russia impacted people, investors, and the markets worldwide. It caused Russia a serious cut in national revenues. The US aim behind the action was to suffocate Russia economically so it would be challenged on matters such as Syria, Iran, and others—forcing it to play ball with the US's front and back channel demands.

And yet, the Saudi decision to significantly increase oil supply overnight was made by one single person: the Crown Prince of Saudi Arabia, Mohammed Bin Salman (also known as MBS). His decision was not purely economic. It was political and geopolitical and served other superpowers' agendas and goals.

US foreign policy strategy is well known for wanting to keep an economic stranglehold on Russia and China through numerous actions (such as sanctions, tariffs, and many other exercisable levers). This is not breaking news. But the decision by Saudi Crown Prince MBS did not serve Saudi economic interest. In fact, it actually cost the oil producing kingdom hundreds of billions of dollars when you consider oil prices dropping to -$37 a barrel. This is at least doubly significant when factoring in the fact that oil exports are the predominant national revenue source of the kingdom.

So, why would a national leader take such action that is clearly damaging to his own nation and economy? And why would he choose an action that happens to serve US strategic foreign policy interest? Keep in mind, while Saudi Arabia is a traditional ally of the US, its decision was counterproductive to its own national economic interest. And that means the Trump administration was successful in getting the Saudis to take an action that does not serve them. Not only that, it actually hurts them.

During private briefings, I dig deeper into the many levers and narratives the US could have used to convince the Saudis to take this self-damaging action. It would be socially irresponsible for me to disclose them here or publicly. Nevertheless, this is an example of how supposed "free markets" operate and trade, and how the markets set the price based on supply and demand.

The bottom line is two people were able to solely directly influence and impact oil prices and stock markets, sending them tumbling worldwide: US President Donald Trump and Saudi Arabian Crown Prince MBS. The first influenced and the second acted. Doesn't this fact warrant at least a few questions? Here are two worth asking:

1. How is that a free market?
2. How can it be called a global market economy?

The US and Western governments are always deafening our ears as to how lucky we are to live where free market economies reign, where supply and demand determine the best price and best allocates society's resources. Really? I'm not so sure. Think of this example as a special template in the way many sectors operate. And ask yourself, does the stock market truly represent a free market place?

It may not if only two men can push it up or down by simply breathing. However, the number of pushes may be a few dozen or a hundred or two at best. Are you still not convinced? Well, what happens when a big fish name just mentions a stock? They can simply cause it to rise or drop like a yo-yo. And they have!

Remember when Elon Musk talked about Dogecoin cryptocurrency, causing its price to soar five times in 2020? How about insider trading and dealings that go uncaught by the regulators? And let's not forget that for 18 years about $2 trillion went unnoticed by the financial regulators in the US and Europe between 1999 and 2017 (the Panama Papers, as mentioned in Part III). I hope you never forget the "amazing" job our political system and its financial regulators did by not being asleep at the wheel while US and Western banks funded war lords, drug traffickers, terrorists, and money launderers.

I do believe in the power and value of supply and demand, and the forces of a marketplace. That said, existing marketplaces are truly the playground of the powerful and the rich. It's a symptom of a broken system that makes the rich richer and the poor poorer, while recruiting the rich, middle, and lower classes to aspire to that "dream" due to that standard, people all over the world continue seeking simply a better life, and riches—and even if they make that dream a reality, they are often doing so by becoming slaves to the "21st-century pharaohs."

Although the original motivation behind capitalism was for resources being best allocated through a marketplace, it was created knowing people will do the right thing to benefit themselves, other people, and society, and to create value. In those days, people had values, they had traditions, they had morals to live up to. Those ideals were more powerful than any dream of getting rich or powerful by any means, at the expense of others, as we see today. Back then, social responsibly was at its core. The original form of capitalism was not intended to give people loopholes and allow others to create wealth without creating anything or any value. Most capitalists from days long gone, including America's founding fathers, were landowners who created wealth by plowing/sowing the land. They lived by honor, they had values, and they acted with the standards of social responsibility of those days. So, how did we get here?

I believe we allowed the deterioration of our values to worsen in the last couple of decades. And it grew so huge, many forgot their values and what we stand for. But we the people allowed this to happen in our name. We became a pop culture of sound bites with no depth or reflection. More and more people got trapped in the pursuit of money and power at any price. Even worse, we celebrated those who made it, regardless of how they made it. Our values kept eroding until we abandoned them completely to our new 21st-century pharaohs while we continued calling it the American dream. The power falls to the "pimps" established in Chapter 19.

Is it any wonder why our political, economic, and democratic models have failed their people? Is it any wonder why all Western governments failed their people on the COVID-19 pandemic as they pointed at others for their failures? Don't we live in continuous elections and marketing campaigns to elect and legitimize new leaders with so much false advertising?

For a functioning democracy to exist, let alone survive, certain fundamentals must be in place:

A. A less disinformed, more informed citizen
B. A high level of ethical journalistic integrity
C. Transparent checks and balances
D. B & C have to be able to effectively hold politicians and public officials to account.

Is anyone willing to challenge me when I say neither A, B, C, nor D exist today? An informed citizen? Who are you kidding? US presidential races and their campaigns are the epitome of misinformation. Is it any wonder American choices for president were the establishment candidate that many Americans believe epitomizes political corruption? Hillary Clinton and a man many other Americans believe is a racist, bigot, misogynist—Donald Trump? Just look at the choices the system produces for us to choose from. Observe the results they deliver to help ordinary Americans, and the impact they cause on lives of people around the world by the time they leave office.

How about in 2020? Was it any better? Did the system give better choices to Americans? Hardly. In fact, as I've said, never before in the history of mankind has man had so much information at his fingertips, and yet, never before has he been so misled and misinformed, especially in the land where freedom reigns as a beacon to people worldwide.

As for ethical journalistic integrity and transparent checks and balances, I think they died a long time ago. All we have left are news channels that use incomplete truths or partial facts to create narratives that suit their political agendas. This is the cyanide that the self-labeled right, left, progressive, and conservative news channels have been forcing down the throats of citizens of Western democracies today.

The system is broken. It is a failed status quo. It is unsustainable and unfixable. It must be overhauled ASAP before humanity pays the ultimate price it cannot afford. We have multiple levels to our food chain, where the bigger fish continue feeding on the fish below them. The truth is that there is no such thing as a real free market. In the case of oil, two people were able to impact the supposed free market, as I shared regarding OPEC, Saudi Arabia, and Russia.

Bear in mind, from Part I, nations that are pursuing a "supremacy" quest—be it cyber, quantum, economic, political, or any other—no longer operate with allies in the traditional sense. Alliances used to be lifelong and based on unshakable trust with transparent and long-standing common values and interests. This is how nations traditionally categorized others as allies, adversaries, or even enemies.

Events in the last decade have shattered all that. They have created a new and unmitigated dynamic that adds a new existential threat to national security, sovereignty, and survivability. Well, the Era of Unprecedented GPCyber™ motivated attacks has ushered in a new reality and created a new dynamic and category that represents a new existential national security threat ...

ALLY-VERSARIES™ (FANGS OF THE LION)

As the proverb goes from Chapter 5, "If you see the fangs of the lion shining brightly, don't assume the lion is smiling at you." Today, nations must determine if and how their allies, adversaries, enemies, or Ally-versaries™ will act on any particular matter.

Nations who treat other nations as enemies know where they stand. An enemy status is binary. You have no dealings with that enemy. You know you need to keep your eyes open and your guard up 24/7. Adversaries, on the other hand, are nations who compete against other nations in different fields and sectors. They often collaborate as well. They do business with each other because it is in their national strategic, political, or economic interest.

Look at the US, Russia, and China, for example. The US imposes trade sanctions on China and Russia in certain areas to exert pressure that is often motivated by political doctrine. Yet, and at the same time, they also have collaborative arrangements on many other fronts.

However, when it comes to being an "ally," this is where we need to throw old definitions in the toilet—and flush twice. Nations expect themselves to always remain vigilant in the activities of enemy states and adversaries. However, they seldom give the same level of attention to their supposed allies. Why should they? They often call each other brothers and label their relationships as "special."

All this has changed. Nations are more likely to get compromised by allies than enemies or adversaries. If you are thinking this is because their guards are much lower, you are right. This is one of the reasons but certainly not the only one.

Remember PRISM (Planning Tool for Resource Integration, Synchronization, and Management)? I've shared about PRISM in Parts I and III. The US National Security Agency (NSA) was not only caught spying on Americans, which is illegal, but also on the world. Their attention was also on leaders of US allies such as Germany's Angela Merkel—all in the name of hunting down terrorists. Clearly, Merkel posed a serious terrorist threat to Americans back home.

How about Israel? American politicians never hesitate to jump to Israel's defense at every opportunity—even when reprimanding it is the appropriate action. Meanwhile, the on-topic issue can be found in Pegasus, which is owned by the Israeli NSO Group. This spyware company was set up by former Israeli security officials. It has been caught spying on people all over the world, including European and world leaders, as well as thousands of government officials and journalists. And it was implicated in the murder of journalist Jamal Khashoggi at the Saudi embassy in Istanbul, Turkey.

Keep in mind that all of the nations and officials Pegasus spied upon were already supporters or allies of the state of Israel. This includes the US, France, and many others. To add insult to injury, it was uncovered that the Israeli government had granted Pegasus the license to sell its spyware software to many countries who are known for having serious records of human rights abuses according to the UN, US, UK, and many other human rights watchdogs.

And how can I forget to mention how brother was turned against brother after a cyberattack on the Qatari information ministry (Chapter 5)? If you're reading this, FBI Director Wray, there was no ransom demanded in this cyberattack. Instead, the perpetrators hacked the system to attribute words to the Qatari ruler on the official Qatari ministry website to make him look like he supported terrorism.

Within hours, a preplanned, highly sophisticated social media campaign kicked off in the Arabian Gulf region. Within days, brothers were at each other's throats. Saudi Arabia and the United Arab Emirates issued an ultimatum to Qatar. Overnight, all ties were severed between historical brothers and allies—with trade sanctions and travel embargoes imposed on Qatar. This cost all nations involved hundreds of billions of dollars.

And one final case study in Ally-versaries™ can be found in the relationship between Turkey and the US in the last few years. They are historical allies and cofounders of NATO. As shared in Chapter 5, Turkey accused the US of plotting the 2015 coup to overthrow Turkish President Erdoğan. And, the US is unlikely to have been innocent in this regard.

Ally-versaries™ is the new reality. It is also a new and unprecedented risk vector that can be highly destabilizing and devasting to governments, nation-states, corporate entities, and people's lives and livelihoods. Yet, it is totally unprepared for, which makes it an ever-growing risk that's 100% unmitigated. If you think I am sensationalizing, just ponder the constant vulnerabilities that exist, or the ones that are routinely discovered in the sector you operate in, or the sectors I addressed in Part II.

Just think how many ways these sectors could become GPCyber™ compromised, and with ease to boot, to serve not just an enemy's agenda but that of an Ally-versary™. Already, many traditional allies are not hesitating in perpetrating GPCyber™ attacks on their supposed allies and "brothers" to advance strategic, political, economic, or other sinister agendas and goals.

This requires a new national and corporate survivability awareness to start with, followed by a specially structured national or corporate survivability mitigation strategy to match.

MY TRIBUTE TO A MENTOR

With all the doom and gloom I have shared, you might think that I believe that hope is dead and that we are stuck with the failed status quo of a truly broken system for generations to come—that no hope exists to save democracy in order to save humanity. To the contrary, I truly believe there is a way out and forward. In fact, it is more than just a hope or a mere prayer. I believe it is actionable now and achievable for us and our children and theirs after to reap its benefits. And I will tell you here in my concluding chapter how we can make it happen and before it is too late.

But first, I want to pay a special tribute to a man who was a great force in guiding me in my life's journey since my early 20s. His influence and impact on my intellectual and philosophical growth has been monumental. This man is Dr. Arthur Laffer, my professor at the University of Southern California in the early 1980s (from Chapter 3).

As he is one of the fathers of supply-side economics and modern capitalism of the 20th century, I am blessed to have learned directly from him. Learning of the Laffer curve in my early years provided me the unique opportunity to stimulate and test my critical thinking and to develop my mind to create constructive models and mechanisms.

Sharpening the critical thinking I was fortunate to inherit from my father through DNA and learning how to better question became key. Dr. Laffer helped me think and develop processes and protocols on how to improve things and make them better. My exposure to his theories and his tolerating my challenging him (I was always respectful but unrelenting) helped me figure out and crystalize how to make improvements to things to benefit others first, not me.

Had Dr. Laffer not exposed me to supply-side economics, I would not have identified its challenges and pitfalls, nor would I have developed the clarity of mind and abilities I have today. I don't know if he realizes how much he mentored me, but I certainly see his influence in much that I do in my life. And his mentorship triggered me to identify "social responsibility" back in the early '80s as the missing critical variable that would seriously compromise modern capitalism, supply-side economics, and society decades later.

I had many feelings when I saw Federal Reserve Chairman Alan Greenspan's testimony before a Senate hearing about the 2008 financial crisis. I was struck by much of what he said, but the following hit where it counted:

- "It is not that humans have become any more greedy than in generations past. It is that the avenues to express greed had grown so enormously."
- "We share the outrage of most Americans at the greed that blinded Wall Street to its civic duty to protect Main Street."
- "I made a mistake in presuming that the self-interest of organizations, specifically banks and others, were such is that they were best capable of protecting their own shareholders and their equity in the firms."

I essentially heard him admitting that "we got it wrong about greed." Overall, this wasn't just a moment of vindication for me; it was a moment of authentication of what I always believed in my core since I was a teenager who could think and rationalize. It was a validation to my theory on "socially responsible capitalism"—it was also a moment of pride that I must share with my mentor and esteemed Professor Laffer. Without him, my vision, realizations, and successes may not have been possible if it were not for his impact on my life.

Dr. Laffer, thank you. I am eternally grateful. Because of you, I was encouraged to become informed, active, engaged, and relentless in all my pursuits to inspire others and my readers in many readers to come.

REAL HOPE (MOBILIZED CRITICAL THINKING CITIZENS IN THE NEW ERA OF THE WHISTLEBLOWER)

And while I'm on the topic of gratitude, I want to draw attention to some of the heroic actions mentioned in my book in light of the death of integrity and objectivity in journalism today, and its unprecedented failure to hold elected officials to account. Many of the people listed below were instrumental in ushering in the new era of whistleblowers—to effectively hold elected officials and top decision makers to account.

- Chris Valasek and Charlie Miller (Sector 7: Transportation, revealed ease of hacking passwords to Jeep)
- Justin Paine (Sector 7: Transportation, revealed vulnerabilities to Honda)
- International Consortium of Investigative Journalists (ICIJ)
- BuzzFeed
- Hervé Falciani (Chapter 20: Swiss Leaks, if he was truly intending to blow the whistle and hoping he was not taking advantage of a broken system)
- Natalie Mayflower Sours Edwards (Chapter 20: FinCEN Leaks)
- Last but not least, Edward Snowden and Julian Assange

Since the death and absence of high integrity journalism to serve as democracies' checks and balances to hold elected politicians accountable, the people named above may have inadvertently created a new era of checks and balances players—the Era of the Whistleblower.

FinCEN, the Panama Papers, and Pandora Papers—and most recently, the Facebook Papers from Frances Haugen—prove that journalism in this day and age has failed to hold our public officials to account regardless of their claims of being "objective, fair, and unbiased." It appears that the age of the whistleblower has emerged. Only whistleblowing has been effective in exposing globally extensive abuses of power by governments and big corporations.

This is good but it is not enough. What is missing are consequences that remedy these exposed lies, deceptions, narratives, and so on. The new world order needs this in place in order to safeguard sovereignty, corporate security, and citizens. Above all, without it, democracy will most certainly die. Is it any wonder that governments worldwide pursue and prosecute whistleblowers with venom? This is done to protect the status quo, which keeps them in power and relevant, in the face of being exposed for crimes and corruption.

But of course, once again, a wakeup call was in store as I approached the final stages of creating my book. The year 2021 brought yet another "gift" for humanity in the first few days of October, when the ICIJ struck uranium one more time with further discoveries of world-leader wealth being hidden in offshore accounts. With the release of the Pandora Papers, more than 600 journalists from over 100 countries shared their analysis of leaked information from 14 offshore financial service firms. From 11.9 million records now debunked, the world has an even clearer idea of how the wealthy hide their assets.

This great feat by ICIJ was followed by the elite scrambling to address the implications. I wonder, will this serve as the long awaited and final nail in the coffin of a broken system? Or will we the people return to the status quo, to our lives and lies with minor tweaks labeled as "real change"? If venturing a guess based on immediate history, I'm sadly confident in the reality of the latter. In that likely case, will you accept their "change"? Or will you rise to the challenge?

For the reader, if you feel a calling to Survivability, I created an opportunity for you to get involved. If you see a value in partnering with MLi Group on any of our initiatives, get in touch via expression of interest through our online resource page (see EOI).

And for those who see or wish to explore a career in Survivability, cyber and non-cyber, with MLi Group or any of our subsidiaries, get in touch and upload your CV through our online resource page (see Survivability Recruitment).

Know this: Securing any form of personal, corporate, or national survivability requires a changed mindset to start with. It then needs to be matched by passionate and motivated leaders and citizens who want to see change happen, and who value acquiring competitive advantages in the 21st century. Do you remember the slogan attributed to Uncle Sam saying "I want you"? Well, as of 2021, Uncle Khaled is saying, "You need me—and I want you!" Get in touch.

But before I thank you for reading my book and say goodbye, I want to leave you with this foundational thought, hoping it will create a eureka moment that anchors in your mind, one that would instigate a proactive action.

Do you remember how the press reported on the FBI Director Wray's words? Let me remind you what he said:

> "There are a lot of parallels [between the recent challenges of ransomware and those posed by the 9/11 attacks], there's a lot of importance, and a lot of focus by us on disruption and prevention. ... There's a shared responsibility, not just across government agencies but across the private sector and even the average American."

Read his words carefully. Nothing in what he said was sensationalistic. Wray was simply drawing comparisons and the key words I believe he wanted everyone to be focused on were *disruption* and *prevention*. But this is not what the media ended up focusing on. Now read again the headlines I shared with you earlier:

- *The New York Times*: "F.B.I. Director Compares Danger of Ransomware to 9/11 Terror Threat"
- *Fox News Business*: "FBI Director Chris Wray Compares Ransomware Attacks to 9/11"
- *The Guardian*: "FBI Director Sees 'Parallels' between Ransomware Threat and 9/11"

- *The Washington Post*: "The Biden Administration Seeks to Rally Allies and the Private Sector against the Ransomware Threat"

Do you now see the sensationalization of his words by all, some more than others? I suggest you read the full articles too. When you do, look to see if any of these reports or any other mainstream or establishment news outlet or publication seriously challenged Director Wray on why, what, how, where, and better still, why now, and why only ransomware. Ponder this for a moment.

In fact, not only did they all misunderstand when he was saying, many quoted him and then added their own sensationalistic twist. You will see how some were spinning their own exaggerations to vindicate their conservative or progressive agendas to show the failure of the other side. Did they do this purely to sell more advertising? Of course not. Regardless, and as a result, most stakeholders were none-the-wiser citizens.

I have yet to see anything specific being offered to decision makers and citizens alike as to what they can do next. And as Wray indicated, I don't see any of them becoming better aware of what their supposedly "shared responsibility" is. The truth is that we must also start holding our news agencies and outlets to a better account.

If we remain willing to accept and tolerate such mediocrity and failures to act at the highest ethical journalistic integrity possible, in turn, they will continue to fail to hold our public officials to account. The result will be our most scared and cherished democracy most certainly dying. I believe this is not an acceptable outcome.

A FINAL MESSAGE (WHEN TO *NEVER* COMPROMISE)

I believe the change we need begins with ordinary citizens and top decision makers recognizing the importance of doing the right thing when faced with a life-changing decision. They need to make that decision be the best not only for themselves, but for their community or society, especially if that decision is key to making a lifelong financial dream or ambition a reality. In essence, I'm saying that if you have not found yourself saying "No" to a career-changing proposition, it means you have not yet been truly tested.

Let me now tell you about a big "No" I needed to give to a major, life-changing proposal I was offered—one that some might sell their mothers for or give their right arm to say "Yes."

As mentioned in the Introduction to this book, I created the investigative program, "the Era of the Unprecedented," in 2016–2017. I set about creating this because I believed there was a critical need to spread awareness about changes to the threat landscape as well as GPCyber™ motivations behind cyberattacks that were already devastating nation-states, governments, elections, and so on. I could only see these events increasing in frequency, damage, and compromisability. While this was already impacting society, businesses, the sovereignty of nations, and above all the lives and livelihoods of citizens around the world, I foresaw this getting significantly worse before it would even remotely get better.

Unique from other investigative programs, I designed mine to create direct citizen engagements after the airing of each episode in each country. At the conclusion of each episode, an event would be hosted and livestreamed from a location such as a university or town hall. It would have high-profile panelists comprised of celebrities, experts, law enforcement officials, and elected politicians, as well as an audience attending the event both in person and online. My team and I identified and researched more than 36 topics to investigate and showcase. They would get covered in 12 to 18 episodes.

If the topic, for example, was on the cyberattack that hit Equifax, the Qatari ministry of information, or any other event, then we would have on the panel experts to discuss that segment and answer questions from the audience about the nature of the attack, motivations (etc.), and what this means for the future if things stay unchanged. The panel would field other questions from the audience in the auditorium and online, questioning and creating debates on what needs to be improved and how.

In essence, I wanted to create the opportunity for healthy, constructive, and intelligent debates, not dumbing-down ones. I wanted to make citizens better informed and more aware, and to give them the opportunity to exercise their critical thinking and civic duties in questioning leaders and decision makers—in order to hold them accountable without prescreenings. I wanted to help bring about real change. I believed that some engagements would be so very heated but valuable and constructive that they would make sincere public officials want to be invited.

Genuine officials would embrace being put on the spot to explain themselves in being held accountable, unlike insincere officials.

The program model was going international. I won't bore you with the intellectual property requirements I insisted on. However, we had great interest expressed from a major North American network. I would have been just as happy if it told me it just wanted a pilot. Instead, it expressed great interest in 13 episodes. You can imagine my exhilaration at the prospect.

We went through the due diligence process. It all came down to agreeing on terms and signing the agreement. At that point, my attorney flagged something he discovered. It turned out the network had injected numerous clauses that gave them 100% editorial control of the program. I had anticipated this to some extent, but I believed this to be resolvable and not a deal breaker. What was a red flag for me was that on top of episode editorial control, it also wanted full editorial control of the public engagement aspect of the program too.

I recall sitting in their boardroom with the network executives, my counterparts. I sat back in my chair, smiled and looked at them and I said, "Are you familiar with an investigative program called *60 Minutes*?"

They looked at me with bewilderment. "Of course—why do you ask?" one of them replied.

"I ask because *60 Minutes* is an international giant in the investigative world." I paused and then added, "Who am I compared to *60 Minutes*? But I can tell you that over the years *60 Minutes* had numerous episodes that were highly explosive in what they were exposing to air. The anticipation of some of these episodes brought serious worry to many people and parties involved, who tried very hard to stop these episodes from airing."

I said, "I know for a fact that when some of these people learned about what *60 Minutes* was investigating, and planning to air, phones started to ring at advertisers' offices, and then advertisers started calling the network threatening sponsorship and advertising would be pulled if the segment(s) in question were allowed to air. To my knowledge ... there have been episodes that may have been put to sleep, and others appropriately diluted before airing."

I smiled when I asked, "How often do you think your network phone will ring before or after we've aired our episodes? How often do you think you will be asked not to let certain debates go in a certain direction?"

The fact was, I fully understood the need for the network to have some editorial control, as they needed to ensure they wouldn't be sued. On that, I was more than happy to cooperate to ensure this by jointly controlling it. But I said to them that under no circumstances would I relinquish control of the panels or debates to anyone else. I added, I would not compromise, nor would I give any network a nuclear button to silence citizens in their ability to exercise their right to free speech. I concluded the negotiations in saying that unless they were willing to drop the control condition on the debate part of the program there would be no deal, and I would be walking away from their offer.

I was raised in a publisher and journalist's household, and I learned invaluable lessons from my dad therein, which I shared with my counterparts. "You never compromise on your values or your integrity." This I did not do. I said "No," and I walked.

All of my efforts and the work of MLi Group aside, society's Era of the Unprecedented will indeed get worse before it gets better, and time is running out for the latter. For any readers who are decision makers and leaders, I wish you well as you consider what you must do moving forward. And for citizens who have taken the time to read my book, I wish you well as you move forward in life, knowing what choices you have awaiting you.

Thank you, all, for reading. We can either accept our new reality or we can accept the consequences. Here's to our survivability.

Farewell, good luck, and may you succeed in helping shape a better present and future for you, your children, and their children.

—Khaled Fattal

Don't forget! I've placed these text boxes throughout the book to provide further reading and opportunities for you to connect with MLi Group, *Survivability News*, and our many subsidiaries and initiatives (survivabilitythebook.com). My intention is to help us all become more engaged citizens, and I hope you find our resources beneficial along the way

ABOUT THE AUTHOR

With a BS in business administration (USC, 1984) and an MBA from CSULA (1987), Khaled Fattal is the founder and chairman of the MLi Group, whose motto is "Cybersecurity Is No Longer the Keyword—Survivability in a Geo-Poli-Cyber™ Threatened World is."

Using the MLi Group Survivability Strategies™ and Solutions, Fattal and his MLi Group help businesses and governments mitigate the latest cyber and non cyber threats—especially Geo-Poli-Cyber™ perpetrators whose motivations are political, ideological, extremist, and "religious," which cyber security, resiliency, and continuity strategies and solutions continue to routinely fail to defend governments and organizations. A key threat is the destruction/devastation-motivated new breed of GPCyber™ hackers and lone wolves, often directed or backed by not only enemies but also presumed allies.

The MLi Group and Fattal have been involved in the global infrastructure of the internet and its resiliency, stability, and security since the mid-1990s; he championed it as, and led the way in making it, the Multilingual Internet it is today through international institutions and forums such as the UN, ITU, ICANN, UNIGF, and many others.

Fattal is frequently invited to keynote, speak at, and chair public and private expos, international conferences, and events, as well as being interviewed on radio and TV. He writes regularly for online and print cyber, internet, political, and defense publications.

REFERENCES

1 The Federal Reserve Board. "Testimony of Chairman Alan Greenspan," July 16, 2002. Accessed May 26, 2022, https://www.federalreserve.gov/boarddocs/hh/2002/july/testimony.htm

2 House of Representatives. "The Financial Crisis and the Role of Federal Regulators," October 23, 2008. Accessed May 26, 2022, https://www.govinfo.gov/content/pkg/CHRG-110hhrg55764/html/CHRG-110hhrg55764.htm

3 Europol. "Convergence of Cyber and Terrorism." Accessed March 29, 2022, https://www.europol.europa.eu/iocta/2016/convergence.html

4 Europol. "Convergence of Cyber and Terrorism." Accessed March 29, 2022, https://www.europol.europa.eu/iocta/2017/THE_CONVERGENCE_OF_CYBER_AND_TERRORISM.html

5 The *Independent*. "Isis-linked hackers attack NHS websites to show gruesome Syrian civil war images." Accessed May 19, 2022. https://www.independent.co.uk/news/uk/crime/isis-islamist-hackers-nhs-websites-cyber-attack-syrian-civil-war-images-islamic-state-a7567236.html

6 The *Washington Post*. "AstraZeneca used 'outdated and potentially misleading data' that overstated the effectiveness of its vaccine, independent panel says." Accessed March 29, 2022, https://www.washingtonpost.com/world/astrazeneca-oxford-vaccine-concerns/2021/03/23/2f931d34-8bc3-11eb-a33e-da28941cb9ac_story.html

7 The *Telegraph*. "Denmark becomes world's first country to stop using AstraZeneca vaccine." Accessed March 29, 2022, https://www.telegraph.co.uk/news/2021/04/14/denmark-permanently-stops-using-astrazeneca-vaccine/

8 CBS News. "Pfizer execs discuss hiking vaccine price after pandemic wanes." Accessed March 29, 2022, https://www.cbsnews.com/news/pfizer-covid-vaccine-price-hike-post-pandemic/

9 *Nature*. "Hello quantum world! Google publishes landmark quantum supremacy claim." Accessed March 29, 2022, https://www.nature.com/articles/d41586-019-03213-z

10 National Cyber Security Centre. "CNI Hub." Accessed March 29, 2022, https://www.ncsc.gov.uk/section/private-sector-cni/cni

11 Cybersecurity & Infrastructure Security Agency. "Critical Infrastructure Sectors." Accessed March 29, 2022, https://www.cisa.gov/critical-infrastructure-sectors

12 Emsisoft. "The State of Ransomware in the US: Report and Statistics 2019." Accessed March 29, 2022, https://blog.emsisoft.com/en/34822/the-state-of-ransomware-in-the-us-report-and-statistics-2019/

13 *Wired.* "How an Entire Nation Became Russia's Test Lab for Cyberwar." Accessed March 29, 2022, www.wired.com/story/russian-hackers-attack-ukraine

14 Mystateline.com. "Winnebago County IT experts talk cyber security amid RPS breach." Accessed March 29, 2022, https://www.mystateline.com/news/local-news/winnebago-county-it-experts-talk-cyber-security-amid-rps-breach/

15 The *Financial Times.* "India confirms cyber attack on nuclear power plant." Accessed April 1, 2022, https://www.ft.com/content/e43a5084-fbbb-11e9-a354-36acbbb0d9b6

16 *Forbes.* "U.S. Government Issues Powerful Cyberattack Warning As Gas Pipeline Forced Into Two Day Shut Down." Accessed March 29, 2022, https://www.forbes.com/sites/kateoflahertyuk/2020/02/19/us-government-issues-powerful-cyberattack-warning-as-gas-pipeline-forced-into-two-day-shut-down

17 House of Commons Committees. "A major cyber attack on the UK is a matter of 'when, not if'." Accessed March 29, 2022, https://houseofcommons.shorthandstories.com/jcnss-cni-report/index.html

18 Infosecurity Group. "A Quarter of UK CNI Firms Have Suffered Cyber-Attack Outages." Accessed March 29, 2022, https://www.infosecurity-magazine.com/news/a-quarter-of-uk-cni-firms/

19 Parliament.uk. "Cyber Security of the UK's Critical National Infrastructure." Accessed March 29, 2022, https://publications.parliament.uk/pa/jt201719/jtselect/jtnatsec/1708/170803.htm

20 Parliament.uk. "Cyber Security of the UK's Critical National Infrastructure." Accessed March 29, 2022, https://publications.parliament.uk/pa/jt201719/jtselect/jtnatsec/1708/170803.htm

21 Parliament.uk. "Protecting CNI against cyber attack: a 'wicked' problem." Accessed March 29, 2022, https://publications.parliament.uk/pa/jt201719/jtselect/jtnatsec/1708/170805.htm

22 The White House. "What We Urge You To Do To Protect Against The Threat of Ransomware." Accessed March 29, 2022, https://www.whitehouse.gov/wp-content/uploads/2021/06/Memo-What-We-Urge-You-To-Do-To-Protect-Against-The-Threat-of-Ransomware.pdf

23 The White House. "Press Briefing by Press Secretary Jen Psaki, June 3, 2021." Accessed March 29, 2022, https://www.whitehouse.gov/briefing-room/press-briefings/2021/06/03/press-briefing-by-press-secretary-jen-psaki-june-3-2021/

24 Click2Houston.com. "Man hacks wireless baby monitor, makes vulgar threats to family." Accessed March 29, 2022, https://www.click2houston.com/news/2018/12/19/man-hacks-wireless-baby-monitor-makes-vulgar-threats-to-family/
25 *Insurance Business America*. "Transportation is now the third most vulnerable sector exposed to cyberattacks." Accessed March 29, 2022, https://www.insurancebusinessmag.com/us/news/cyber/transportation-is-now-the-third-most-vulnerable-sector-exposed-to-cyberattacks-106900.aspx
26 BleepingComputer. "Zero-Day Vulnerabilities Leave Smart Buildings Open to Cyber Attacks." Accessed March 29, 2022, https://www.bleepingcomputer.com/news/security/zero-day-vulnerabilities-leave-smart-buildings-open-to-cyber-attacks/
27 Sonic Wall. "Linear eMerge E3 access controller actively being exploited." Accessed March 29, 2022, https://securitynews.sonicwall.com/xmlpost/linear-emerge-e3-access-controller-actively-being-exploited/
28 Intersoft Consulting. "General Data Protection Regulation." Accessed March 29, 2022, https://gdpr-info.eu/
29 Capital One. "Capital One Announces Data Security Incident." Accessed March 29, 2022, https://www.capitalone.com/about/newsroom/capital-one-announces-data-security-incident/
30 Capital One. "Capital One Announces Data Security Incident." Accessed March 29, 2022, https://www.capitalone.com/about/newsroom/capital-one-announces-data-security-incident/
31 Scribd. "Data Breach Prevention and Compensation Act of 2018 (Final)." Accessed March 29, 2022, https://www.scribd.com/document/368838846/Data-Breach-Prevention-and-Compensation-Act-of-2018-Final?campaign=VigLink&ad_group=xxc1xx&source=hp_affiliate&medium=affiliate
32 *The Guardian*. "Deloitte hit by cyber-attack revealing clients' secret emails." Accessed March 29, 2022, https://www.theguardian.com/business/2017/sep/25/deloitte-hit-by-cyber-attack-revealing-clients-secret-emails
33 Senate Committee on Homeland Security & Governmental Affairs. "Testimony of Arne Sorenson, President & CEO, Marriott International." Accessed March 29, 2022, https://www.hsgac.senate.gov/imo/media/doc/Soresnson%20Testimony.pdf
34 Mobile World Live. "MWC19 LA Keynote 1: FCC." Accessed March 29, 2022, https://www.mobileworldlive.com/on-stage/mwc/mwc19-la-keynote-1-fcc/.
35 SAMENA Telecommunications Council. "SAMENA Trends." Accessed March 29, 2022, https://www.samenacouncil.org/samena_trends/files/SAMENA_Trends_June_2019.pdf
36 Gallagher. "Compliance Consulting: Key Considerations in Avoiding & Calculating Penalties Pursuant to the Employer Shared Responsibility Mandate." Accessed March 29, 2022, https://www.ajg.com/us/news-and-insights/2018/01/whitepaper-employer-shared-responsibility/
37 BBC News. "Hackers hit San Francisco transport systems." Accessed March 29, 2022, https://www.bbc.co.uk/news/technology-38127096

38 *TechCrunch*. "Security lapse exposed weak points on Honda's internal network." Accessed March 29, 2022, https://techcrunch.com/2019/07/31/security-lapse-exposed-weak-points-on-hondas-internal-network/

39 U.S. Department of Homeland Security. "Homeland Threat Assessment October 2020." Accessed March 29, 2022, https://www.dhs.gov/sites/default/files/publications/2020_10_06_homeland-threat-assessment.pdf (page 18)

40 Centre for Strategic & International Studies. "The War Comes Home: The Evolution of Domestic Terrorism in the United States." Accessed March 29, 2022, https://www.csis.org/analysis/war-comes-home-evolution-domestic-terrorism-united-states

41 *Cyber Defense Magazine*. "Maersk reinstalled 45,000 PCs and 4,000 Servers after NotPetya Attack." Accessed April 21, 2022, https://www.cyberdefensemagazine.com/maersk-reinstalled-45000-pcs-and-4000-servers-after-notpetya-attack/

42 *Forbes*. "NotPetya Ransomware Attack Cost Shipping Giant Maersk Over $200 Million." Accessed March 29, 2022, https://www.forbes.com/sites/leemathews/2017/08/16/notpetya-ransomware-attack-cost-shipping-giant-maersk-over-200-million/?sh=9a49d104f9ae

43 Futurenautics. "2017 Waypoint Digital Survey Report." Accessed March 29, 2022, https://www.futurenautics.com/product/2017-waypoint-digital-survey-report/

44 *Ship Technology*. "Did the Maersk cyber attack reveal an industry dangerously unprepared?" Accessed March 29, 2022, https://www.ship-technology.com/features/maersk-cyber-attack-reveal-industry-dangerously-unprepared/

45 Pen Test Partners. "Hacking, tracking, stealing and sinking ships." Accessed March 29, 2022, https://www.pentestpartners.com/security-blog/hacking-tracking-stealing-and-sinking-ships/

46 MarineLink. "KR Certifies First Cyber Security Compliant Vessel." Accessed May 19, 2022. https://www.marinelink.com/news/kr-certifies-first-cyber-security-476352

47 BBC News. "Russian plane crash: What we know." Accessed March 29, 2022, https://www.bbc.co.uk/news/world-middle-east-34687990

48 *Infosecurity*. "BA's Magecart Breach Lands it £183m GDPR Fine." Accessed May 19, 2022. https://www.infosecurity-magazine.com/news/bas-magecart-breach-lands-it-183m/

49 BBC News. "British Airways faces record £183m fine for data breach." Accessed March 29, 2022, https://www.bbc.co.uk/news/business-48905907

50 History. "September 11 Attacks." Accessed March 29, 2022, https://www.history.com/topics/21st-century/9-11-attacks

51 yahoo! Finance. "White House Also Blames Russia for NotPetya Attacks." Accessed July 15, 2022, www.finance.yahoo.com/news/2018-02-16-white-house-blames-russia-for-notpetya.html

52 Wikipedia. "Lloyd's of London." Accessed March 29, 2022, https://en.wikipedia.org/wiki/Lloyd%27s_of_London

53 YouTube. "What Are the Panama Papers?" https://www.youtube.com/watch?time_continue=41&v=FX6-0FvwjF0&feature=emb_logo
54 OpenSecrets. "Incumbent Advantage." Accessed March 29, 2022, https://www.opensecrets.org/elections-overview/incumbent-advantage
55 Quora. "How many credit card transactions are there in the average month in the US?" Accessed March 29, 2022, https://www.quora.com/How-many-credit-card-transactions-are-there-in-the-average-month-in-the-US
56 *International Consortium of Investigative Journalists.* "The Panama Papers: Exposing the Rogue Offshore Finance Industry." Accessed July 15, 2022, www.icij.org/investigations/panama-papers/the-power-players/
57 Internet World Stats. "World Internet Users and 2022 Population Stats." Accessed March 29, 2022, https://www.internetworldstats.com/stats.htm
58 Bureau of Economic Analysis. "Gross Domestic Product, 2nd Quarter 2020 (Advance Estimate) and Annual Update." Accessed March 29, 2022, https://www.bea.gov/news/2020/gross-domestic-product-2nd-quarter-2020-advance-estimate-and-annual-update
59 ABC News. "George W. Bush in 2005: 'If we wait for a pandemic to appear, it will be too late to prepare'." Accessed March 29, 2022, https://abcnews.go.com/Politics/george-bush-2005-wait-pandemic-late-prepare/story?id=69979013
60 The White House. "President Outlines Pandemic Influenza Preparations and Response." Accessed March 29, 2022, https://georgewbush-whitehouse.archives.gov/news/releases/2005/11/20051101-1.html
61 The White House. "'A Test of Our Character as a Nation': President Obama on What We Need in the Fight Against Ebola." Accessed March 29, 2022, https://obamawhitehouse.archives.gov/blog/2014/12/02/test-our-character-nation-president-obama-what-we-need-fight-against-ebola
62 National Library of Medicine. "Bush announces US plan for flu pandemic." Accessed March 29, 2022, https://www.ncbi.nlm.nih.gov/pmc/articles/PMC1283304/
63 Congress of the United States Congressional Budget Office. "U.S. Policy Regarding Pandemic-Influenza Vaccines." Accessed March 29, 2022, https://www.cbo.gov/sites/default/files/110th-congress-2007-2008/reports/09-15-pandemicflu.pdf
64 Propublica. "How Tea Party Budget Battles Left the National Emergency Medical Stockpile Unprepared for Coronavirus." Accessed March 29, 2022, http://www.propublica.org/article/us-emergency-medical-stockpile-funding-unprepared-coronavirus
65 The Federal Reserve Board. "Testimony of Chairman Alan Greenspan," July 16, 2002. Accessed May 26, 2022, https://www.federalreserve.gov/boarddocs/hh/2002/july/testimony.htm
66 House of Representatives. "The Financial Crisis and the Role of Federal Regulators," October 23, 2008. Accessed May 26, 2022, https://www.govinfo.gov/content/pkg/CHRG-110hhrg55764/html/CHRG-110hhrg55764.htm
67 United Nations. "The Paris Agreement." Accessed March 29, 2022, https://www.un.org/en/climatechange/paris-agreement

68 *The Conversation*. "New Zealand gun owners invoke NRA-style tropes in response to fast-tracked law change." Accessed March 29, 2022, https://theconversation.com/new-zealand-gun-owners-invoke-nra-style-tropes-in-response-to-fast-tracked-law-change-114430

69 NBCNews. "NRA chief: If putting armed police in schools is crazy, 'then call me crazy'." Accessed May 19, 2022. https://www.nbcnews.com/politics/politics-news/nra-chief-if-putting-armed-police-schools-crazy-then-call-flna1c7721801

70 The *Washington Post*. "An NRA board member blamed the pastor killed in Charleston for the deaths of his members." Accessed May 19, 2022. https://www.washingtonpost.com/news/wonk/wp/2015/06/19/an-nra-board-member-blamed-a-murdered-pastor-for-the-deaths-in-charleston-yes-really/

71 *USA Today*. "Gun laws don't deter terrorists: Opposing view." Accessed March 29, 2022, https://www.usatoday.com/story/opinion/2016/06/13/gun-laws-deter-terrorists-opposing-view/85844946/

72 *Salon*. "Texas Lt. Gov. Dan Patrick: Video games, abortion to blame for school shootings—but not guns." Accessed May 19, 2022. https://www.salon.com/2018/05/21/texas-lt-gov-dan-patrick-video-games-abortion-to-blame-for-school-shootings-but-not-guns/

73 The *Washington Post*. "President Trump says arming teachers would be up to states and 'very inexpensive'." Accessed May 19, 2022. https://www.washingtonpost.com/news/post-politics/wp/2018/02/24/president-trump-says-arming-teachers-would-be-up-to-states-and-very-inexpensive/

74 *Wikipedia*. "Lobbying in the United States." Accessed July 15, 2022, https://en.wikipedia.org/wiki/Lobbying_in_the_United_States

75 National Archives. "Milestone Documents." Accessed March 29, 2022, https://www.ourdocuments.gov/doc.php?flash=false&doc=90&page=transcript

76 The *Washington Post*. "Text: President Bush Addresses the Nation." Accessed March 29, 2022, https://www.washingtonpost.com/wp-srv/nation/specials/attacked/transcripts/bushaddress_092001.html

77 Statista. "Total lobbying spending in the United States from 1998 to 2021." Accessed March 29, 2022, https://www.statista.com/statistics/257337/total-lobbying-spending-in-the-us/

78 Investopedia. "Why Lobbying Is Legal and Important in the U.S." Accessed March 29, 2022, https://www.investopedia.com/articles/investing/043015/why-lobbying-legal-and-important-us.asp#:~:text=Lobbying%20is%20an%20important%20lever,to%20gain%20power%20in%20numbers

79 Statista. "Number of registered active lobbyists in the United States from 2000 to 2021." Accessed March 29, 2022, https://www.statista.com/statistics/257340/number-of-lobbyists-in-the-us/#:~:text=This%20statistic%20shows%20the%20number,actively%20lobbied%20amounted%20to%2011%2C862

80 BBC News. "The man who thinks Europe has been invaded." Accessed March 29, 2022, https://www.bbc.co.uk/news/resources/idt-sh/Viktor_Orban

81 France 24. "Hungary's Orban blames foreigners, migration for coronavirus spread." Accessed March 29, 2022, https://www.france24.com/en/20200313-

hungary-s-pm-orban-blames-foreign-students-migration-for-coronavirus-spread

82 The *New York Times*. "The Money Farmers: How Oligarchs and Populists Milk the E.U. for Millions." Accessed March 29, 2022, https://www.nytimes.com/2019/11/03/world/europe/eu-farm-subsidy-hungary.html

83 Reuters. "How Viktor Orban will tap Europe's taxpayers and bankroll his friends and family." Accessed March 29, 2022, https://www.reuters.com/investigates/special-report/hungary-orban-balaton/

84 Reuters. "Brazil's Bolsonaro accommodates interest groups behind his rise." Accessed March 29, 2022, https://uk.reuters.com/article/brazil-election/brazils-bolsonaro-accommodates-interest-groups-behind-his-rise-idUSL2N1X42IS

85 The *Guardian*. "Fires are devouring the Amazon. And Jair Bolsonaro is to blame." Accessed March 29, 2022, https://www.theguardian.com/commentisfree/2019/aug/26/fires-are-devouring-the-amazon-and-jair-bolsonaro-is-to-blame

86 BBC News. "How Narendra Modi has reinvented Indian politics." Accessed March 29, 2022, https://www.bbc.co.uk/news/world-asia-india-48293048

87 *The Guardian*. "How Hindu supremacists are tearing India apart." Accessed March 29, 2022, https://www.theguardian.com/world/2020/feb/20/hindu-supremacists-nationalism-tearing-india-apart-modi-bjp-rss-jnu-attacks

88 *The Guardian*. "India plans to fell ancient forest to create 40 new coalfields." Accessed March 29, 2022, https://www.theguardian.com/world/2020/aug/08/india-prime-minister-narendra-modi-plans-to-fell-ancient-forest-to-create-40-new-coal-fields

89 NPR. "Minnesota Congresswoman Ignites Debate On Israel And Anti-Semitism." Accessed March 29, 2022, https://www.npr.org/2019/03/07/700901834/minnesota-congresswoman-ignites-debate-on-israel-and-anti-semitism

90 BBC News. "Gaza crisis: Toll of operations in Gaza." Accessed March 29, 2022, https://www.bbc.co.uk/news/world-middle-east-28439404

91 Wikipedia. "Hervé Falciani." Accessed March 29, 2022, https://en.wikipedia.org/wiki/Herv%C3%A9_Falciani

92 International Consortium of Investigative Journalists. "Swiss Leaks." Accessed March 29, 2022, https://projects.icij.org/swiss-leaks/countries/rankings#money

93 International Consortium of Investigative Journalists. "Swiss Leaks." Accessed March 29, 2022, https://projects.icij.org/swiss-leaks/countries/rankings#clients

94 *BuzzFeed News*. "We Got Our Hands On Thousands Of Secret Documents. Let's Break Them Down." Accessed March 29, 2022, https://www.buzzfeednews.com/article/jsvine/fincen-files-explainer-data-money-transactions

95 United States Department of Justice. "Former Senior FinCEN Employee Sentenced To Six Months In Prison For Unlawfully Disclosing Suspicious Activity Reports." Accessed March 29, 2022, https://www.justice.gov/

usao-sdny/pr/former-senior-fincen-employee-sentenced-six-months-prison-unlawfully-disclosing

96 National Archives. "Federal Register." Accessed March 29, 2022, https://www.govinfo.gov/content/pkg/FR-2019-07-10/pdf/FR-2019-07-10.pdf

97 Wikipedia. "Pandemic and All-Hazards Preparedness and Advancing Innovation Act." Accessed March 29, 2022, https://en.wikipedia.org/wiki/Pandemic_and_All-Hazards_Preparedness_and_Advancing_Innovation_Act

98 The *Guardian*. "What was Exercise Cygnus and what did it find?" Accessed March 29, 2022, https://www.theguardian.com/world/2020/may/07/what-was-exercise-cygnus-and-what-did-it-find

99 The *Guardian*. "Labour urges UK government to publish findings of 2016 pandemic drill." Accessed March 29, 2022, https://www.theguardian.com/world/2020/apr/02/labour-urges-government-publish-findings-2016-pandemic-drill

100 *Metro*. "Pandemic simulation 'killed' 65,000,000 months before real outbreak." Accessed March 29, 2022, https://metro.co.uk/2020/02/28/pandemic-simulation-killed-65000000-months-real-outbreak-12318182/

101 The *BMJ*. "Pandemic preparedness: Government must release 2016 report, says information commissioner." Accessed March 29, 2022, https://www.bmj.com/content/371/bmj.m3953

102 Center for Health Security. "Public-private cooperation for pandemic preparedness and response." Accessed March 29, 2022, https://www.centerforhealthsecurity.org/event201/recommendations.html

103 *The Times of Israel*. "Netanyahu: Trump right about building wall, 'great success' in Israel." Accessed March 29, 2022, https://www.timesofisrael.com/netanyahu-trump-right-about-building-wall-great-success-in-israel/

104 BBC News. "Trump's Middle East peace plan: 'Deal of the century' is huge gamble." Accessed March 29, 2022, https://www.bbc.com/news/world-middle-east-51263815

105 *The Times*. "Growing risk of attacks as world order crumbles." Accessed March 29, 2022, https://www.thetimes.co.uk/article/growing-risk-of-attacks-as-world-order-crumbles-rhhqv6fhm

106 https://publications.parliament.uk/pa/cm5802/cmselect/cmsctech/92/9203.htm

107 The *Wall Street Journal*. "FBI Director Compares Ransomware Challenge to 9/11." Accessed March 29, 2022, https://www.wsj.com/articles/fbi-director-compares-ransomware-challenge-to-9-11-11622799003

ABOUT THE AUTHOR

THE BOOK WEBSITE

Milton Keynes UK
Ingram Content Group UK Ltd.
UKHW011427250823
427489UK00014B/76/J

9 781636 982267